The Ethics of Technology

Philosophy, Technology and Society

Series Editor: Sven Ove Hansson

Technological change has deep and often unexpected impacts on our societies. Sometimes new technologies liberate us and improve our quality of life, sometimes they bring severe social and environmental problems, sometimes they do both. This book series reflects philosophically on what new and emerging technologies do to our lives and how we can use them more wisely. It provides new insights on how technology continuously changes the basic conditions of human existence: relationships among ourselves, our relations to nature, the knowledge we can obtain, our thought patterns, our ethical difficulties, and our views of the world.

Title in the Series:

The Ethics of Technology: Methods and Approaches, edited by Sven Ove Hansson

The Ethics of Technology

Methods and Approaches

Edited by
Sven Ove Hansson

ROWMAN &
LITTLEFIELD
——————INTERNATIONAL

London • New York

Published by Rowman & Littlefield International, Ltd.
Unit A, Whitacre Mews, 26-34 Stannary Street, London SE11 4AB
www.rowmaninternational.com

Rowman & Littlefield International, Ltd. is an affiliate of Rowman & Littlefield
4501 Forbes Boulevard, Suite 200, Lanham, Maryland 20706, USA
With additional offices in Boulder, New York, Toronto (Canada), and Plymouth (UK)
www.rowman.com

British Library Cataloguing in Publication Data

A catalogue record for this book is available from the British Library

ISBN: HB 978-1-7834-8657-1
     PB 978-1-7834-8658-8

Library of Congress Cataloging-in-Publication Data

Names: Hansson, Sven Ove, 1951- editor.
Title: The ethics of technology: methods and approaches/edited by Sven Ove Hansson.
Description: London; New York: Rowman & Littlefield International, Ltd., [2017] |
    Series: Philosophy, technology and society | Includes bibliographical references and
    index.
Identifiers: LCCN 2016052347 (print) | LCCN 2016059514 (ebook) |
    ISBN 9781783486571 (cloth: alk. paper) | ISBN 9781783486588 (pbk.: alk. paper) |
    ISBN 9781783486595 (Electronic)
Subjects: LCSH: Technology—Moral and ethical aspects.
Classification: LCC T14 .E78 2017 (print) | LCC T14 (ebook) | DDC 174/.96—dc23
LC record available at https://lccn.loc.gov/2016052347

♾ ™The paper used in this publication meets the minimum requirements of American
National Standard for Information Sciences—Permanence of Paper for Printed Library
Materials, ANSI/NISO Z39.48-1992.

Printed in the United States of America

Contents

Preface

What is the task of a professional ethicist? Is it to find out what is morally right and wrong, and tell people what they are morally obliged to do? Or is it to provide them with a list of ethical standpoints that they can choose from? Is it the task of ethicists to investigate and sort out the relevant empirical facts? To find out what people in general think about the issue? To work out the practical implications of fundamental moral theories? These are questions that almost all students of ethics ask themselves at one point in time or other.

For students in the ethics of technology, there are additional complications. How can you distinguish the ethically relevant effects of a technology from the effects of other social forces? And how can you make an ethical appraisal of an emerging technology whose social effects are not yet there to be seen?

This book is a broad methodological introduction to the ethics of technology. It addresses the general questions raised above and offers a wide selection of methods, tools, concepts, and perspectives for ethical investigations of technology. The book is primarily intended for graduate and advanced undergraduate students in the ethics of technology, but most of its chapters are also highly relevant for students in other areas of applied ethics.

The ethics of technology and its sister disciplines are methodologically pluralistic and should so remain. It is hoped that this book will widen the readers' methodological awareness and extend their range of methodological choices.

I would like to thank all the contributing authors and Sarah Campbell and her colleagues at Rowman & Littlefield International for their dedication to this project and for making the editor's task both intellectually and personally rewarding.

Stockholm, August 29, 2016
Sven Ove Hansson

Preview

Sven Ove Hansson

Researchers in other fields have often been surprised by the sparsity of methodological discussions in ethics and other philosophical disciplines. This books aims at promoting such discussions by introducing methodological approaches, tools, and perspectives that are useful for ethical studies of technology. It has been composed primarily for the needs of graduate students in the ethics of technology, but the methodological overview that it provides can also be useful for other students and researchers in the various subdisciplines of applied ethics.

Chapter 1, *Introduction: Theories and Methods for the Ethics of Technology* (Sven Ove Hansson), begins with a discussion of the meanings of the two key terms "technology" and "ethics." It is argued that "technology" should be used in a wide sense that includes not only material objects such as machines and computers, but also their social embedding and the practices they are associated with. A warning is issued against the conception of "applied ethics" as the straightforward application of theories from fundamental moral philosophy. The ethics of technology requires creativity and theoretical innovations, and the same applies to other branches of applied (or area-specific) ethics. Various more constructive ways of interacting with fundamental moral theory are introduced and discussed, and finally, the roles of empirical input and normative standpoints in the ethics of technology are discussed.

PERSPECTIVES

The requirements of sustainable development are, unavoidably, a central topic in the ethics of technology. In Chapter 2, *Ethics of Sustainability— An Analytical Approach*, Christine Rösch provides a broad perspective on the notion of sustainability. Starting out from the definitions used by the

Brundtland Commission and some of its most important followers, she discusses the various dimensions and aspects of sustainability and how they can be operationalized. The social component of sustainability, which has often been conceived as unclear, is spelt out in a concrete way that will facilitate its analysis in relation to various technological practices. The chapter also reminds us that both inter- and intragenerational justice are essential components of sustainable development.

New technology is almost exclusively developed for industrialized countries. Technological development in the Third World is often seen as a simple process consisting mainly in making machines and other material devices available. In Chapter 3, *International Technology Transfer*, Anthony I. Akubue shows that this is very far from the truth. Western technology is often not exactly what Third World countries need, and even when it is, just transporting material objects does not make them functional in a new setting. Much of what makes technology work is imbedded in people, who have the knowledge and experience needed to use, repair, modify, and adapt it. Colonialism and its aftermath have impeded the development in Third World countries of the competences and capacities needed for the successful use and development of technology. This is a necessary perspective to keep in mind in all studies of the effects of technology on an international scale.

Chapter 4, *Technology and Distributive Justice* (Sven Ove Hansson), discusses the various roles that technologies can have in relation to social injustice. Economic and social inequities invariably lead to unfair distributions of technological goods and services. There are also cases when a technology has a causative role in producing or aggravating injustice. On the other hand, some technologies can have the opposite role of promoting justice, as exemplified by enabling technologies that alleviate the impacts of disease or disability. The chapter closes with a brief introduction to some major concepts, distinctions, and criteria of justice that are useful in the ethical analysis of technologies.

Phenomenological approaches to ethics have proven to be particularly fruitful in studies of technology. In Chapter 5, *Phenomenological Approaches to Technological Ethics*, Robert Rosenberger introduces this branch of ethics and, in particular, its application to human-technology relations. He shows how we can distinguish between phenomenologically different relations between humans and technologies, such as embodiment relations, hermeneutic relations, alterity relations, background relations, and cyborg relations. Illustrative examples of the various types of relations are given, and the major approaches in modern phenomenological ethics are introduced.

Engineering ethics is usually treated as a subfield of the ethics of technology. In Chapter 6, *Profession as a Lens for Studying Technology*, Michael Davis emphasizes that it is also a subfield of the ethics of professions. The chapter starts out by clarifying what is meant by a profession (in contradistinction to an occupation), thereby clarifying some of the important features that engineering has in common with other professions. The author shows that it is highly useful to study the ethics of technology through the lens of the engineering profession. The chapter closes with seven pieces of advice for studies of the ethics of engineering. Its final recommendation is that research groups performing such studies should contain at least one philosopher and at least one engineer.

TOOLS

To "perform a case study" is often seen as just another phrase for "studying a case." In Chapter 7, *Case Study Methodologies*, Gertrude Hirsch Hadorn shows that it means much more. There is a long tradition of case study methodologies that ethicists need to be well informed about. Hirsch Hadorn distinguishes between four major types of case studies that are useful in the ethics of technology: narrative case studies, applied research case studies, grounded theory studies, and transdisciplinary case studies. Although the distinction between these forms of case studies is not always razor-sharp, it is often useful to relate one's own work to one of these established methodologies. The chapter provides practical advice for the selection and delineation of case studies, the collection and documentation of data, and the use of content analysis to summarize and structure a material.

A large number of tools for ethical analysis have been put forward, for instance, in the forms of checklists, matrices, flowcharts, and various ways to organize and structure a discussion. In Chapter 8, *Ethical Tools*, Payam Moula and Per Sandin give an overview of different types of ethical tools and discuss their advantages and disadvantages. They also provide a framework for choosing an ethical tool, emphasizing that this choice will have to depend on the purpose of the investigation. Ethical tools may serve different purposes, such as to elicit expert opinion, to include laypersons in a decision process, to achieve consensus, and so on. Different tools will be needed for these different purposes.

Issues of responsibility arise almost invariably in discussions of the ethics of technology, not least in engineering ethics. But our everyday concept of responsibility is too vague and not very useful in ethical analysis. In Chapter 9, *Responsibility Analysis*, Jessica Nihlén Fahlquist provides us with more precise and therefore also more serviceable concepts of responsibility. She shows how we can distinguish between backward- and forward-looking responsibilities, and discusses what is required for responsibility ascriptions in these different senses. In many cases, it is both rational and fair to ascribe forward-looking responsibility for solving a problem to someone who does not have backward-looking responsibility for the past events that gave rise to the problem. The chapter also discusses the nature of collective responsibility, and throws some light on the coordination problems arising when several persons have moral responsibility in some matter.

In the last few decades, information technology has made privacy infringements possible on a scale that was previously almost unthinkable. Therefore, privacy and data protection are major issues in the ethics of technology. A new discipline, privacy impact assessment, has been introduced for that purpose. It is the topic of Chapter 10, *Privacy Analysis—Privacy Impact Assessment*, by Stefan Strauß. The chapter begins by clarifying the notion of privacy and the scope of privacy impact assessment. This is followed by a presentation of the dimensions of privacy that have to be included in such an assessment. Privacy impact assessments are useful, not least since they often reveal that technologies have been designed in a way that leads to unnecessary storage, distribution, and disclosure of privacy sensitive information.

In the discipline of risk analysis, risks are characterized in terms of their objective features such as the probabilities of adverse events, the damages that these events would lead to, etc. However, risk-taking also has an ethical component. From an ethical point of view it is important to know, for instance, whether the benefits of the risk exposure accrues to the risk-exposed or to someone else, and whether the risk exposure is decided by the risk-exposed or by someone else. Chapter 11, *Ethical Risk Analysis* (Sven Ove Hansson), provides a tool for analyzing these and other ethical aspects of risk, based on a three-party model focusing on the three risk roles of risk-exposed, beneficiary, and decision maker.

EMERGING TECHNOLOGIES

The social effects of new and emerging technologies have been at the center of ethical investigations for quite some time, but the difficulties involved in predicting these effects have often made the ethical analysis precarious. In Chapter 12, *Ethics of Emerging Technology*, Philip Brey provides a broad overview over the methodologies that are available for ethical studies of emerging technologies. He distinguishes between five major types of such approaches, namely, generic, anticipatory, risk-analytic, experimental, and participatory or deliberative methodologies. Examples of each of these approaches are introduced, and their advantages and disadvantages are summarized. The chapter also provides an overview of the many methodologies for technology foresight that can potentially provide support for ethical investigations.

The design of technology has mostly been a male prerogative, and in many cases this has led to design and development decisions that reflect typical perspectives, interests, and needs of men or are even disadvantageous to women. In Chapter 13, *Designing Differently: Toward a Methodology for an Ethics of Feminist Technology Design*, Diane P. Michelfelder, Galit Wellner, and Heather Wiltse show how gender norms have been embodied in the design of technologies. They provide an overview of feminist approaches to technology, and based on that they identify some starting points for designing technology in ways that are not biased against women and are more inclusive and diverse with respect to both design processes and outcomes. Achieving this may also require other changes in society; as the authors point out in their concluding section, "the persistent underrepresentation of women in engineering design and leadership roles in technology companies . . . represents a substantial obstacle to taking women's needs and interests as seriously as those of men in the development of new technologies."

Traditionally, ethical analyses of technological development have taken place when the new technology is already in place. Often, values have influenced the design choices in ways that have not been sufficiently discussed. In the new approach of value-sensitive design, values are explicitly discussed and probed in the early stages of technological development in order to make technological design align better with shared societal values. In the related approach of responsible research and innovation, endorsed by the European Commission, socially responsible research and innovation are promoted. In Chapter 14, *Value-Sensitive Design and Responsible Research and Innovation*, Judith Simon provides an overview over these two areas, discusses their potentials and limitations, and clarifies how they are related to each other.

ETHICAL REFLECTIONS

In the final chapter—Chapter 15, *The Ethics of Doing Ethics of Technology* (Sven Ove Hansson)—it is argued that as ethicists we should attend not only to the ethical issues of other professions but also to those of our own. The chapter provides an overview over ethical issues that can arise in research on the ethics of technology, such as: the choice of research topics, (ethically) negative consequences of ethics research, how we should treat the human subjects that we study, for instance, through questionnaires, interviews and focus groups, and how to deal with conflicts of interest. Various forms of misconduct in research are discussed, such as data fabrication and manipulation, plagiarism, inappropriate duplicate publication, and incorrect authorship attributions. In conclusion, it is proposed that it may be helpful for the profession to develop and adopt a code of ethics for the ethics of technology.

Chapter 1

Theories and Methods for the Ethics of Technology

Sven Ove Hansson

Before we delve into the various approaches and research methods in the ethics of technology, it is useful to reflect on what we mean by the two key terms "ethics" and "technology." That is the subject of the next two sections. We will then turn to the relationship between the ethics of technology and the ethical theories that are taught in philosophy departments. Should the ethics of technology be conducted as an application of these theories, or should we choose some other way to systematize our investigations? Principlism and reflective equilibria are two of the main alternatives. The chapter closes with a discussion of the role of normative statements in the ethics of technology and the relationship between ethical analysis and ethical activism.

1. WHAT IS TECHNOLOGY?

Although the word "technology" is of ancient Greek origin, it did not become widely used in European languages until it began to be used in the early nineteenth century to denote knowledge about the skills and devices of craftspeople (Hansson 2015). For instance, in 1829 the American physician and scientist Jacob Bigelow (1787–1879) published a book titled *Elements of Technology*, in which he delineated the subject matter of technology as "the principles, processes, and nomenclatures of the more conspicuous arts, particularly those which involve applications of science" (Tulley 2008; Sebestik 1983). In a similar vein, the 1909 *Webster's Second New International Dictionary* characterized technology as "the science or systematic knowledge of industrial arts, especially of the more important manufactures, as spinning, weaving, metallurgy, etc." (Tulley 2008).

The more precise delineation of the word "technology" seems to have been influenced by the curricula of the new engineering educations that emerged in Europe in the early nineteenth century. Originally, these were schools for young craftsmen in the towns. Therefore, their education had its focus on the tools, machines, and work processes employed by this class of people. For the most part this excluded the tools, machines, and processes that were used by farmers and farm workers, women, and members of the "higher" professions such as pharmacists and surgeons. The usage of the word "technology" followed the same pattern. We still do not consider farming, fishing, cooking, cleaning, pharmacy, dentistry, or surgery as technological occupations, although they involve equally extensive and sophisticated use of tools and machines as many of the occupations so classified. And importantly, in discussions on the ethics of technology, these activities are usually not included (though perhaps they should).

In the nineteenth century, "technology" denoted systematic knowledge about tools and their use, just as "biology" denotes systematic knowledge about living creatures. However, this changed in the English language in the first half of the twentieth century. Increasingly often, "technology" referred to the actual tools, machines, and procedures, rather than to knowledge about them. The earliest example of this usage recorded in the *Oxford English Dictionary* (*OED*) is a text from 1898 about the coal-oil industry, according to which "a number of patents were granted for improvements in this technology, mainly for improved methods of distillation" (Peckham 1898, p. 119). Today this is the dominant meaning of the word in English. As Joost Mertens noted, "In English usage, 'technology' normally refers to instrumental practices or their rules and only exceptionally to the scientific description, explication or explanation of these practices" (Mertens 2002). In the second half of the twentieth century, this usage became increasingly common in other languages, such as French, Spanish, German, Dutch, and the Scandinavian languages. (Several of these languages also have a shorter word such as the French *technique* and the German *Technik* that refers to the actual tools, machines, and practices.)

In more recent years, the meaning of "technology" has been expanded in a way that seems to have followed the development of curricula in engineering schools. With the introduction of computer and information technology, a wide range of programming and other software-related activities became recognized as technological. Similarly, following the development of biotechnology, many activities based on biological knowledge are now considered technological. However, there are still activities, such as farming and surgery, which we do not usually call technological although they have as much focus on the use of tools and machines as most of the areas that we call technological.

It is important to note that "technology" does not only refer to material objects such as tools, machines, buildings, and computers, but also to the social practices that are associated with these objects. For instance, aeronautical technology does not just cover the physical equipment used in air traffic. It also includes the skills, practices, and rules involved in the use of that equipment. The social embedding of the hardware is part and parcel of what we mean by technology. If we restrict our attention to the physical objects per se we cannot understand the impact they have in society—in particular not the ethical aspects of that impact.

2. THE BRANCHES OF ETHICS

In all probability, thoughts and discussions about what is morally right and wrong antedate written history by many thousands of years. In most of human history, religion was the major vehicle for a coherent account of morality, and for a large part of the world's population, it still is. But in academic contexts, the dominant approach to morality is that provided by a secular discipline, moral philosophy.

Moral philosophy has a strong emphasis on the search for comprehensive basic principles for morality. It is dominated by the idea that our moral thinking needs the support of a moral theory, an account of the fundamental principles on which all our ethical judgments should be based. Two of the most important groups of such theories are the utilitarian and the deontological ones. In utilitarian theories it is assumed that the goodness or badness of alternative courses of action can be measured with some number, and that acting rightly consists in choosing an alternative with a maximal degree of goodness. According to deontological theories, morality is based on a set of duties or obligations, and acting rightly consists in fulfilling one's duties. Both deontological and (in particular) utilitarian theories come in many variants, and there are also several additional classes of moral theories, such as those based on rights and on contractual relationships.

There is also another type of ethical discourse that starts out from the practical ethical issues arising in various areas of human activities, mostly areas constituted by the activities of a profession. The oldest such area-specific ethical tradition is medical ethics that dates back to antiquity. Some of the issues alluded to in the Hippocratic oath are still topics of importance in today's medical ethics. The engineering profession also has a fairly long tradition of ethical discussions. Codes of ethics for engineers were already written in the early twentieth century (Davis 2001). However, it was only in the 1960s and 1970s that these fields were established as subjects of specialized studies. Several other branches of area-specific ethics got off the ground in the same period, including research ethics, business ethics, and computer ethics. These developments were mostly initiated by members of the respective professions, but beginning in the 1970s moral philosophers have become increasingly involved. In the 1970s, the term "applied ethics" emerged as the established designation of what I have called here "area-specific" discourses on ethics (Beauchamp 2003, p. 1).

In some of these disciplines, the discourse has been considerably expanded when professional ethicists entered the debate. For instance, nonphysicians studying ethical issues related to health and disease have brought up topics that do not concern the professional conduct of physicians. The term "bioethics" is often used to indicate a wider range of topics than those centering on the physician-patient relationship (Reich 1995). Similarly, the ethics of technology has grown out of engineering ethics from which it differs in adding perspectives on technology other than those of engineering. But, in spite of these broadenings beyond professional affairs, the system of "applied ethics" disciplines is still remarkably dominated by a number of professions whose members have felt a need to clarify and take joint responsibility for their professional duties. With few exceptions, area-specific ethics has only risen to importance as a consequence of such professional involvement. (Arguably, animal and environmental ethics are the most prominent exceptions.) In consequence, these disciplines cover only a small fraction of the human activities that have ethical issues in need of investigation and systematic discussion (Hansson 2009). Welfare provision, social insurance, and foreign aid are examples of areas with at most a rudimentary ethical discussion. Among the virtually unchartered territories on the ethical map we also find important subareas of the ethics of technology. Rescue services, radiation protection, and traffic safety are among the most prominent of these (see Sandin 2009 and Hansson 2007; 2014a for some inroads into those areas). In the ethics of technology there is no lack of unexplored areas, lying open for pioneering work.

3. IS APPLIED ETHICS THE APPLICATION
OF ETHICAL THEORIES?

What does the term "applied" in "applied ethics" signify? It can be instructively compared to other applied disciplines. In applied mathematics, a mathematical theory is used to solve some problem outside of pure mathematics. The theory itself is not changed or significantly extended in the process of its application (Kopelman 1990). Similarly, applied physics makes extensive use of physical theory but does not aim at contributing to its development. In the same way, applied ethics can be seen as a discipline, or collection of disciplines, in which moral theory is used as a tool to solve moral problems in various practical areas. Some moral philosophers have indeed furthered that approach. Bernard Gert (1982, p. 51) defined applied ethics as "the application of an ethical theory to some particular moral problems or set of problems." The most renowned proponent of this view is Peter Singer, who advocates the use of utilitarian moral theory to determine what is right and wrong in bioethics and other areas of applied ethics. However, most researchers in the various areas of applied ethics, including the ethics of technology, do not seem to concur (Beauchamp 1984; MacIntyre 1984; Pihlström 1999).

There are at least three serious problems with the idea that area-specific ethics should consist in the application of an ethical theory. The first of these is the *theory choice* problem. There are quite a few moral theories around, and despite centuries of discussion moral philosophers have not managed to agree on which of them is right. To put it somewhat bluntly, moral philosophers tend to agree that one of the available moral theories is the one and only, correct theory. However, they do not agree on which that theory is. Therefore, the project of basing practical ethics on moral theory faces essentially the same problem as that of basing it on religion. Proponents of different religions tend to agree that there is one particular religion to which we should turn for guidance on moral and other issues, but they disagree on which that religion is. For applied ethicists, the prevailing disagreement on which is the right moral theory can make the approach of "applying moral theory" seem arbitrary. This is in sharp contrast to applied mathematics and physics, both of which build on thoroughly validated theories that are not subject to serious doubt.

The second problem is the *derivation problem.* For a moral theory to be useful in the intended way for applications, it would have to provide sufficient information for determining what is right and wrong in the various practical cases that applied ethicists are expected to analyze. When we have the facts of a case, it should be possible to combine these facts with the theory in question and derive univocally a determinate answer to our moral questions. However, this type of derivation does not usually work in practice since fundamental moral theories have surprisingly little to say on the problems that are the focus in applied ethics. This has become particularly evident in biomedical ethics. Experience shows that the moral theory a philosopher adheres to has little or no predictive power for her standpoints on concrete bioethical issues (Kymlicka 1993; Heyd 1996). You can for instance find a utilitarian and a deontologist who agree on most of the ethical issues in health care, although they have different underpinnings for their standpoints. Similarly, two adherents of the same moral theory can disagree vehemently on practical moral issues since they apply it in different ways. The reason for this is that moral theories operate on an abstract level, and most practical moral problems cannot be connected in an unequivocal way to principles or standpoints on that level. For instance, deontologists can disagree on what duties we have and how they should be interpreted, and utilitarians can disagree in multifarious ways on the utilities of different outcomes (Hansson 2014b). The upshot is that even if we manage to choose one of the many available moral theories as the basis for applied ethics, that theory will not provide us with clear-cut answers to our ethical questions. This, again, is very different from the application of mathematical or physical theories that are essentially devoid of such ambiguities.

Thirdly, we have the *moral novelty problem*. Ideally, moral theories are thought of as timeless. If there is a unique, correct moral theory, then a sufficiently sagacious ancient thinker should—in principle—have been able to discover it. But the timelessness of moral theories can be put to serious doubt. Developments in human society unceasingly provide us with moral novelties, that is, new problems that cannot be solved with the existing moral theories. Some of the most pressing problems in modern medical ethics, such as brain death and human enhancement, require considerations of issues that had not been covered in previously presented moral theories. The problem of moral novelties is also pervasive in the ethics of technology, due to its strong focus on new and emerging technologies, some of which have aspects that preexisting moral theories do not cover. This can be seen, for instance, from the discussions on information technology, virtual reality, space travel, and biotechnology, all of which refer to issues not foreseen in preexisting moral theories. Here as well we can note a stark contrast to mathematical and physical theory, both of which have a strong claim to timelessness.

Applied ethics is far from the only applied discipline that fails to satisfy the strict definition of application referred to above. Most forms of applied science include the creation of genuinely new theory, for the simple reason that the theories developed in the basic sciences do not suffice for solving the applied problems. This is true, for instance, of applied linguistics and applied psychology. Arguably, application in the strict sense of using a theory as a tool without changing it is only possible if the theory in question is broad and exceptionless enough to cover unaided a whole area of knowledge. Major mathematical and physical theories answer to that description, but they seem to be the exception rather than the rule. As we have seen, a strong case can be made that ethical theory in its current form is not suitable for pure application.

This does not necessarily mean that we should give up the *term* "applied ethics," but we may have to define it differently than what we did above. The word "apply" also has the more general meaning of putting something to use. The ethics of technology is certainly ethics put to use, and the same is true of medical ethics, research ethics, etc. If application is interpreted in this way, as putting to use, then the term "applied ethics" is uncommitted on what role—if any—moral theory should have.

However, before throwing moral theories overboard, we need to consider carefully what we want to put in their place. Academic ethics should be able to provide a systematized account of our well-considered moral judgments and their implications. Moral theories are highly useful to achieve such systematicity. Presumably, we do not wish to be thrown back to just collecting and reporting prevailing moral opinions on the various issues we are studying. If we give up the idea of conducting applied ethics as a straightforward application of moral theory, then we need to find either some other way to use moral theories, or some other means than moral theories to achieve systematicity and cohesion. The next two sections will be devoted to these two approaches.

4. TEMPERED USES OF MORAL THEORIES

At the very minimum, we can use concepts developed in various moral theories as tools in our moral analysis. This will provide us with conceptual tools to express moral issues and standpoints with more precision than by using what is available in everyday language. Terms such as prima facie rights, residual obligations, supererogatory actions, moral luck, and a host of others can be used to describe issues and standpoints more accurately and to characterize the similarities and differences between different cases. This is one of the reasons why studies of moral philosophy are a necessary prerequisite for professional competence in applied ethics.

Stepping up our usage of moral theories, we can employ their central thought patterns as tools in our moral analysis, without assigning absolute precedence to any of these thought patterns (Hansson 2007; 2013). For instance, utilitarianism can be seen as a precisified and exclusivized version of a common thought pattern in colloquial moral reasoning—namely, that of weighing advantages and disadvantages against each other. Even if we do not put such weighings on top of all moral considerations, we have use for important distinctions from utilitarian theory about the conduct of weighings, for instance: Should only material consequences of our options be put on the scale, or should they be joined by nonmaterial effects such as rights infringements? Should the weights be determined by the individual concerned or by uninvolved observers? Should the interests of all persons be included (as required by utilitarianism) or only those of particularly concerned persons (such as patients in medical ethics) (Hansson 2004)? Similarly, deontology systematizes the everyday concept of limits to what one may or may not do, contract theory the everyday notion of adhering to agreements and commitments, and virtue ethics the everyday ideal of developing one's moral character and doing what one's best self would do. Even if we do not give one of these thought patterns priority over all the others, we have much use for their more rigorous versions that have been developed in moral theories.

Moral theories are given an even more important role in the method of searching for a *reflective equilibrium* (Daniels 1996). In a general sense, a reflective equilibrium is a state of mind that is sufficiently thought through so that additional thinking will not lead to any changes in standpoints. It can be described as a stable state or a state in which coherence has been achieved (Goodman 1954). In ethics, the area in which the notion of a reflective equilibrium has been most influential, the focus is on the relationship between our judgments on individual cases and our more general moral standpoints as expressed in moral theories. Proponents of a reflective equilibrium maintain that our specific and general judgments should be adjusted to each other, rather than one of them being given precedence over the other.

The term "reflective equilibrium" was coined by John Rawls (1971), who also put this method to effective use in developing his theory of social justice. In subsequent discussions, distinctions have been made between several variants of reflective equilibria, most importantly between narrow and wide reflective equilibria (Rawls 1974). A narrow reflective equilibrium is achieved when we deliberate on a single case or a small group of (real or hypothetical) cases in relation to a moral theory, arriving through mutual adjustment at a coherent theoretical account of these cases. A wide reflective equilibrium covers our moral beliefs in full generality, and will therefore have to be based on deliberations potentially including all our ethical judgments and principles. In applied ethics, the focus is usually on narrow reflective equilibria.

Unsurprisingly, appeals to reflective equilibria have been criticized by proponents of moral theories, who deny that our intuitive judgments about particular cases should induce adjustments of fundamental moral theory. Reflective equilibria have also been denounced by moral particularists, who dismiss moral theories altogether. Even some philosophers who recognize the pertinence of both particular and general moral judgments have pronounced severe doubts about reflective equilibria. It is unclear what type of coherence is called for among the judgments included in an equilibrium. (Presumably, logical consistency is insufficient, but exactly what more is required?) And even if coherence is achieved, it does not necessarily guarantee moral unassailability. (Even repulsive moral theories such as moral egoism can be coherent; cf. Bass 2006.) It may also be problematic for the method that, as Rawls later recognized, rational persons with access to the same information may arrive at different reflective equilibria (Rawls 1993). However, in spite of these limitations, many researchers in applied ethics have found the ideal of a reflective equilibrium to be a useful tool for dealing with disaccord between particular judgments and general moral principles.

5. REPLACEMENTS FOR MORAL THEORIES

Another response to the difficulties in using moral theories in area-specific work is to replace them by principles that provide more distinct guidance in the respective areas. This is the approach commonly taken in medical ethics, whose "standard" approach is based on the following four principles:

> *Autonomy*: "Personal autonomy is, at a minimum, self-rule that is free from both controlling interferences by others and from limitations, such as inadequate understanding, that prevent a meaningful choice."
> *Non-maleficence*: "The principle of nonmaleficence asserts an obligation not to inflict harm on others."
> *Beneficence*: "Morality requires not only that we treat persons autonomously and refrain from harming them, but also that we contribute to their welfare."
> *Justice* is "fair, equitable, and appropriate treatment in light of what is due or owed to persons." (Beauchamp and Childress 2001, pp. 58, 113, 165, 226)

Various practices and rules in medical ethics can be justified by these four principles. For instance, the requirement of the patient's informed consent for medical interventions is based on the principle of autonomy, and the requirement to offer treatment to all in need is based on the principle of justice. These principles form the basis of the ethical education of most physicians and other health-care personnel, and they are continuously referred to in ethical committees around the globe. The term "principlism" was introduced by Clouser and Gert (1990) to denote the ethical discourse that is based on them (Beauchamp 1995, p. 186).

The four principles are usually conceived as intermediate between "low-level" particular judgments and "high-level" moral theories such as utilitarianism and deontology. However, the practical employment of the four principles does not hinge on their inclusion in a larger structure that also includes some moral theory. Probably, most users of the principles lack a determinate opinion on which—if any—higher-level criterion they should be combined with.

As should be fairly obvious, there are situations in which the four principles run into conflict. There are no generally accepted guidelines for how to deal with such conflicts. Consequently, principlism differs from moral theories in lacking an all-encompassing mechanism for adjudicating between competing moral arguments. Instead, case-based intuitions about the relative importance of the principles will have to be resorted to. Largely for that reason, principlism tends to be less popular among moral philosophers than among practicing physicians. The following is a forceful expression of that criticism:

> Our general contention is that the so-called "principles" function neither as adequate surrogates for moral theories nor as directives or guides for determining the morally correct action. Rather they are primarily chapter headings for a discussion of some concepts which are often only superficially related to each other. . . . The principles of Rawls and Mill are effective summaries of their theories; they are shorthand for the theories that generated them. However, this is not the case with principlism, because principlism often has two, three, or even four competing "principles" involved in a given case, for example, principles of autonomy, justice, beneficence, and nonmaleficence. This is tantamount to using two, three, or four conflicting moral theories to decide a case. Indeed some of the "principles"—for example, the "principle" of justice—contain within themselves several competing theories. (Clouser and Gert 1990, p. 221)

Some ethicists have wished to apply principlism to the ethics of technology. However, it has not always been realized that—with the possible exception of the ethics of medical technology—this will require extensive reworking of the principles. A major reason for this is that clinical decision making has its focus on an individual patient, whereas decisions on technology often concern large and diverse groups of people who may well have conflicting interests. For instance, the practice of informed consent cannot be transferred from clinical medicine to the context of technological innovation and development, since it would give single individuals veto power to stop projects with large advantages for many others (Hansson 2006). The formulation of principlism for (various forms of) technology remains to be performed. It may very well be a worthwhile undertaking.

6. IMPARTIAL ANALYSIS OR ETHICAL ACTIVISM?

It is part of the ethos of science, and academic research in general, that investigations should aim at finding out what is, rather than postulating what ought to be. According to Robert K. Merton's classic description of the value base of science, scientists are supposed to engage in an impersonal and disinterested search for the truth, and academic organizations should embody a form of organized skepticism that rectifies individual shortcomings in this respect (Merton [1942] 1973). For our present purposes we can leave it as an open question whether this ideal is desirable and feasible in other disciplines.

Ethics is different since its subject matter consists of normative standpoints and their underpinnings. We cannot avoid talking about normative issues. However, this does not license us to present our own ethical standpoints as truths that every rational person must subscribe to.

Statements made in ethics can be divided into four major categories:

Type 1: Empirical statements about nonnormative matter.

Type 2: Empirical statements about normative standpoints (such as psychological, sociological and historical reports about people's normative attitudes).

Type 3: Analytical statements about normative standpoints (such as assertions about their implications and how they relate to other such standpoints).

Type 4: Advocacy of normative statements.

Statements of type 1 are important in ethics, since our ethical standpoints in concrete issues depend crucially on our factual beliefs about the world. For instance, in order to discuss the ethical aspects of climate policies we need to have a solid basis in climate science. Although it is not a task for ethicists to determine the validity of such statements, it is up to ethicists to summarize and present them in ways that clarify their ethical implications. Statements of type 2 are also important since many forms of ethical reasoning require adjustments to the standpoints of others. However, although statements of types 1 and 2 have important roles in ethics, they draw primarily on other competences than those of ethicists.

In contrast, statements of type 3 appertain to the core competences of ethicists. As ethicists we can identify normative issues and separate them out from complexes that have both normative and nonnormative components. We can dig out hidden assumptions and nonobvious implications, and we can point out alternative standpoints and clarify the differences. All of this can have an impact on the ethical judgments of those who take our counsel, but it can nevertheless be performed in the traditional academic spirit of striving to be as fair as possible to all standpoints and trying to identify one's own biases and discuss them openly.

Statements of type 4 are different. When advocating normative standpoints we transcend the traditional limits of scholarship. Obviously there is nothing wrong with advocacy or activism in ethical issues, but in some circumstances it can reduce the credibility and therefore, also the impact of scholarly work that is reported in the same text or presentation. A common countermeasure is to clearly distinguish between what one says as a scholar, striving to be impartial between different standpoints, and as a proponent of one of these standpoints.

However, there are two categories of normative statements that can usually be made without reservations. One is the category of uncontroversial ethical statements. When assuming that infanticide, rape, or discrimination is morally wrong, we need not signal that we are making normative statements; these are assumptions that we can expect to be shared by all reasonable discussants. (This approach to uncontroversial norms is paralleled in other academic disciplines. Legal scholars usually take adherence to the rule of law for granted, and political scientists tend to do the same with human rights and basic democratic principles.)

The other exception is normative statements that follow from the consensus view in an area with well-established ethical canons. There are two such areas, namely, medical ethics and research ethics. For instance, we can without hesitation say that it is unethical to administer a drug surreptitiously in a mentally competent person's food, or to expose an unprepared research subject to an incident that makes her fear for her life. In a professional ethics context, the proviso "according to the consensus in medical/research ethics" is mostly self-evident and therefore superfluous.

As ethicists we have a valid claim to expertise in norm-related issues of type 3, that is, analytical issues concerning norms. In contrast, we have no such claim in issues of type 4, that is, the actual choice of a normative standpoint. However, we have the same right as everyone else to express our opinions in those issues. We should feel perfectly free to do so, but it is a matter of professional responsibility never to profess an expertise that we do not possess.

REFERENCES

Bass, Robert H. (2006) "Egoism versus Rights," *Journal of Ayn Rand Studies* 7:329–49.

Beauchamp, Tom L. (1984) "On Eliminating the Distinction between Applied Ethics and Ethical Theory," *Monist* 67:514–31.

Beauchamp, Tom L. (1995) "Principlism and its Alleged Competitors," *Kennedy Institute of Ethics Journal* 5(3):181–98.

Beauchamp, Tom L. (2003) "The Nature of Applied Ethics," pp. 1–16 in R. G. Frey and Christopher Heath Wellman, *A Companion to Applied Ethics*. Malden: Blackwell.

Beauchamp, Tom L., and James F. Childress (2001) *Principles of Biomedical Ethics*, 5th ed. New York: Oxford University Press.

Clouser, K. Danner, and Bernard Gert (1990) "A Critique of Principlism," *Journal of Medicine and Philosophy* 15:219–36.

Daniels, Norman (1996) *Justice and Justification: Reflective Equilibrium in Theory and Practice*. Cambridge: Cambridge University Press.

Davis, Michael (2001) "Three Myths about Codes of Engineering Ethics," *IEEE Technology and Society Magazine* 20(3):8–14 and 22.

Gert, Bernard (1982) "Licensing Professions: Preliminary Considerations," *Business and Professional Ethics Journal* 1(4):51–60.

Goodman, Nelson (1954) *Fact, Fiction and Forecast*. London: Athlone Press.

Hansson, Sven Ove (2004) "Weighing Risks and Benefits," *Topoi* 23:145–52.

Hansson, Sven Ove (2006) "Informed Consent Out of Context," *Journal of Business Ethics* 63:149–54.

Hansson, Sven Ove (2007) "Ethics and Radiation Protection," *Journal of Radiological Protection* 27:147–56.

Hansson, Sven Ove (2009) "Ethics Beyond Application," pp. 19–28 in T. Takala, P. Herissone-Kelly, and S. Holm (eds.), *Cutting Through the Surface: Philosophical Approaches to Bioethics*. Amsterdam: Rodopi.

Hansson, Sven Ove (2013) "Moral Thinking and Radiation Protection," pp. 33–52 in Deborah Oughton and Sven Ove Hansson (eds.), *Social and Ethical Aspects of Radiation Risk Management*. Elsevier Science.

Hansson, Sven Ove (2014a) "Making Road Traffic Safer: Reply to Ori," *Philosophical Papers* 43:365–75.

Hansson, Sven Ove (2014b) "The Moral Oracle's Test," *Ethical Theory and Moral Practice* 17:643–51.

Hansson, Sven Ove (2015) "Science and technology: What they are and why their relation matters," pp. 11–23 in Sven Ove Hansson (ed.), *The Role of Technology in Science: Philosophical Perspectives*. Dordrecht: Springer.

Heyd, David (1996) "Experimenting with Embryos: Can Philosophy Help?" *Bioethics* 10:292–309.

Kopelman, Loretta (1990) "What is Applied About 'Applied' Philosophy?" *Journal of Medicine and Philosophy* 15:199–218.

Kymlicka, Will (1993) "Moral Philosophy and Public Policy: The Case of the New Reproductive Technologies," *Bioethics* 7:1–26.

MacIntyre, Alasdair (1984) "Does Applied Ethics Rest on a Mistake?" *Monist* 67:498–513.

Mertens, Joost (2002) "Technology as the Science of the Industrial Arts: Louis-Sébastien Lenormand (1757–1837) and the Popularization of Technology," *History and Technology* 18:203–31.

Merton, R. K. ([1942] 1973) "Science and Technology in a Democratic Order," *Journal of Legal and Political Sociology* 1: 115–26, 1942. Reprinted as "The Normative Structure of Science," pp. 267–78 in Robert K. Merton, *The Sociology of Science: Theoretical and Empirical Investigations*. Chicago: University of Chicago Press.

Peckham, S. F. (1898) "The Genesis of Bitumens, as Related to Chemical Geology," *Proceedings of the American Philosophical Society* 37:108–39.

Pihlström, Sami (1999) "Applied Philosophy: Problems and Applications," *International Journal of Applied Philosophy* 13:121–33.

Rawls, John (1971) *A Theory of Justice*. Cambridge, MA: Belknap Press of Harvard University Press.

Rawls, John (1974) "The Independence of Moral Theory," *Proceedings and Addresses of the American Philosophical Association* 48:5–22.

Rawls, John (1993) *Political Liberalism*. New York, NY: Columbia University Press.

Reich, W. T. (1995) "The Word 'Bioethics': The Struggle Over its Earliest Meanings," *Kennedy Institute of Ethics Journal* 5:19–34.

Sandin, Per (2009) "Supreme Emergencies without the Bad Guys," *Philosophia* 37:153–67.

Sebestik, Jan (1983) "The Rise of the Technological Science," *History and Technology* 1:25–43.

Tulley, Ronald Jerome (2008) "Is There Techne in My Logos? On the Origins and Evolution of the Ideographic Term–Technology," *International Journal of Technology, Knowledge and Society* 4:93–104.

Part I

PERSPECTIVES

Chapter 2

Ethics of Sustainability—
An Analytical Approach

Christine Rösch

1. HISTORICAL BACKGROUND

The idea of sustainability emerged gradually as a key concept for environmental and social analytical and decision-making processes. It has its roots in the history of Western ideas about the relation between nature and culture and reflections on the impact of resource use on the availability of natural resources. Two famous documents illustrate the negative influence of past (non-sustainable) utilization practices on forest resources, as well as the needs of future generations for continued use of these resources: John Evelyn's *Silva or a discourse on forest trees* from 1664 and Colbert's *French Forest Ordinance* from 1669. These documents are considered as important starting points in the development of forestry science. Forestry may therefore be considered as the first science that explicitly incorporated concerns about safeguarding finite natural resources for future generations. The concept of sustainability was for the first time explicitly formulated as the "Nachhaltigkeitsprinzip" in the eighteenth-century German forestry literature (Peters and Wiebecke 1983; Rubner 1992).

The term *sustainability* (German: *Nachhaltigkeit*) was coined by the Royal Saxon chief mining official Hans Carl von Carlowitz in 1713 in the face of a cross-regional wood shortage that had been precipitated by the mining and refining of iron ore. In his fundamental work on forestry, "Sylvicultura oeconomica oder Haußwirthliche Nachricht und Naturmäßige Anweisung zur wilden Baum-Zucht," Carlowitz is calling for forests to be exploited in a "consistent, lasting and sustainable way, as man cannot act against nature" (von Carlowitz 1713). In 1804, Georg Ludwig Hartig, appointed privy counsellor and chief inspector of forests in Berlin, further developed this term to ensure that forest resources are still available for future generations as follows: "Every wise forest director has to have evaluated the forest stands without losing time, to utilize them to the greatest possible extent, but still in a way that future generations will have at least as much benefit from as the living generation" (Mantel 1966). Since that time, the concept of sustainability has been elaborated in forestry as the principle of sustained yield. Although the concept of sustainability has for a long time been one of the central principles in forestry, up to the present forestry scientists have pondered upon the precise meaning and operational definition of the concept.

In its modern form—decisively shaped by the report from the so-called UN Brundtland Commission in 1987 (United Nations Group World Commission on Environment and Development)—the definition of sustainable development is a broad ethical principle with three key components. First, it comprises the ethical principle that the needs of the present generations have to be met without compromising the ability of future generations to meet their own needs. This statement makes an explicit commitment to future generations. It clarifies that the quality of today's living should not be at the expense of the future generation's quality of life (generational equity). Second, the definition of sustainable development includes the normative principle of global justice. This means that here and now, in all parts of the world, a good quality of life should be possible, and that resources should not only be used responsibly, but also be fairly distributed. The requirements of sustainability are not satisfied if some regions live in abundance while others suffer from deficiency. Last but not least, the definition is clearly based on the philosophical approach in environmental ethics that has been associated with anthropocentrism, or the view that protection of the environment should be based primarily (if not exclusively) on benefits that humans derive from utilizing natural resources.

The Brundtland definition amounts to a comprehensive ethical responsibility for people, living today as well as those in the future, to use the resources and the environment so that everybody can experience a good quality of life today and tomorrow. The operational implementation of this sustainability vision is an enormous challenge for society which requires significant changes in thinking, policy, lifestyles, and economy. For the present, it would mean that wealthier, more technologically sophisticated societies would have to contribute materially and through a wide range of assistance programs to increase the wealth of poorer nations, to aid them in developing the capability to provide for the basic needs of their populations. For future generations, it means ensuring the availability of a wide range of resources: natural, mineral, food, clean air and water, genetic diversity, cultural, educational, and numerous others that support a good quality of life. Beyond that it has to be ensured that the environmental impacts of human societies do not threaten the resilience of nature.

The Brundtland definition of sustainable development is widely recognized and referenced. Yet, because of its complexity it remains inherently difficult to apply it in analytical approaches, assessments, and policy consultations. The implementation of sustainable lifestyles is also difficult due to the enormous shifts in thinking and behavior that it requires. In the decade after the Brundtland report, numerous attempts have been made to specify and quantify its general commitments in more precise language that could be used in analytical and decision-making contexts. In the first decade of the new millennium, a highly technical debate over indicators and specification of the Brundtland approach took place. Indicator sets have been developed to specify the Brundtland definition and to monitor and assess progress in sustainable development in various contexts and at different scales.

At the global level, the United Nations Commission on Sustainable Development (CSD) and the Global Reporting Initiative (GRI), an international independent standards organization founded in 1997, are the best-known institutions that have developed sustainability goals and indicators. The CSD, established in 1992, commissioned the development of an indicator set by a group of experts from developing and developed countries and international organizations in 1996. After implementing and extensively testing the CSD indicators, they have been revised in 2001 and 2006. The revised edition comprises 96 indicators, including a subset of 50 core indicators. This set of global indicators is applied to follow up and review the goals and targets of the vision "Transforming our World." The indicators have to be complemented by indicators at the regional and national levels, which will be developed by member states. In 2015, the CSD announced 17 Sustainable Development Goals (SDG) and 169 targets, which are regarded as integrated and indivisible and balance the three dimensions of sustainable development: the economic, social, and environmental. The GRI has developed an indicator-based standard for sustainability reporting in order to enable businesses, governments, and other organizations to measure and understand their most critical impacts on the environment, society, and the economy as well as to communicate their impacts on issues such as climate change, human rights, and corruption.

With the work of the CSD and GRI the meaning of sustainable development has been substantiated and defined at the global level. It is apparent that discrepancies, mismatches, and even contradictions are arising when the SDG are transferred and implemented on the national and regional levels and applied in different contexts. This is related to the varying meaning and definition of sustainability and the differences in existing indicator sets. Hence, if sustainability eludes a more precise definition than the one from the Brundtland report, then the question arises as to how it can serve as a basis for measuring and monitoring sustainability as well as in formulating appropriate recommendations for decision-making processes. There is considerable need for orientation knowledge on how to define sustainable development in a substantial and conclusive way, so that it can guide the transformation of societal systems. To gain practical relevance, some essential criteria have to be fulfilled:

1. a clear object relation, that is, it must be defined what the term applies to and what not, and which are the subjects to which assessments should be ascribed;
2. the power of differentiation, that is, clear and comprehensible differentiations between "sustainable" and "non-sustainable" practices must be possible, and concrete ascriptions of these judgments to societal developments have to be made possible beyond arbitrariness;
3. the possibility to operationalize, that is, the definition has to be substantial enough to define sustainability indicators, to determine target values for them and to allow for empirical "measurements" of sustainability.

The Integrative Sustainability Concept (Kopfmüller et al. 2001) claims to meet these criteria. It provides a theoretically well-founded approach to operationalize the vision of sustainable development and an operable analytical tool for sustainability analyses. The concept has been applied in various research projects (Kopfmüller 2006).

2. THE INTEGRATIVE SUSTAINABILITY CONCEPT

Based on the Brundtland report with its well-known sustainability definition and on essential documents of the sustainability debate, such as the Rio Declaration and the Agenda 21, the starting points of the Integrative Sustainability Concept are not the different dimensions of sustainability, but three constitutive elements (Kopfmüller et al. 2001):

1. inter- and intra-generational justice, equal in weight;
2. the global perspective regarding goals and actions; and
3. an anthropocentric approach with a self-interested obligation of mankind to interact cautiously with nature. This acknowledges that long-term preservation of nature and a healthy, sustainable environment are necessary for the well-being of humans.

The guiding principle of sustainability comprises two objectives of justice: justice between different people of the present generation (intra-generational justice), and justice between people of different generations (intergenerational justice), with equal normative importance being attached to both objectives of justice (WCED 1987). Accordingly, people living today and people living in the future have equal rights to certain basic goods, including ecosystems and their services (e.g., Feinberg 1981; Visser't Hooft 2007). Accepting these normative elements requires a comprehensive and integrative understanding and implementation of sustainable development; in particular because justice is a cross-dimensional issue. The constitutive elements of the Integrative Sustainability Concept are translated into three general sustainability goals:

1. Securing human existence;
2. Maintaining society's productive potential;
3. Preserving society's options for development and action.

These goals are specified by substantial sustainability rules (Table 2.1) forming the core elements of the concept (Kopfmüller et al. 2001). The substantial

Table 2.1   Rules of the Integrative Sustainability Concept (Kopfmüller et al. 2001)

Substantial Rules

Securing human existence	Maintaining society's productive potential	Preserving society's options for development and action
1. Protection of human health	6. Sustainable use of renewable resources	11. Equal access for all to information, education and occupation
2. Addressing basic human needs	7. Sustainable use of non-renewable resources	12. Enabling participation in societal decision-making processes
3. Enabling all people to secure their own livelihood	8. Sustaining ecosystem services	13. Preserving cultural heritage and cultural diversity
4. Equal chances of using nature's capital and ecosystem services	9. Avoiding unacceptable technological risks	14. Conserving nature and landscape as cultural assets
5. Reducing excessive income and wealth inequalities	10. Sustainable development of man-made, human and knowledge capital	15. Maintaining social cohesion

Instrumental Rules

1. Internalization of external social and ecological costs	6. Society's ability to respond
2. Adequate discounting	7. Society's ability of reflexivity
3. Limitation of public debt	8. Society's capability of government
4. Fair international economic framework conditions	9. Society's ability of self-organization
5. Promotion of international cooperation	10. Balance of power between societal actors

rules describe the minimum conditions for sustainable development that need to be assured for all people living in the present as well as those who will live in future generations. Sustainability, at least with respect to environmental concerns, results from a sense that certain activities constitute a threat to human well-being through the destruction of environmental integrity. In addition to these substantial rules, instrumental rules were defined. They describe essential framework conditions to fulfil the substantial rules. More information about the Integrative Sustainability Concept and further explanation of the rules and their derivation can be found in Kopfmüller et al. (2001).

Whereas ideal theories of sustainability and justice do not recognize interdependencies between intra-generational and intergenerational justice, the Integrative Sustainability Concept acknowledges that trade-offs and conflicts between rules can possibly arise in the design and implementation of sustainability policies. Identifying and preventing such conflicts is fundamental to devise an ethically legitimate, politically consistent, and actually effective sustainability policy. In the following sections the rules of the Integrative Sustainability Concept will be explained. The relevance of the rules will be exemplified within the context of the energy system.

2.1 Securing Human Existence

Human health should not be exposed to or put at risk through any harmful influences. Instead, human health has to be protected for instance, by reducing the emission of chemical substances damaging to health, by improving protection against harmful radiation, and by avoiding increasing noise pollution. In poor, developing country households, wood, charcoal, and other solid fuels (mainly agricultural residues and coal) are often burned in open fires or poorly functioning stoves for cooking and heating. Incomplete combustion leads to the release of small particles and other constituents that have been shown to be damaging to human health in the household environment. A WHO risk assessment indicates that solid fuel use (mainly biomass) may be responsible for up to 2.4 million premature deaths each year (Smith et al. 2004). Also, in industrialized countries energy-related emissions of particulate matter, cadmium and mercury are harmful to human's health because the energy system is still a major contributor to total emissions of these substances that cause a wide range of serious health problems. Production and use of energy can have other impacts which can negatively affect human health both in the short and long term. This includes accident hazards in industrial production, but also in everyday use of technology, for example, fatalities caused by motorized road traffic. Besides, there are upstream and downstream health impacts of the energy system which can cause harmful medium- or long-term health effects.

These impacts can be revealed only by comprehensive life cycle assessment (LCA). Of particular note in the field of energy supply are coal accidents and fatalities during mining activities (Burgherr and Hirschberg 2014).

Addressing Basic Human Needs

A minimum level of basic services as well as protection against key life risks must be guaranteed for all members of society. Every person must at least have access to minimum standards of accommodation, food, clothing, and health care, and needs assistance in case of illness or incapacity to work. Access to modern and clean energy is crucial for improving the health and livelihoods of billions of people around the world. Technical infrastructure such as grids is a core requirement for the supply of modern energy (electricity and heat). Still about 1.1 billion people representing 15 percent of the world's population do not have access to electricity, and about 2.9 billion people representing 41 percent of the global population do not have access to non-solid fuels as a primary source for cooking (World Bank 2015). Besides the physical and technical access to energy services, they should be affordable for all households. However, this is not the case even in industrialized countries, where many households lack adequate heating or other energy services in their homes at affordable costs due to rising energy prices, low incomes, and poor energy efficiency (Pye et al. 2015).

Enabling All People to Secure their Own Livelihood

Sustainable development must include the best possible preparation for individuals to plan their lives themselves in an active and productive manner, and to secure an adequate and stable existence by an occupation chosen of their own free will. This rule, formulated according to Sen (1998), is directed at the presuppositions for a self-determined life. Everyone should have the opportunity to secure a decent living for themselves and their family through their own work and without having to rely on welfare payments. Work in this context refers not only to "gainful employment" in the traditional sense, but also to, for example, raising children, household work, and caring for relatives. There is growing evidence linking socioeconomic benefits with access to a reliable and affordable supply of energy, particularly electricity as energy consumption is correlated with the number of jobs for a couple of reasons. Jobs often involve using vehicles or machines that require energy. In addition, people with jobs have the income to buy goods that need energy for their production. Besides, in industrialized countries, the energy sector is an important employer and thus contributes directly to secure human livelihood. Jobs are provided by traditional energy industries, including production, transmission, distribution, and storage as well as low-carbon energy enterprises including renewable energy and nuclear energy and companies established in the energy efficiency sector. By the use of agricultural resources in biogas, bioethanol, or biodiesel plants, jobs in the area of agriculture could be safeguarded, which would also result in a contribution to the creation of added value. For example, in Germany, 128,000 jobs representing 34 percent of all employments in the renewable energy sector are related to bioenergy (FNR 2015). By this, the autonomous self-support of farmers as well as the economic sustainability of rural areas is supported.

Equal Opportunities of Using Nature's Capital and Ecosystem Services

The use of nature's capital and ecosystem services has to be distributed according to principles of fairness and justice (inter- and intra-generationally) and it has to be decided by participatory procedures involving all people affected. Providing the basis for an independent livelihood presupposes, in its turn, that access to the necessary resources is assured. A necessary condition for this purpose is a just distribution of the opportunities for making use of the globally accessible environmental goods (the earth's atmosphere, the oceans, water, biodiversity, etc.) with the fair participation of all concerned. Currently, the opportunities to use nature's capital and ecosystem services are unfairly distributed among industrialized and developing countries. This is especially true for the use of energy resources. The energy consumption per capita differs significantly between industrialized and developing countries because high and rising living standards lead to increasing energy consumption. In 1998 the Swiss Federal Institute of Technology (ETH) proposed the 2000 Watt Society (representing roughly the world average per capita energy consumption) as global guideline for an equal distribution of energy use (Imboden et al. 1999). For Switzerland and other industrialized countries, this means a dramatic reduction in their future energy use to only one-third of their present energy consumption. The use of ecosystem services is also unequally distributed. For example, per capita carbon dioxide emissions from burning of fossil fuels and cement manufacture differ significantly between industrialized and poor, developing countries (The World Bank 2016).

Reducing Excessive Income and Wealth Inequalities

While some people in the world live in abundance, other parts of the population live below the poverty threshold. Wealth is unevenly distributed, especially between developing and industrialized countries. The uneven distribution of goods is at the root of many global as well as national problems. Excessive wealth and income imbalances are to be avoided or reduced because they are the main cause of poverty and social marginalization. In the energy sector as in many other industrialized sectors there are large pay gaps between the technical workforce and managers. For example, Germany's big energy suppliers have in average a relation of 1:79 between the salary of the technical workforce and managers (NRW 2015). This ever-widening pay gap creates disparities between levels of prosperity.

2.2 Maintaining Society's Productive Potential

Renewable resources are a part of the Earth's natural environment and the largest components of its ecosphere. Human well-being depends on the natural resources and services provided by ecosystems, such as energy and food, purification of water, protection from soil erosion, and recreation sites. Yet, humans substantially exploit resources and degrade the world's ecosystems, not only to secure their existence but to live in abundance and prosperity. Renewable natural resources such as water, soil, and forests are neither inexhaustible nor capable of indefinite exploitation but are endangered by nonregulated industrial developments and growth. They must be carefully managed to avoid exceeding the natural world's capacity to replenish them through natural processes. Renewable resources may be more critical to sustainability than finite resources because they could be exploited well beyond their ability to recover, without triggering a significant price increase. Sustainable use of renewable resources means that no more is taken from nature than what nature is able to restore. The energy system requires land to produce conventional (e.g., mining of brown coal) as well as renewable energy (e.g., open space solar energy, wind farms, energy cropping), transmission lines and energy storages. Bioenergy is a classical form of renewable energy that represents with 62 percent the largest share of European Union's renewable energy use in 2012. However, a debate is ongoing about the environmental impacts of bioenergy and of its limitation to levels that can be supplied sustainably (Fern 2015).

Sustainable Use of Nonrenewable Resources

The reserves of proven nonrenewable exhaustible natural resources such as fossil fuel are limited and have to be preserved over time so that future generation can benefit from them. The consumption of nonrenewable resources can be called sustainable, if the available remaining supply of the resource does not decline in the future. This is possible if technological progress leads to an increase in resource efficiency that fully compensates for the reduction of the reserves. As scarcity grows, the price of nonrenewable resources will provide incentives for progress in resource efficiency, reduced consumption, and greater conservation as well as an intensive search for alternatives. Besides, wealth acquired over the short term will give people the ability to substitute new resources including currently unknown technological capabilities in the future. Finally, the economic practice of discounting costs and benefits in the future tends to make impacts less and less significant for present-day decision making, the further into the future they occur (Solow 1993). However, discounting does not contribute to sustainability. If we discount future losses with a high discount rate, then that may lead to a loss in resources that future generations cannot compensate for. In the energy system, the majority of the nonrenewable resources used are fossil and nuclear energy carriers. Their ranges can be extended by improving energy efficiency and productivity as well as a reduction in consumption.

Sustaining Ecosystem Services

Ecosystem services are indispensable for the well-being of all people in all places. They are the benefits that people obtain from ecosystems, including food, natural fibers, a steady supply of clean water, regulation of pests and diseases, medicinal substances, recreation, and protection from natural disasters such as floods. Despite their obvious importance, ecosystem services are in decline in many places around the world. However, some services are increasing in some areas, such as food production in managed ecosystems. The reasons for the ongoing decline are basically human activities. Especially the extraction of natural resources, transport, production and disposal processes, and manifold forms of resource use generate emissions and wastes which are released into the environment. The release of substances—for example, greenhouse gas emissions—can exceed the absorption capacities and endanger the resilience of ecosystems and thereby create serious problems, especially concerning the quality of air, water, biodiversity, and other ecosystem services. The energy system plays a major role in strategies for solving these problems because they can increase resource and energy efficiency and reduce the emissions, for example, by carbon capture and storage.

Avoiding Unacceptable Technological Risks

Technological risks with potentially disastrous impacts for human well-being and the environment have to be avoided. There are three different categories of technological risks: (1) risks with comparatively high occurrence probability where the extent of the potential damage is locally or regionally limited, for example, transport accidents; (2) risks with a low probability of occurrence but a high risk potential for human beings and the environment, for example, a severe nuclear reactor accident; and (3) risks that are fraught with high uncertainty, since neither the possibility of occurrence nor the extent of the damage can currently be sufficiently and adequately estimated, for example, by the release of genetically modified microalgae used for the improved production of biofuels.

Sustainable Development of Man-Made, Human and Knowledge Capital

Future generations should be able to manage and take care of themselves. The man-made, human and knowledge capital needs to be developed in such a way that the production capabilities (e.g., plants, grids, infrastructure, training and research facilities, and competencies) can effectively support sustainable development. This means that the production plants and their fittings (machines, tools) as well as the technical infrastructure should be maintained in an appropriate amount and quality. In addition, skills and knowledge should be sustained. Research investments that add value should be undertaken when appropriate.

2.3 Preserving Society's Options for Development and Action

All members of a society must enjoy equal opportunities to exercise their personal liberty and their political rights. They must also be able to develop their own talents and realize their life ambitions. All should have or receive equal access to basic social necessities, namely, self-confidence and self-respect as well as access to education, information, employment opportunities, political office, and positions. This applies in particular to those social groups hitherto disadvantaged and still suffering disadvantages. Differences in gender, national, or ethnic origin, skin color, culture, age, and sexual orientation should not restrict access to basic social necessities. The availability of energy is often a crucial precondition for being able to have access to information, education, and occupation at all, for example, for having access to information and communication technologies which need energy or mobility which is also impossible without energy. The lack of a regular energy supply in developing countries considerably restricts the access possibilities of people living there. In industrialized countries, substantial obstacles for social equality remain primarily related to equality between gender, ethnicity, and cultural background, and especially regarding employment and income conditions. An example here is the gender pay gap in the energy sector. For the German energy sector as a whole, women's gross hourly earnings are on average significantly below those of men. The gender pay gap is a consequence of structural differences and various inequalities in the labor market such as differences in working patterns, institutional mechanisms, and systems of wage setting. Consequently, the pay gap is linked to a number of legal, social, and economic factors which go far beyond the issue of equal pay for equal work.

Enabling Participation in Social Decision-making Processes

A society may only develop sustainably if the interests and knowledge of its members have some influence on the political opinion-forming process, and if everybody is able to take part in societal decision making. In a modern democracy, this is made possible through the right to vote and to run for public office, freedom of opinion and assembly, and through further forms of civil participation such as citizens' bureaus, citizens' conferences, and Internet platforms for debates on societal issues. In the energy system, transparency, openness of procedures, and access to suitable information as well as enabling institutional structures for deliberation and participation formats tailored to energy issues should be sustained. Modern participation formats and public dialogues are important to reach public consensus on major energy infrastructure projects, such as the expansion of the grid. This makes it possible for everyone to voice their particular concerns at a very early stage, so that their inputs can be fed into the planning process.

Preserving Cultural Heritage and Cultural Diversity

Culture is reflected not only in the historic buildings and other attractions of a country, but also in the diversity of its lifestyles, customs, languages, and other traditions. Cultural diversity and cultural heritage are important sources of creativity, and must therefore be preserved. However, culture is ever-changing and therefore, subject to the tensions between tradition and modernity. Historic buildings are an integral part of our cultural heritage. However, they are energy guzzlers and must be changed and adapted to retain their values and usefulness to people. Heritage preservation and energy efficiency need not be conflicting aims. Many energy efficiency measures even support the preservation of the historic substance. Moisture-related structural damage and mold growth are a frequent problem in historic buildings that are subject to modern usage conditions. Energy efficiency measures such as thermal insulation, improved airtightness, and heat recovery ventilation can stop moisture accumulation that causes structural damage (Changeworks 2016). Energy efficiency measures also improve the usability of historic buildings by enhancing thermal comfort, preventing health risks, and dramatically lowering energy costs. This is a good basis for ensuring that the building will be used and maintained in the future.

Conserving Nature and Landscape as Cultural Assets

We need nature not only to survive but also for our gratification. Our children and grandchildren should also be able to enjoy nature—in keeping with the principle of intergenerational equity. It is necessary to conserve at least those landscapes which are particularly valuable. These include not only untouched (wildlife) landscapes but also some of those shaped by the human hand. Cultural and natural landscapes or parts of landscapes of particular characteristic and beauty have to be conserved. A concept of sustainability only geared toward the significance of resource economics of nature would ignore additional aspects of the "life-enriching significance" of nature. Nature can be a lot more than just an economic resource, for example, it can also be a subject of sensual, contemplative, spiritual, religious, and aesthetic experience. Energy infrastructures can impair recreational values, spiritual, and sensual meanings or aesthetic contemplation potentials of nature and can thus be perceived as negative and have negative effects on tourism and the residents' quality of life. By concentrating energy plants, it can be avoided that the total landscape looks like an asparagus field. In this way, nature and landscape as cultural assets can be maintained.

Maintaining Social Cohesion

A society thrives if its members stand together, if nobody is excluded, and if a common development can take place. Trust and good relationships among people contribute to a peaceful social coexistence. Existing social networks must therefore be strengthened and new ones created to support these elements. With this in mind, members must be open to new and different ways of life. Education plays an important role in encouraging unprejudiced relations. It ensures that social and cultural issues are understood. Overall, a sense of justice and fairness, tolerance, solidarity, and public interest orientation should be strengthened. In order to improve the sustainability of the energy transition process, the issue of social cohesion should be taken systematically into account in the design of transition strategies.

2.4 Instrumental Sustainability Rules

The so-called instrumental sustainability rules define essential framework conditions which need to be achieved to fulfil the substantial sustainability rules (tables 2.2 and 2.3). They concern the economic, societal, and institutional conditions that must be achieved in order to implement sustainable development. Ten instrumental sustainability rules are defined within the framework of the Integrative Sustainability Concept (Kopfmüller et al. 2001). The instrumental rules for sustainable economic conditions refer to the economic issues that need to be solved in order to achieve a sustained a sustainable development (table 2.2).

For example, the limitation of public debts is necessary to provide enough financial leeway for the implementation of sustainable development. In the

Christine Rösch

Table 2.2 Instrumental Rules for Sustainable Economic Conditions

Instrumental rule	Explanation
Internalization of external social and environmental costs	Prices have to reflect the external environmental and social costs arising through the economic process.
Adequate discounting	Neither future nor present generations should be discriminated through discounting.
Limitation of public debts	In order to avoid restricting the state's future, freedom of action, its current consumption expenditures have to be financed, as a matter of principle, by current income.
Fair international economic relations	International economic relations have to be organized in a way that fair participation in the economic process is possible for economic actors of all nations.
Encouragement of international cooperation	The various actors (government, private enterprises, nongovernmental organizations) have to work together in the spirit of global partnership with the aim of establishing the prerequisites for the initiation and realization of sustainable development.

Table 2.3 Instrumental Rules for Sustainable Societal and Institutional Conditions

Instrumental rule	Explanation
Society's ability to respond	Society's ability to react to problems in the natural and human sphere has to be improved by means of the appropriate institutional innovations.
Society's reflexivity	Institutional arrangements have to be developed, which make a reflection of options of societal action possible, which extend beyond the limits of particular problem areas and individual aspects of problems.
Self-management	Society's ability to lead itself in the direction of future development has to be improved.
Self-organization	The potentials of societal actors for self-organization have to be increased.
Balance of power	Processes of opinion formation, negotiation, and decision making have to be organized in a manner which distributes fairly the opportunities of the various actors to express their opinions and to take influence, and makes the procedures employed to this purpose transparent.

majority of countries, public debt is accumulating and is still considered as a major obstacle for macroeconomic stability. In many countries, especially those that have experienced debt crises, public debts cause fears of economic breakdown (Švaljek 2002).

The instrumental rules for societal conditions define the capabilities and qualities of societies and institutions that are required to implement strategies and measures targeting for sustainable development (table 2.3).

The transformation of the energy system and thus the expansion of renewable energies imply deep changes for the overall system, the technologies, and the infrastructure as well as for society. The institutions have to ensure that households can become producers or so-called prosumers or decide which type of energy they like to purchase. This can, for example, be achieved by making it possible for households to produce renewable electricity or to buy renewable electricity from certified green energy suppliers.

2.5 Conflicts of Sustainability Goals

Conflicts between sustainability rules can exist on different levels. First of all, it cannot be excluded that the hypothesis of a simultaneous satisfiability of all rules will be falsified. Undiminished population growth, for instance, could make it impossible. Other conflict potentials can arise when the guiding principles are translated into concrete responsibilities of action for societal actors. In such conflicts, each rule can be valid only within the limits set by the others. The Integrative Sustainability Concept includes a weighing principle by distinguishing between a core scope for each rule which always has to be fulfilled and may not be weighed against other rules, and a rather peripheral scope where weighing is possible. For example, the core scope of the rule "Ensuring satisfaction of basic needs" would be the survival of everyone. The peripheral scope would have to be defined to a certain extent according to particular regional contexts.

The conflict potential included in the sustainability rules shows that even an integrative concept is not free of conflicts. Rather, the integrative nature of sustainability increases the number of relevant trade-offs and conflicts. This approach is able to uncover otherwise hidden conflicts in defining and implementing sustainable development. Thus, conflicts are by no means to be avoided, but rather are at the heart of any activities to make sustainability work. Rational conflict management and deliberation are essential. Sustainable development remains a political and normative notion also in the scientific attempts of clarifying and operationalizing. Therefore, it will not be possible to provide a kind of "algorithm" for sustainability assessments allowing for calculating objectively a single "best solution" to sustainability challenges. What can be done, however, is to clarify the framework for assessments and societal decision making to support transparent, well-informed, and normatively orientated societal processes of deliberation on sustainability.

3. CONCLUSIONS AND OUTLOOK

The integrative approach brings forth the wide spectrum of aspects that have to be considered in comprehensive sustainability assessment. The well-being of humans belonging to present generations plays a crucial role. However, this is not just a matter of satisfying basic needs such as food, health care, and shelter. It's rather a question of ensuring appropriate social conditions that facilitate and encourage a self-reliant and responsible life, equality of all people regardless of their ethnic origin, gender, age, religion, sexual orientation, or disability, reflexive societal decision-making processes, and public participation in decision-making processes. These sustainability criteria are of growing importance to maintain and strengthen social cohesion in modern societies. As a consequence, it has to be recognized that social sciences must be more closely involved in the sustainability analysis and assessment.

Human well-being and the manufacturing of products depend on natural resources and services provided by ecosystems. That is why ecological aspects are highly important to societies. In the integrative approach the role of nature goes far beyond the mere preservation of resources, aiming to cover as many ecosystem services as possible. For example, nature and landscapes that are valuable due to their beauty or cultural assets need to be sustained.

Sustainability assessment in industrialized countries are often narrowed down, reduced to questions of security of supply and compatibility with the environment (i.e., the climate), at the utmost supplemented by aspects of economic development and social acceptance of the products and decisions made. In order to get the whole picture, the sustainability of products and systems has to be measured against a much larger spectrum of criteria and indicators than what is often assumed. Only then can the meaning of sustainable development be adequately substantiated and operationalized. However, the expansion of the assessment framework aggravates the well-known challenges of dealing with trade-offs and conflicts of goals and interests. The interlinkages, interdependencies, synergies, and trade-offs between sustainability criteria increase the demand for methods to cope with multicriteria evaluation and integrated decision making.

The integrative approach presented in this chapter provides a coherent and comprehensive concept of sustainability rules to be considered in assessments, but no systematic quantitative tool to be used. Classical analytical instruments like environmental life cycle assessment (LCA), life cycle costing (LCC), and social life cycle assessment (S-LCA) are techniques with similar methodological frameworks which can be applied to evaluate impacts throughout the entire life cycle of a product or service, but this is by no means sufficient for sustainability assessment of systems. The tools have to be developed to include the full range of sustainability criteria and to assess sociotechnical systems, such as the energy system. Approaches like the life cycle sustainability assessment (LCSA) developed by the United Nations Environment Program (UNEP) have shown that it is possible to combine them into an integrated assessment, but are still in their infancy.

In practice, only a subset of the relevant impacts tend to be taken into account. Reasons for this are, inter alia, that a clearer picture can be created that is easier to communicate and that some impacts are hard to grasp and operationalize, such as land use or acceptance, and are therefore omitted for practicality reasons. Sustainability criteria that cannot be quantified will have to be analyzed with qualitative procedures of deliberation. The Integrative Sustainability Concept introduced in this chapter does not solve these methodological problems, but nevertheless it provides a well-founded conceptual framework for the further development of such methods of assessment on a transparent basis.

REFERENCES

Burgherr, P., & Hirschberg, S. 2014. Comparative Risk Assessment of Severe Accidents in the Energy Sector. *Energy Policy* 74(1), pp. 35–56.

Changeworks 2016. *Energy Heritage: A guide to improving energy efficiency in traditional and historic homes.* http://www.changeworks.org.uk/sites/default/files/Energy_Heritage.pdf.

Feinberg, J. 1981. The Rights of Animals and Unborn Generations. In *Responsibilities to Future Generations.* Edited by E. Partridge. New York: Prometheus Books.

Fern 2015. *Pitfalls and Potentials: The Role of Bioenergy in the EU Climate and Energy Policy Post 2020.* http://www.fern.org/sites/fern.org/files/Biomass%20post%202020%20NGO%20recommendations.pdf.

FNR (Fachagentur für nachwachsende Rohstoffe) 2015. *Basisdaten Bioenergie Deutschland 2014.* https://mediathek.fnr.de/media/downloadable/files/samples/b/a/basisdaten_9x16_2014_web.pdf.

Gee, D., & Greenberg, M. 2002. Asbestos: From 'Magic' to Malevolent Mineral. In Harremoes, P., Gee, D., MacGarvin, M., Stirling, A., Keys, J., Wynne, B., Guedes Vaz, S. (Hg.), *The Precaution-ary Principle in the 20th century: Late Lessons from Early Warnings.* London, pp. 49–63.

Imboden, D., Schlatter, H. P., & Bossert, P. 1999. 2000-Watt-Gesellschaft—Klärung der Begriffe. Zur Zuschrift in SI+A 44, 5.11.1999 (1), (2) und (3). In *Schweitzer Ingenieur und Architekt.* Nr. 48, 3. Dezember 1999, pp. 29–30.

Kopfmüller, J. (ed.) 2006. Ein Konzept auf dem Prüfstand. Das integrative Nachhaltigkeitskonzept in der Forschungspraxis. Berlin.

Kopfmüller, J., Brandl, V., Jörissen, J., Paetau, M., Banse, G., Coenen, R., & Grunwald, A. 2001. Nachhaltige Entwicklung integrativ betrachtet. Konstitutive Elemente, Regeln, Indikatoren. Berlin.

Ludwig, D. 1993. Environmental Sustainability: Magic, Science, and Religion in Natural Resource Management. *Ecological Applications* 3(4), pp. 555–58.

Ludwig, D., Walker, B., & Holling. C. S. 1997. Sustainability, Stability, and Resilience. *Conservation Ecology* [online] 1, p. 7.

Mantel, Kurt, "Hartig, Georg Ludwig" 1966. *Neue Deutsche Biographie* 7, pp. 711–12, http://www.deutsche-biographie.de/pnd118978764.html.

Peter, W., & Wiebecke, C. 1983. Die Nachhaltigkeit als Grundsatz der Forstwirtschaft. *Forstarchiv* 54(5), pp. 172–78.

Pye, S., & Dobbins, A. 2015. Energy Poverty and Vulnerable Consumers in the Energy Sector across the EU: Analysis of Policies and Measures. *Policy Report Insight_E*, pp. 1–77.

Rubner, H. 1992. Early Conceptions of Sustained Yield for Managed Woodlands in Central Europe, pp. 2–8 in Proceedings IUFRO Centennial, Interdivisional and Divisional Sessions of Division 6 and 4, Berlin-Eberswald, Germany.

Sen, A. 1998. Ausgrenzung und Politische Ökonomie. *Zeitschrift für Sozialreform* 44(4–6), pp. 234–47.

Smith, K. R., Mehta, S., & Maeusezahl-Feuz, M. 2004. Indoor Smoke from Household Solid Fuels. In M. Ezzati, A. Lopez, A. Rodgers, S. Vander Hoorn, & C. Murray, eds. *Comparative Quantification of Health Risks: Global and Regional Burden of Disease Due to Selected Major Risk Factors*, pp. 1435–93. Geneva, Switzerland, WHO.

Švaljek, S. 2002. *Public Debt Boundaries: A Review of Theories and Methods of the Assessment of Public Debt Sustainability*. http://hrcak.srce.hr/file/9649.

The World Bank 2015. *Sustainable Energy for All 2015: Progress Toward Sustainable Energy*. Washington, DC: World Bank. © World Bank; International Energy Agency. https://openknowledge.worldbank.org/handle/10986/22148.

The World Bank 2016. *CO2 Emissions (Metric Tons per Capita)*. http://data.worldbank.org/indicator/EN.ATM.CO2E.PC.

Visser't Hooft, H. P. 2007. *Justice to Future Generations and the Environment*. Berlin, NY: Springer.

von Carlowitz, H. C. 1713. Sylvicultura Oeconomica. Hausswirthliche Nachricht und Naturmäßige Anweisung zur Wilden Baum-Zucht. http://www.forstbuch.de/CarlowitzLeseprobe.pdf.

WCED—World Commission on Environment and Development 1987. *Our Common Future*. Oxford: Oxford University Press.

Chapter 3

International Technology Transfer

Anthony I. Akubue

International technology transfer, especially from the developed to developing countries, is often seen as a process that automatically leads to the technological, social, and economic development of recipient Third World countries. For too long now, technology transfer to the Third World has been aggressively pushed by major Western industrial countries, who enjoy almost total monopoly on generating the technology desperately craved or coveted by Third World countries themselves. Both the industrially advanced and Third World countries assume, albeit for motives of different self-interests, that technology transfer from the advanced nations is of paramount importance or essential for Third World endogenous infrastructure development, industrialization, diversified economies, employment creation, poverty alleviation, basic needs fulfillment, growing inequality gap abridgement, and environmental sustainability. There is no doubt that this is possible, but only when Third World countries rid themselves of their current Western-induced understanding of what constitutes technology and aspire to attain the technological mastery needed to use technology to spur their development.

INAPPROPRIATENESS OF WESTERN TECHNOLOGY

It is clear that years of mass acquisition of capital-intensive Western technologies, that is, technologies only compatible with Western conditions, based on the aforementioned assumption have been in most cases without much validation. The appropriateness of such technologies have been frequently questioned over the years. Nonetheless, the practice of relocation of inappropriate Western technological artifacts has proceeded relentlessly in the false hope of achieving different results. I can only point out here that this behavior

35

fits quite well with Albert Einstein's definition of insanity. It is naïve, and even disingenuous, to hold onto the notion that technologies that work well in the West, where they were designed and developed with obvious meticulous attention to the West's peculiar circumstances in mind, would work as well in Third World countries. Western countries have the necessary human resource capital rich with technological, innovative, and absorptive capabilities as generally displayed by their citizens in their entrepreneurial, technical, engineering, manufacturing, construction, architectural, and science-based expertise and undertakings. Consequently, Western countries can and do transform both domestic and foreign acquired raw materials into a variety of manufactured consumer products, capital goods, and spare parts to build and maintain different infrastructural systems that serve their economies' diverse industrial base. It is not surprising—in fact, it is rather obvious—that the absence of these coveted human capabilities and technological systems in Third World countries makes it abundantly clear that what works in the Western industrialized countries would not necessarily work in most Third World countries.

TECHNOLOGY MEANS MORE THAN PHYSICAL OBJECTS

The notion of technology transfer to the Third World as it is currently practiced guarantees increasing wealth for Western countries, as it is based incorrectly on the narrow definition of technology as a physical object or artifact. Most people know that the very aspect of technology that is embodied in people is what enabled the development of object-embodied forms of technology, including machines of various types and uses, equipment for various operations, industrial structures, instruments, and tools. This limited view of technology that leaves out technological and scientific knowledge, ideas, expertise, skills, attitude, understanding, etc., has contributed enormously to the dependency of Third World countries on the Western world. Third World countries are handicapped because most of them lack the indigenous innovative and technological capability to create machines, set up their own production processes, and extract and transform their plentiful supply of raw materials into manufactured products independent of Western presence and assistance. This limited availability of local know-how is also preventing many Third World countries from transforming their great endowment of raw material into durable products needed to set up necessary infrastructure that supports industrialization. For example, the extraction of iron ore, which many Third World countries have in abundance, the process of iron smelting, the production of steel, the manufacture of steel rails and related parts with which to construct railroad tracks are mostly accomplished through Western and/or Chinese operatives. They do not have the skills to construct their own railroad tracks, not to talk about having the capability of manufacturing the train itself. Some examples of failed projects in the Third World based on the transfer of Western technology will be presented later in the chapter.

THE FOCUS OF THIS CHAPTER

This chapter discusses issues limiting industrialization and why technology transfer as currently practiced has done little or nothing to promote sustainable technological, social, and economic development in most Third World countries. It addresses the role that colonialism and neocolonialism have played and are still playing in limiting the ability of most Third World countries to utilize technology to independently raise the level of their development. It delves into some of the tactics used by the Western industrialized countries to keep Third World countries from achieving self-reliance and endogenous technological, social, and economic development. The chapter also presents a definition of technology in the hope of providing a better understanding of the process of technology transfer that leads to indigenous creation and application of technology to spur self-sustained socioeconomic development in recipient Third World countries. The necessity for a definition of technology that delineates its composition is to direct attention to the current misleading conceptualization and practice of technology transfer. The chapter also points out that while colonialism by European powers discouraged domestic technological development in the colonies, neocolonialism by Western advanced nations has kept this colonial legacy alive long after the colonies gained their independence as nation-states. Finally, the issue of technology assessment (TA) conducted in the West, which does not take into consideration the appropriateness of Western technology in Third World countries, is addressed as well.

ABOUT TECHNOLOGY AND ITS TRANSFER
TO THE THIRD WORLD

Much has been written about technology transfer to the Third World for socioeconomic development. Unfortunately, much of what has been promoted as technology transfer to the Third World has been mostly the sale and relocation there of only the physical or material forms of technology. Technology entails, but is not synonymous with machines, equipment, plants, tools, or instruments. The purchase and relocation of the physical version of technology, what erroneously is termed technology transfer, does not involve the active capacity transfer that would bring about the development of indigenous technological capability in the human capital of the Third World. Emmanuel (1982) contends that the relocation of a machine from the environment where and for which it was created to a new environment "rather constitutes a substitute for the transfer of the technology that would have been necessary in order to produce it locally, and is a sort of non-transfer" (p. 22). He was referring to the knowledge that made the development of the machine possible. In other words, the purchase of a machine or equipment by a Third World country neither bestows upon the citizens of the country the scientific and technological knowledge essential to its domestic reproduction, nor the ability to incorporate it in efficient production processes. This point underlies the statement by Jequier (1976) on the importation of object-embodied technologies:

> The symbols of modernity, in the form of steel mills, chemical plants, automobile factories or squadrons of military aircrafts can be purchased on the international markets, but development is a complex social process, which rests in large part upon the internal innovative capabilities of a society. Imports of foreign ideas, values and technologies have a major part to play, but few societies in history have developed exclusively on the basis of such imports. (p. 16)

The development of indigenous technological capability would stimulate local production of capital goods, technology, and continued innovation for self-reliance, self-sustained development, and make Third World countries less dependent in their relationship with the industrial countries. Additionally, its acquisition will enable Third World countries to establish the imperative support systems that technological artifacts require to function. Indigenous technological capability affords a country the absorptive capacity to assimilate, adapt, modify, and generate technology domestically. Capacity technology transfer is the class of technology transfer that enables a Third World country to build its indigenous technological capability, develop self-reliance, and self-sustained socioeconomic development. It is often referred to as the active transfer because capacity transfer allows the recipient to reproduce the knowledge and change it, adapting it to different conditions (Aharoni, 1991). Capacity transfer develops the human capital and technological capability of the recipient Third World country or firm. Among the attributes of a society that has acquired indigenous technological capability are: an understanding of its technological needs; an effective policy on technology and its acquisition; effective global scanning and search procedures for identifying and selecting the most beneficial technology and suppliers; the ability to evaluate the appropriateness of the technology to be imported; a strong bargaining or negotiating expertise needed for technological acquisitions; technical and organizational skills to use imported technology; the ability to adapt imported technology to local conditions; the availability of requisite infrastructure and raw materials; and the capacity to solve its technological and development problems using its resources. These attributes are the basis for the statement by the United Nations (1983) that indigenous technological capability is not an alternative to a successful technology transfer but a necessary condition for it.

THE UNDERMINING ROLE OF EUROPEAN COLONIALISM

It is my observation that this apparent distortion of the real meaning of technology transfer is deliberate and intended to work mostly in favor of the rich and powerful nations. In fact, this perversion of the essence of technology transfer was preceded in time by the formulation and implementation of self-serving policies during European colonialism. These policies were aimed primarily at preventing local development of technological and innovative mastery to drive industrialization and self-sustained socioeconomic development in the colonies.

Take the practice of colonial deindustrialization in the colonies for example. Imperial colonial policies did not favor industrialization in most European colonies. Allowing industrialization to take place in the colonies would have meant enabling the growth of domestic manufacturing and innovative capability locally. The development of such capability in the colonies would have been in direct conflict with the colonial objective of exploitation and fostering vertical integration, in which cheap raw materials produced with cheap labor from the colonies could only be converted into manufactured goods in the metropolitan factories of Europe. It was to carry out this objective, among other things, that the economies of the colonies were purposely structured to rely solely on the provision of cheap raw materials coveted by European factories. Transportation infrastructure, especially railroads, established with cheap—in some instances forced—domestic labor served the interest of the colonizer by facilitating the convergence of raw materials and minerals from locations in the hinterland in urban centers and harbors for export to Europe and European factories. In addition, the colonies served as vital markets for the manufactured products from Europe. In other words, fostering technological, industrial, and socioeconomic development was not the driving force that necessitated European imperial expansion and its accompanying colonization of foreign lands.

Precolonial industries based on indigenous technologies were destroyed with the inception of colonialism. For example, a wide variety of consumer goods made locally with African production processes and feedstock existed before the "Balkanization of Africa." As Settles (1996) pointed out, socioeconomic and technological progress in Africa would have probably been comparatively better than it is today had colonial policies not undermined its industrialization to create a society dependent on manufactured goods from Europe. This motive was accomplished in some cases by direct physical destruction of production facilities, but generally by flooding the colonies with manufactures from Europe, a strategy still in common use in today's Western-imposed globalization.

THE UNDERMINING ROLE OF WESTERN NEOCOLONIALISM

After the European colonies in Africa and Asia joined their Latin American counterparts following their independence as nation-states, certain policies articulated and established by the advanced nations facilitated the transition from colonialism by Europe to neocolonialism by the West. Following the end of the first United Nations Development Decade from 1960 to 1969, Third World countries, who became worse off in terms of deteriorating terms of trade and unfavorably fluctuating commodity prices, went through the United Nations to press for the establishment of a New International Economic Order (NIEO). Majority votes cast by mostly Third World countries at the Special Session of the UN General Assembly in favor of the Charter of Economic Rights and Duties of States on December 12, 1974, approved the establishment of the NIEO (Akubue, 2012). The aim of the NIEO was to initiate "what was considered a fairer distribution of global wealth by negotiating a new set of rules for economic relations in the field of commodities, world finance, industry, trade, and technology transfer" (Welsh and Butorin, 1990, p. 710). Those who either abstained or voted against the measure were the industrialized countries, whose contributions constituted 95 percent of the UN budget (Akubue, 2012). The NIEO was never implemented because the advanced industrial nations were vehemently against it; they insisted on the status quo that was to their advantage.

Meanwhile, these new nations, obviously lacking in economic independence, were surreptitiously saddled with a debt burden they could never hope to completely repay. Third World debt of about $4.08 trillion in 2010 (Wright and Boorse, 2014) owed to the West, left these countries vulnerable and subservient to the West. Consequently, these new nations were left with no other choice but to do as they are told, acquiescing to the dictates of countries such as the United States and Britain.

An instance of this debt-induced vulnerability was when these new nations were coerced into a new world of globalization, the evolution of which was intensified and accelerated by Britain and the United States during the regimes of Prime Minister Margaret Thatcher and President Ronald Reagan in the 1980s. With globalization involving free trade based on comparative advantage, these new countries were not only forced to continue their roles in colonial times as raw material providers, but also pressured by the World Bank and the International Monetary Fund (IMF), through the prescription of premature trade liberalization and privatization, into opening their economies to foreign multinational corporations of developed countries. These two multilateral agencies, with the urging of the United States and the European Union, carried out the implementation of the so-called Washington Consensus: a set of ten broadly stated free market economic policy prescriptions put together in Washington, DC, for implementation mostly in the Third World countries with zero input from them. Joseph Stiglitz, a former World Bank economist, was, and is still, a staunch critic of the Washington Consensus, which enriches the advanced nations, while doing nothing to encourage self-sustained technological and socioeconomic development in the Third World.

TECHNOLOGICAL LEAPFROGGING INVOLVES WESTERN TECHNOLOGY

Lacking indigenous technological capabilities, which kept them from creating wealth by means of domestic capital goods production, Third World countries became heavily dependent on the West for capital goods, technology, Western technical and engineering consultants, and other factors. They were referred to as late comers to development, as countries that did not have to reinvent the wheel but simply acquire capital goods and expert technical personnel from the West to transform themselves into developed countries. This is about leapfrogging, which essentially has to do with bypassing necessary indigenous development and mastery of foundational technical developments in response to foreign pressure to allow the introduction of highly advanced technology. For Third World countries it meant skipping the development of a necessary prerequisite for sustained endogenous technological and socioeconomic capabilities of their citizens, for their citizen, and by their citizens. It is without dispute that in order for technology transfer to be successful the citizens of the recipient country must have various indispensable skills to be able to provide the complementary products or systems that the technology needs to be functional. Leapfrogging involving the import of foreign technologies may work to a certain degree. However, one must not ignore the fact that leapfrogging may work only as long as the foreign creators of the technologies are around to maintain them and to ensure that they continue to work. Technologies for leapfrogging also happen to require their own special infrastructure, too. The reason why technology transfer was often more successful in colonial times than it is today is that the process was coordinated by colonial personnel who ordered technologies in their European country (Kebede and Mulder, 2008). This author recalls a coal-fired power plant built at Oji River in southeastern Nigeria by British colonial authorities to serve their power needs. This plant fell apart a few years later with the departure of the British at independence for lack of skilled citizens and spare parts to maintain it.

The cell phone, which is often cited by the West in support of leapfrogging in the Third World, is not without its associated special infrastructure. Besides, there is also the issue of who owns, controls, maintains, and operates the technological system in Third World countries of which the cell phone itself is only a part. In most cases, the cell phone and its infrastructure are owned and operated by companies located in the developed world. Noting that the leapfrogging involving the cell phone was an exception, Volti (2014) wrote that "more often than not, the successful use of advanced technologies depends on the preparation that comes through involvement with well-established technologies" (p. 84). Even the now technologically advanced countries did not start out with advanced technologies; they evolved historically with simple technologies that corresponded with their level of development and factor endowment. For example, the capital stock of the United States in the late eighteenth century consisted of hand pumps, Franklin stoves, wooden plows, and draft animals (Norwine and Gonzalez, 1988). As "The Economist" (2008) observed:

> It would be great if you could always jump straight to the high-tech solution, as you can with mobile phones. But with technology . . . such short-cuts are rare. Most of the time, to go high-tech, you need to have gone medium-tech first. (p. 2)

Suffice it to say that leapfrogging generally has not done much to enhance the human capital of most Third World countries, nor has it helped them to create and apply technology to serve their own development needs.

However, the purchase of machines, equipment, plants, and other physical forms of technology by the Third World from the West unethically gained acceptance as what constitutes technology transfer. In their eagerness to import technologies from the West, many Third World countries signed contracts out of ignorance that has left them victims of "technological colonialism." In these agreements, the transfer of technology was often linked to the right to build, operate, and maintain the manufacturing plants. As a result, Third World countries neither got much technology transferred to them, nor developed necessary indigenous technological capacity (Haug, 1992). Developed-country multinational corporations now operate out of many

Third World countries, where they have continued the exploitation of cheap raw materials and labor. Products from these foreign multinational corporations are exported to their developed-country markets where they are reaping great profit margins.

INCEPTION OF IMPORT-SUBSTITUTION AND EXPORT-ORIENTED INDUSTRIALIZATION

Strategies for industrialization, articulated solely in the West, were deemed proper for the new countries. These were the strategies of import-substitution industrialization and export-oriented industrialization. It was even suggested that a country could pursue both strategies simultaneously and successfully. With import-substitution industrialization a new Third World country would concentrate on the local manufacture of products it used to import from the West for local consumption. Export-oriented industrialization concerned domestic manufacture of products that meet international market standards for export to other countries, including Western industrialized countries. Of course, these standards were established by the West without input from the new countries. The capital goods, technologies, and technical personnel needed for both trajectories of industrialization all would have to come from the West at prohibitive costs to the Third World. Lack of progress in the pursuit of industrialization was blamed on the countries for maintaining import-substitution industrialization and protectionist policies without transitioning to export-oriented industrialization. Interestingly, disseminating misleading information and blaming the victim by the World Bank and the IMF, both of which work in the interests of the West, became and have continued to be the rule rather than the exception.

Many decades after independence, development continues to elude most Third World countries despite the deluge of artifacts of technology being acquired from the West. Without the required infrastructure in place and the development of indigenous technological capability, these artifacts of technology can be seen littering the landscape of many Third World countries, because they are inappropriate.

What this tells us is that technology transfer is definitely more than the simple act of geographical relocation of products from their source of manufacture in the West to Third World countries. To understand the process of technology transfer one must first of all develop a clear understanding of what is meant by technology, which consists of material and nonmaterial aspects. The physical aspect of technology is the outcome of scientific and general knowledge, skills, ideas, education, training, expertise, experience, entrepreneurship; all of which are aspects of technology embodied in people. To illustrate, the successful economic recovery of both Europe and Japan after World War II, with the assistance of Marshall, Norwegian, and other plans, was called an "economic miracle" by those with a narrow view of technology as just objects such as computers, television, cell phones, or devices commonly referred to as artifacts of technology. The fact is that physical structures or techniques of production represent only the visible (material) character of technology, or metaphorically a tip of the iceberg. The submerged base of the iceberg, or the invisible aspect of technology, including knowledge, skills, and organization, remained intact after the physical industrial structures were smashed to pieces during World War II. It was this invisible form of technology (nonmaterial technology) of which people are the carriers that enabled the countries to rebuild their economies as rapidly as they did after the war. Europe and Japan were already developed and possessed the technological and scientific knowledge base lacking in most Third World countries that enabled them to rebuild quickly with the added assistance of the different plans involving grants. In the absence or limited presence of this aspect of technology in the human capital of Third World countries most of the countries are very likely to remain indefinitely vital sources of wealth for the West. The effort to understand the process of technology transfer, in my opinion, should begin with the meaning of technology. I completely endorse Volti (2014) when he says that "gaining an understanding of the meaning of words is often the beginning of knowledge" (p. 3).

DEFINING TECHNOLOGY AND TECHNOLOGY TRANSFER

From this author's perspective, technology refers to an intellectually based human process that gives rise to the synthesis and accumulation of knowledge from which skills, ideas, processes, techniques, technical devices, and more knowledge are generated to augment human capacity to solve practical problems. Volti (2014) defines technology as "a system created by humans that uses knowledge and organization to produce objects and techniques for the attainment of specific goals" (p. 6). These definitions, and others similar to them, not only present the two aspects of technology, but also disclose that it is the knowledge that people possess that gives rise to technical devices.

The problem with equating technology with physical devices is that so much is often assumed as the given. It is often assumed that if a machine or a technique of production works perfectly well in the country and circumstances in which it was created and nurtured, it should do just fine in any other locale. First, technology does not function in a social vacuum as this line of reasoning seems to suggest; it depends on factors such as the prevailing social relations, physical as well as human infrastructure, and access to raw material.

Artifacts of technology belong to larger technological and social systems, without which they cannot function away from their countries of origin where such technological and social systems are profusely available. Kebede and Mulder (2008) also expressed a similar idea in paraphrasing the statement by the International Environmental Technology Center, Osaka, Japan:

> Beyond "hard" technological characteristics, a lot of factors must be considered which include the total system in which a technology is intended to function, skills to handle the equipment, spare parts of the technology, along with maintenance know-how, organizational and managerial procedures. (p. 85)

Take the automobile for instance. The automobile is an artifact of technology that cannot operate in the absence of auto mechanic workshops, auto parts stores, good roads, oil industry, gas stations, auto body shops, tow truck companies, mechanical engineers, government agencies, etc. Many wells drilled and equipped with water-pumping machines in parts of the Third World by developed-country operatives ceased to function after the foreign operative left, because the natives had neither the skills to reproduce the machines, nor the spare parts to maintain them.

The suggestion is also made that the transfer of technology provides all that Third World countries need for technological, social, and economic development, when they purchase machines and other technology artifacts from the advanced countries. This notion of technology transfer is exaggerated and misleading. It is even false, because several of the elements implied have no basis in reality. As Lall (1982) affirms, it is not true that Third World countries have no problem absorbing these acquired technical means, that these acquisitions do not require adaptations, all companies remain equally efficient, and that firm-specific learning or technical effort is unnecessary and irrelevant. In fact, capital goods such as machines, equipment, and plants embody but do not by themselves constitute all that technology is; these are products or physical objects that anyone with the financial capability can purchase freely on the international market. If indeed the import of such capital goods were all that it took, many Third World countries would be as industrialized today as their counterparts in Europe and North America. A Third World country like Saudi Arabia can be cited as an example to explain this point. With all its oil wealth and billions of dollars in foreign exchange, Saudi Arabia is able to buy state-of-the-art machines and equipment from Europe, North America, and Japan; however, the quality of the country's telephone system, for instance, is not as efficient and reliable across the nation as they are in the West and Japan. This is in part because the country is heavily dependent on foreign workers and companies for whom Saudi Arabia is a continuous source of revenue or income.

Third World countries can never realize their development potential, achieve self-reliance, and become less dependent on the West by purchasing product-embodied forms of technology from the West and retaining Western technical experts to integrate them in production processes, ensure their maintenance and operational continuity. Material transfer that involves just machines, equipment, and chemicals will last as long as the creators of the materials are around. What is needed "is the training of people in skills and technologies to allow people to creatively adapt, innovate and invent new technologies appropriate to their needs and societies" (Pearce, 1992, p. 2). Technology transfer is not about giving a man or woman a fish, but teaching him or her all there is to know about fishing, from developing the fishing paraphernalia, including the making and improving of the fishing rod, the fishing line, the hook, and knowing the spot to fish, and not threatening sustainability.

Technology transfer, among other things, involves "the movement of knowledge, skill, organization, values and capital from the point of generation to the site of adaptation and application" (Mittelman and Pasha, 1997, p. 60). Technology transfer is the useful exchange of ideas and innovations in such a way that allows the receiving country to expand on and utilize the knowledge. A critical test of technology transfers, therefore, is whether they stimulate further innovations by the citizens of the recipient country. For instance, the transmission of information about the invention of gunpowder and some basic gun-like devices in China stimulated the invention of the formidable cannon in Europe. Information about transistor technology from the United States provoked the development of new kinds of consumer products in Japan (Pacey, 1990). This is not happening in most Third World countries to the extent expected despite decades of massive importation of technological artifacts from the industrialized world. As Schumacher (1973) aptly observed, "Development does not start with goods; it starts with people and their education, organization, and discipline; without these three, all resources remain latent, untapped, potential" (p. 168). The primacy of people as the ultimate basis for the wealth of a nation is indisputable. As the active participants in an economy, human beings accumulate capital, exploit natural resources, build social, economic, and political organizations, and affect national development. Capital and natural resources, on the other hand, are passive factors of production that depend on human manipulation to be useful. As Meier (1984) aptly observed, "Clearly, a country which is unable to develop the skills and knowledge of its people and utilize them effectively in the national economy will be unable to develop anything else" (p. 3). Obviously, most Third World countries are not developing the human as well as the physical capital that they need to build and enhance their national stock of capital, which would enable them to take charge of their own development.

Unless all Third World countries develop the indigenous technological capability discussed extensively earlier, most of them are likely to remain the milk cows of advanced industrial nations in perpetuity.

INCLUSIVE AND ETHICAL TECHNOLOGY ASSESSMENT

Western TA is an attempt to find out before any technology is unleashed into that society what secondary and tertiary consequences could occur from its use. Coates (1971) defined this Western-based TA as the "systematic study of the effects on society that may occur when a technology is introduced, extended, or modified, with special emphasis on the impacts that are unintended, indirect, and delayed" (p. 225). The necessity is that TA should become a global imperative insofar as inventions, innovations, and discoveries by scientists, technologists, and engineers are targeted for diffusion to the global community at large and not limited in their use to the community of technocrats alone. Neutrality and objectivity guide ethical TA. Toffler (1970) echoed this sentiment when he wrote:

> We cannot permit technological decisions to be made haphazardly, independently of one another. We cannot permit them to be dictated by short-run economic considerations alone. We cannot permit them to be made in a policy vacuum. And we cannot casually delegate responsibility for such decisions to businesspersons, scientists, engineers, or administrators who are unaware of the profound consequences of their own actions. (pp. 436–37)

However, the Western notion of TA is disproportionately dominated by short-term profit motive, with little or no ethical consideration of its relevance or appropriateness to Third World countries. The Western traditional TA of the 1970s and 1980s was fashioned to serve the interests of Western countries without regard to the interests of the majority of Third World countries. This was affirmed by Palm and Hansson (2006), who stated that these traditional "TA practices . . . are formed by a relatively homogenous social, political, and economic climate," adding that "the interests of non-Western nations are seldom taken into consideration" (2006, p. 544). Any ethically sound evaluation of technology for suitability must involve an interdisciplinary approach and must attend to the interests of non-Western countries. Questions of how the technology intended for transfer will affect Third World countries must be addressed. For instance, will the technology build indigenous technological capacity in the human resource of Third World countries, allowing them to create and apply their own technology? Will the technology perpetuate or minimize the dependence of Third World countries on the developed world? Will the technology create many jobs in very high unemployment rates found in most Third World countries? Will the technology utilize raw materials present in Third World countries? Will the technology pollute or contaminate the soil and water that many in the Third World depend on to make a living? Will the technology promote self-reliance and self-sustained technological and socioeconomic development of Third World countries? Will the technology diminish gender disparity or exacerbate it in Third World countries? Will the technology be affordable enough to reduce the income disparity between the haves and the have-nots? Questions like these, in addition to those that address the circumstances found in Western countries, will go a long way to promote better international relations.

CONCLUDING REMARKS

In conclusion, this chapter has been an attempt to shed some light on the concept of technology as a prerequisite for a better understanding of the process of technology transfer. What has been termed technology transfer has erroneously been based on the conception of technology as technical devices. This interpretation of technology has for many decades ignored the sharing of knowledge, ideas, attitude, and expertise, which are all embodied in people. It is this aspect of technology in most cases that give rise to the technical devices that we mistake for the whole meaning of technology. The limited level of people-embodied technology in Third World countries has continued to foster their dependency on the advanced industrial nations. Before technology can be used as an agent of change to serve the well-being of people and promote their technological and socioeconomic development, they must acquire indigenous technological capability that allows them to shape their own destiny. The developed countries must assume the responsibility of acting in good faith with Third World countries in their quest for self-reliance and partnerships of mutual interdependence.

REFERENCES

Aharoni, Y. (1991). Education and technology transfer: Recipient point of view. In T. Agmon and M. A. Von Glinow (Eds.), *Technology Transfer in International Business* (pp. 79–102). New York, NY: Oxford University Press, Inc.

Akubue, A. I. (2012). *Technological and Socioeconomic Development: A Third World Perspective* (3rd ed.). St. Cloud, MN: Sunray Publishing.

Coates, J. F. (1971, December). Technology assessment: The benefits . . . the costs . . . the consequences. *The Futurist* 5, 225–31.

The Economist (2008, February 7). *The Limits of Leapfrogging.* Retrieved February 26, 2016, from http://www.economist.com/node/10650775.

Emmanuel, A. (1982). *Appropriate or Underdeveloped Technology?* New York: John Wiley & Sons.

Haug, D. M. (1992). The international transfer of technology: Lessens that East Europe can learn from the failed Third World experience. *Harvard Journal of Law and Technology* 5(Spring Issue), 210–40.

Kebede, K. Y., & Mulder, K. F. (2008). Needs assessment and technology assessment: Crucial steps in technology transfer to developing countries. *Revista Internacional Sustenibilidad, Tecnoloia y Humanismo*, #3.

Lall, S. (1992). Technological capabilities and industrialization. *World Development* 20(2), 165–86.

Meier, G. M. (1984). *Emerging from Poverty: The Economics that Really Matters.* New York, NY: Oxford University Press, Inc.

Mittelman, J. H., & Pasha, M. K. (1997). *Out from Under-Development Revisited: Changing Global Structures and Remaking of the Third World.* New York, NY: St. Martin's Press.

Norwine, J. & Gonzalez, A. (1988). Introduction. In J. Norwine and A. Gonzalez (Eds.), *The Third World: States of Mind and Being*, 1–5. London, England: Unwin Hyman, Limited.

Pacey, A. (1990). *Technology in World Civilization: A Thousand-Year History.* Cambridge, MA: The MIT Press.

Palm, E. & Hansson, S. O. (2006, June). The case for ethical technology Assessment (eTA). *Technological Forecasting and Social Chance* 73(5), 543–58.

Pearce, F. (1992, May 9). The hidden cost of technology transfer: The developing world demands economic growth. But that is no excuse for rich industrial nations to transfer technology destined to bring social chaos and environmental ruin. *The New Scientist* 1820, 1–4.

Settles, J. D. (1996). The impact of colonialism on African economic development. *University of Tennessee Honors Thesis Project.* From http://tennessee.edu/utk_chanhonoproj/182.

United Nations (1983). Transnational Corporations in World Development (ST/CTC/46). New York: Author.

Volti, R. (2014). *Society and Technological Change* (7th ed.). New York, NY: Worth Publisher, A Macmillan Higher Education Company.

Toffler, A. (1970). *Future Shock.* New York, NY: Random House, Inc.

Welsh, W. W., & Butorin, P. (Eds.). *Dictionary of Development: Third World Economy, Environment, Society* (Vols. 1–2). New York, NY: Garland Publishing, Inc.

Wright, R. T., & Boorse, D. F. (2014). *Environmental Science: Toward a Sustainable Future* (12th ed.). Upper Saddle River, NJ: Pearson Education, Inc.

Chapter 4

Technology and Distributive Justice

Sven Ove Hansson

The term "distributive justice" refers to the moral qualities of the distribution of advantages and disadvantages among human beings. The word "distribution" is ambiguous in an important sense. It can refer to how something is dealt out through some conscious action, such as when members of a voluntary organization divide up tasks among themselves or when a parliament apportions the tax burden among those eligible to pay taxes in the country. However, it can also refer to how something is dispersed among people, irrespective of how that pattern came about. In the latter sense we can, for instance, refer to the injustice in how abilities and talents are distributed, without necessarily implying that this distribution results from some human act or decision. In discussions on distributive justice, usage vacillates between these two senses of the term.

Furtherance of the morally good has many other aspects than how it is apportioned among people. The total amount of good is of crucial importance, and so are the respect for rights, the fulfillment of obligations, and the promotion of virtues. It is important to keep in mind that distributive justice does not cover everything that is morally important. Sometimes a too narrow-minded focus on distributive justice can make us overlook moral issues that it does not cover. To avoid such omissions, we often need to complement studies of distributive justice with other considerations.

Codes of ethics for engineers have usually not mentioned issues of distributive justice (Baum et al. 1985), but such issues have a prominent role in both academic and popular discussions on technology. There are many connections between technology and distributive justice. Technological resources are among the assets that can be justly or unjustly distributed among people. Perhaps more importantly, technologies sometimes have a more active role, as drivers of justice or injustice.

51

The purpose of this chapter is to introduce concepts and tools for the investigation of how technology-related advantages and disadvantages are distributed. In what follows, the first section makes it clear that technologies are inequitably distributed as a consequence of the way in which social resources are distributed in general. The following two sections are devoted to the special cases when the introduction and development of a technology is a causal factor that thwarts or boosts distributive justice. The remaining three sections provide a brief account of major distinctions and standpoints in the ethical studies of distributive justice, focusing on the three issues among whom the distribution takes place (Section 4), what is distributed (Section 5), and how it is distributed (Section 6).

1. SOCIAL INJUSTICE IN THE DISTRIBUTION OF TECHNOLOGIES

There are huge differences in people's access to technologies, both within countries and even more on an international scale. While some of us can easily afford the latest electronic gadgets, large parts of the world's population still lack the most elementary technologies for everyday life. About 500 million people do not have access to safe drinking water, and about 1,600 million lack adequate sanitation (Cumming et al. 2014). It has been estimated that around 500,000 deaths in diarrhea are caused every year by unhealthy drinking water and about 280,000 by inadequate sanitation (Prüss-Ustün et al. 2014). About 2.8 billion people live in households that cook their food indoors over an open fire or in a simple stove (Bonjour et al. 2013). The resulting indoor air pollution has been estimated to cause around 3.5 million deaths every year, mostly from cancer and cardiovascular diseases (Lim 2012, p. 2238).

Hopefully, no one would even think of blaming the large differences in living conditions on modern stoves, water closets, water purification, or sewage treatment. These are beneficial technologies. There is nothing inherent in them that gives rise to social injustices. Instead, their inequitable distribution in the world is an effect of how resources are in general distributed.

However, other technologies have been portrayed as the causes of inequitable distributions. This applies in particular to expensive new medical technologies that have often been described as taking away resources from more important tasks in health care (Fein 1969). Similar arguments have occasionally been heard about other technologies. For instance, several authors have claimed that the development of nanotechnology will create a "nano divide," that is, a gap between those who have and those who lack access to nanotechnology (Moore 2002, p. 10).

There is little doubt that access to future nanotechnology will be unequally distributed for the same reasons as access to currently available technologies. In fact, this applies to any potential new technology. However, from this it does not follow that the technology itself creates or worsens social injustices. We need to distinguish cases when technologies are inequitably distributed as a manifestation of social injustices from cases when the introduction of a technology causes or worsens social injustices.

It is also important to see the distributive patterns of new technologies in a time perspective longer than the initial period of introduction. Typically, technological products become gradually less expensive, and this often makes them accessible to a much larger audience than those who could afford them from the start. Cars, televisions, computers, and smartphones are examples of technologies that were first only available for a wealthy minority but have increasingly become accessible to larger parts of the world's population. Similarly, many medical interventions that were originally much too expensive for routine health care have successively become less expensive and are now widely used all over the world. This is, for instance, true of transplantations, renal dialysis, and tomographic diagnostic imaging.

2. TECHNOLOGY AS A CAUSE OF SOCIAL INJUSTICE

Unfortunately we still lack a general account of which technologies contribute causally to distributive injustices. In this section, four categories of potentially injustice-creating technologies will be presented. When analyzing the social consequences of a technology, it is useful to check if it belongs to one of these classes, but it is also important to consider whether it might contribute to injustices by some other mechanism.

Technologies creating permanent advantages for a privileged minority. As we saw in the previous section, many technologies that were initially only accessible to a privileged minority have subsequently become available to much larger parts of the world's population. David Hunter (2013) has pointed out that this may not be true of technologies that confer "multi-generational and transferable" advantages to their first users. He mentioned two classes of technologies that may potentially have such effects. The first are genetic enhancements that give rise to advantages that pass on to future generations, potentially giving rise to a genetic superclass. The other are radically life-extending technologies. A resourceful minority that can afford a life-extending technology that is economically inaccessible to everyone else can achieve "such a significant head start in acquiring resources that they cannot be caught up with" (Hunter 2013). The result may be a society in which a longevous minority rules over a population with much shorter lifespans.

Richard Dees (2007) has pointed out that enhancements of cognitive and social abilities could have similar effects. A wealthy, intellectually enhanced minority could gain a strong hold on positions of power in society and pass on these positions to their children, thereby also controlling the distribution of other social advantages. We would "end up with two classes of citizens: the neuroenhanced rich and the normal poor."

Technologies creating permanent disadvantages for underprivileged groups. Conversely, technological choices can create disadvantages for underprivileged groups in society. As shown by Michelfelder et al. (2016) there are many examples of technologies that put women at a disadvantage, including seat belts that are unsafe for pregnant women, artificial hearts that are unsuitable for most women, and health software that neglects women's health issues. The effects of technological development on job demands are particularly important from the viewpoint of social justice. In the transition from industrial to postindustrial occupations, demands of physical strength have decreased significantly on the labor market, but on the other hand, intellectual demands have increased (Goldin 1990, p. 59). This is positive for gender equality, since men have on average more muscular power than women but not more intellectual power. However, the decreasing number of jobs with limited intellectual job demands may lead to increased difficulties on the labor market for individuals with disabilities that affect their mental abilities. This is problem that can to a large extent be coped with, for instance with specific job-creating policies.

Technologies promoting prejudice. Some of the most appalling social injustices take the form of discrimination of people with certain "racial" physical characteristics.[1] Technologies and medical procedures have been developed for removing or reducing such traits, for instance "surgeries to shrink 'Jewish-looking' noses and reshape Asian eyes, and hair straighteners and skin bleaches to make African-Americans appear more 'white'" (Lamkin 2011, p. 186). Reportedly, some cosmetics companies have spent considerable resources on developing technology that turns off or reduces the production of melanin, thereby making it possible for people born dark-skinned to become light-skinned (Obasogie 2007). Matt Lampkin has pointed out that the use and promotion of such technologies can reinforce racist sentiments:

> Allowing wealthy individuals to purchase such services on the market could compound the disadvantage experienced by those who either could not afford such procedures, or who declined to undergo them. Extensive use of such technologies would likely validate and further entrench racist appearance standards, further disadvantaging many of the worst-off members of society. (Lamkin 2011, p. 190)

He concluded that "justice may require limiting access to this type of enhancement because of its potential to increase racial disparities" (pp. 186–87). The same type of problem can arise—or may already have arisen—through other types of cosmetic interventions. Perhaps the clearest example is breast implants. Their availability and active promotion can reinforce oppressive conceptions of female beauty and thereby put pressure on women to undergo operations that are associated with non-negligible medical risks but which confer no medical advantage (Jacobson 1998).

Technological change with an unfair distribution of transition costs. A technological development that is socially beneficial in the long run may nevertheless have negative consequences in the short run. Such transition costs are often unevenly distributed. In particular, technological change affects workers in the industries making the products that are to be replaced. The replacement of occupations and employment opportunities by new ones is a continuous process that can only be understood in a long historical perspective. A large part of the work tasks that people were hired to perform a hundred years ago are no longer in demand, but others have replaced them. Many of these changes have been rather frictionless, but there have also been large layoffs that could not be absorbed by local labor markets. This happened, for instance, when the manufacture of typewriters, mechanical calculators, tape recorders, and telephone switchboards came to an end.

Despite gloomy prophesies, technological development has not led to increased levels of unemployment, but it has undoubtedly cost many workers their jobs. Those affected carry a high cost for technological changes, and their plight must be taken seriously, even if these changes are advantageous for society at large in the long run. The burden of technological transformations need not be carried by those directly affected alone. That burden can be shared by all who benefit from those changes, for instance with various tax-funded policy measures ranging from social welfare programs to subsidized job creation measures.

3. TECHNOLOGY THAT PROMOTES JUSTICE

Just as technologies can in some cases promote injustice, there are other cases in which specific technologies promote justice. Sometimes this happens when a less expensive variant of a useful technology becomes available, so that more people gain access to it. Arguably, the most interesting cases are those in which a new technology effaces or compensates for preexisting differences in living conditions. Oral contraception that became available to women in the 1960s and 1970s is a major example of this. "The pill" provided women with freedoms that had previously been male prerogatives. This had important effects on society, one of which was increased female participation in higher education (Goldin and Katz 2002). A more recent example is the way in which electronic communication evens out geographical disadvantages, for instance, in access to medical expertise:

> Many rural hospitals in the developed world and most hospitals in the developing world do not have the resources or the trained personnel to provide 24 h[ours] in-house intensivist care. Through the use of this new technology patients in all hospitals can receive state-of-the-art care. . . . [Telemedicine in intensive care] holds enormous potential for a fairer distribution of limited healthcare resources. (Nesher and Jotkowitz 2011, p. 656)

Another important way in which technology can promote justice is by making social functions and services accessible to people with various disabilities, who were previously excluded from them. At least since the 1970s, handicap activists have pointed out that handicap should not be seen as a medical problem but rather as a consequence of social exclusion that is often mediated by technology:

> If I lived in a society where being in a wheelchair was no more remarkable than wearing glasses and if the community was completely accepting and accessible, my disability would be an inconvenience and not much more than that. It is society which handicaps me, far more seriously and completely than the fact that I have spina bifida. (Newell 1999, p. 172)

(A disability is an impairment of a bodily or mental function. A handicap is an obstacle that persons with disabilities are subject to in society; hence it is not a property of the person but a relation between a person and her environment.)

We can use the term *enabling technology* as a general designation of technology that alleviates the impact of disease or disability (Hansson 2007). Such technologies can be divided into four categories according to how their impact is distributed between the individual and the surrounding society: therapeutic, compensatory, assistive, and universal technology. *Therapeutic technology* has its focus entirely on the individual and restores or saves the original biological function. *Compensatory technology* replaces (fully or in part) a lost biological function by some external technological device. Some examples of compensatory technology are eyeglasses, hearing aids, speech synthesis systems, walking sticks, crutches, wheelchairs, and orthotic appliances. *Assistive technology* makes it possible for the individual to perform a task or activity despite an (uncompensated) lack of function. Typical examples are knives that require less strength than standard kitchen knives, plates and dishes that do not slide on the table, appliances for dressing, toileting, and bathing, remote controls for doors, and reading machines for the visually impaired.

Universal technology, the fourth and final category, is technology intended for general use, not only for persons with a specific disease or disability. The difference between assistive and (adjusted) universal technology is often social rather than physical. Hence, a ramp that is used to enter a building either walking or in a wheel chair is universal technology; a wheelchair ramp at the back of the building intended only for those who cannot use the stairs at the front is assistive technology.

All these forms of enabling technologies can contribute to social justice. Obviously, from the viewpoint of social inclusion, universal technology is superior to both compensatory and assistive technology. In the ethical analysis of technology it is important to find out whom it includes and whom it excludes. Those excluded can be disabled persons, but they can also be members of other groups. In this analysis, we should ask questions such as:

- Why does the new building have a main entrance that is inaccessible with a wheelchair?
- Why is the parkway so dark that many women do not dare to use it in evenings?
- Why is the tool so heavy that many workers cannot use it?
- Why does the computer program only contain white male characters, so that female and nonwhite players do not feel included?

By systematically asking questions like these, much can be learned about social power relationships and how the access to technologies is distributed in society.

4. JUSTICE AMONG WHOM?

In the remainder of this chapter, conceptual tools for the analysis of distributive justice will be introduced. One section each will be devoted to the three fundamental issues:

- Among whom does the distribution take place?
- What is distributed?
- How is it distributed?

Justice among groups or individuals. The "justice among whom" question can be answered either with reference to groups or individuals. Most of the public discussion concerns *justice among groups*. For instance, women earn on average less than men, certain ethnic groups have on aver-age shorter educations than others, and adherents of some religions have less than proportionate representation in parliament. In a discussion of *justice among individuals*, we refer to the differences between more and less advantaged individuals without paying attention to what groups these individuals belong to. For instance, we may discuss the overall differences in income without paying attention to who the people with high respectively low incomes are.

If the differences among individuals are small, then there is not much scope for differences among groups. But on the other hand it is possible, at least in principle, for a country to have large differences between rich and poor while at the same time men and women, different ethnic groups, religions etc. are about equally represented in the various income classes. For someone who has considerably less resources than most other members of society it may not be much of a consolation that her unfortunate situation does not depend on her membership in one or other disadvantaged group.

But on the other hand, injustices among groups are often particularly vicious and persistent. This is largely because group injustices tend to be closely related to discrimination. By discrimination is meant that people belonging to some particular group(s) receive a worse treatment, or less of some advantage, than others. Discrimination has usually affected women and the members of ethnic, religious, linguistic, disabled, and sexual minori-ties. Historical evidence shows that discriminatory thought patterns tend to become rooted in minds and in cultural traditions, and transferred from generation to generation. Each act of discrimination contributes to establish-ing or perpetuating a social pattern that will give rise to further wrongdo-ings. "All blacks have a chance of being discriminated against in future by a bigot whose racism is learned or reinforced by witnessing a discriminatory action" (Brooks 1983). In addition, since discrimination expresses a negative appraisal of a group, an act of discrimination can be seen as a wrongdoing against all members of that group (Woodruff 1976). It follows from all this that all analyses of distributive justice have to pay close attention to group inequalities, in particular pertaining to groups that are known to be subject to discrimination.

Geographical limitations. Distributional justice is often discussed sepa-rately for each nation or state. This is undoubtedly a legitimate perspective. Decisions affecting social justice, including decisions on taxation, education, health care, and welfare policies, are made for each particular nation, and the citizens of one country do not have much influence on distributional issues in other countries. But in an increasingly globalized economy, distributional issues are often transnational. National taxation decisions are often evaded by individuals and companies who have the capacity to move their assets and transactions to other countries (Slemrod and Weber 2012). National regulations of a service or technology can often be bypassed by inhabitants with sufficient means to obtain it in some other country. For instance, if a country decides to prohibit an enhancement technology or a method for assisted reproduction, then those sufficiently moneyed can often obtain these services in some other country. What was intended as a general prohibition will then in practice become a prohibition only for those with limited economic means (Murphy 2007). With the growth of Internet-based businesses, the effectiveness of national regulations is decreasing in many areas. Consequently, analyses of the distributional effects of such regulations will have to go beyond national borders.

It is a contested issue in political philosophy, whether the notion of distributive justice should be applied on a global or an exclusively national scale. According to what is often called the cosmopolitan view, the world is now so tightly knit by trade and cooperation that considerations of justice have to be extended from a national to an international scope (Beitz 1979; Pogge 2002). Opponents of that view emphasize that justice cannot be effectuated without the power of legitimate coercion that states have over their inhabitants but international organizations do not have (Nagel 2005).

Temporal limitations. Some of the decisions that we make today will have implications in coming decades and centuries. This applies not least to decisions on environmental and climate policies, but also for instance to many decisions on infrastructure and spatial planning. In long-term decisions, not only those living but also future generations will be affected. For policies to be sustainable, future generations should be included in considerations of justice, and their interests should be counted as equal to those of us now living. To achieve this, analysis of social justice will have to be combined with sustainability analysis (Rösch 2016).

5. JUSTICE IN TERMS OF WHAT?

Partial or total distributions. In a *partial* approach to distributive justice, we investigate the distribution of some particular social advantage or disadvantage, for instance, sanitation technology, access to electricity, or exposure to violent crime. In a *total* approach, we decide on a measure of what is good for human beings, and investigate how that measure is distributed.

The total approach has the obvious advantage of providing us with an overall picture of distributive justice. However, some political philosophers maintain that different goods should be distributed according to different principles (Walzer 1983). If the distribution patterns for health care, education, and income should ideally be different, then it is misleading to look for justice in some sort of total distribution that adds up all three of them. Instead, we would have to investigate each of these distributions separately.

Studies in the ethics of technology usually have a partial approach since they focus on particular technology-related goods such as means of transportation or Internet access. However, the interpretation of such partial distributions is often influenced by theories of total distributions. The rest of this section is devoted to some major features of such theories.

Material or mental welfare. The overall good referred to in a total approach is often called "welfare." Unfortunately this is a notoriously ambiguous term. According to one view, a person's welfare is determined by her material conditions, such as access to food, shelter, health care, etc. According to another view, welfare is a matter of the inner, or mental state of the person, such as happiness or satisfaction. Both the material and the mental view of welfare have ardent proponents, but they also both have severe problems.

First, consider a person who has all the material resources anyone can wish, but is still deeply unhappy and frequently on the verge of suicide. It would be strange to claim that this person has a high level of welfare. But on the other hand, consider a person who is happy in spite of living under deplorable material conditions. A claim that she has a high degree of welfare would be equally implausible. In the words of Amartya Sen:

> The battered slave, the broken unemployed, the hopeless destitute, the tamed housewife, may have the courage to desire little, but the fulfilment of those disciplined desires is not a sign of great success and cannot be treated in the same way as the fulfilment of the confident and demanding desires of the better placed. (Sen 1985, p. 11)

In summary, both the material and the mental account of welfare have considerable problems. From a practical point of view the material account has the considerable advantage of being more directly accessible to empirical studies.

Opportunities and luck. It has often been pointed out that if various commodities are distributed to those in need of them, then this could remove incentives to work and to contribute to the common good. A common attempt to solve this problem is to focus on the distribution of opportunities to various advantages rather than on the distribution of these advantages themselves. Proponents of equal opportunity maintain that it is unproblematic if two persons who had equal opportunities end up in under widely different circumstances, provided that each of them decided her- or himself how to use these opportunities.

Critics have maintained that formally equal opportunities may not have the same value for people with different background conditions. For instance, even if all students have the same opportunity to qualify for admission to a university program, doing so will be much easier for students with supportive and resourceful parents. In order for opportunities to be really equal, the argument goes, such differences would have to be compensated for. This would imply much more radical egalitarian policies than what is usually associated with "equal opportunities" (Hansson 2004).

According to another common criticism, when people who had equal opportunities end up in widely different living conditions, this often depends on luck rather than their own choices. Much of the recent discussion on social justice has focused on the extent to which social justice requires that individuals be compensated for bad luck. Ronald Dworkin introduced a highly influential distinction between option luck and brute luck. Option luck is a matter of "whether someone gains or loses through accepting an isolated risk he or she should have anticipated and might have declined." In contrast, brute luck concerns "how risks fall out that are not in that sense deliberate gambles" (Dworkin 1981, p. 293). Being hit by a meteor is a clear case of bad brute luck, and losing money on the stock exchange an equally clear case of bad option luck. It is commonly claimed that social justice requires compensation for bad brute luck but not for bad option luck. However, many cases of bad luck seem to be complex combinations of the two. For instance, the risk of many diseases can be decreased but far from eliminated by individual lifestyle changes. Several attempts have been made to further develop this distinction in ways that are helpful for assessments of distributive justice (Hansson 2016; Lippert-Rasmussen 2014).

Two influential answers to the question "justice in terms of what."
According to John Rawls's theory of justice, a just social distribution consists in a fair distribution of primary social goods. These are "things which it is supposed a rational man wants whatever else he wants," such as rights and liberties, opportunities and powers, income, and wealth (Rawls 1972, p. 92). That they are social goods means that they are under social control and can be distributed through social decisions. Other resources, such as health and intelligence, cannot be moved between people and are therefore not included in the discussion on social distribution. That these goods are primary means that every rational being wants to have more rather than less of them. There are other social goods, such as parachute jumps, that are desired by some but not by others. Rawls's definition implies "an agreement to compare men's situations solely by reference to things which it is assumed they all prefer more of" (ibid., p. 95). Critics have pointed out that Rawls's notion of primary social goods fails to take into account that different people have different needs due to their health and other factors over which they have no influence.

Amartya Sen has proposed a theory of social distribution based on the notions of functionings and capabilities. Functionings are activities like eating or seeing, or states of existence such as being well nourished or free from malaria. A person's capabilities are determined by the functionings that she has the freedom or opportunity to realize. Hence, a fasting person has the capability to be well nourished, whereas a starving person lacks that capability (Sen 1985b). Since there are many different capabilities, they have to be weighed with an index, just as the primary social goods. According to Sen, such an index should give priority to the capabilities that are most important for human well-being, but he has not worked out the details. In practical applications, Martha Nussbaum's list of ten central human capabilities have been much referred to. (Life. Bodily health. Bodily integrity. Senses, imagination, and thought. Emotions. Practical reason. Affiliation. Other species. Play. Control over one's environment.) (Nussbaum 2003)

6. CRITERIA OF JUSTICE

Finally, there are different views on what is the appropriate or ideal distribution pattern for that which is up for distribution. According to an *egalitarian* view, the ideal distribution is one that allocates an equal amount to everyone. Most egalitarians endorse an equal distribution of the satisfaction of needs rather than an equal distribution of resources. Hence they advocate that medical resources be distributed according to need, which implies a highly unequal distribution of medical resources.

According to a *sufficientarian* view, what is important is that everyone has a sufficient amount of the available resources. Once everyone has enough, sufficientarians do not see the need for any further leveling of wealth or other resources.

According to the Rawlsian *difference principle*, redistribution is desirable if it improves the situation of those who are worst off. This view differs from the egalitarian one in emphasizing that if a redistribution from the rich to the poor worsens the positions of the poor, then it should not be performed. (This may occur if the redistribution has negative effects on the economy as a whole.)

According to *desert-based principles*, social goods should be distributed in proportion to what people deserve, based on some criterion such as effort or actual contribution. Some desert-based principles can also be expressed in terms of equality, for instance as equal remuneration per work unit performed.

Two major views on justice deny the need for special consideration of distributive issues. According to the *entitlement view*, justice is essentially backward-looking. In order to determine if individual holdings are just, we need to find out whether or not they resulted from just acquisitions and transfers. The current pattern of distribution can only be just or unjust in consequence of how it came about (Nozick 1974).

According to classical *utilitarianism*, it is the sum of welfare that counts, and the distribution that results in the highest total sum is the best one. If the marginal utility of wealth is rapidly decreasing, then this may lead to conclusions compatible with egalitarianism, but only as a secondary effect of maximizing of the sum. *Prioritarianism* is an adjusted form of utilitarianism, in which one maximizes the sum of weighted welfare, with higher weights being assigned to the lower levels of welfare (Parfit 1997).

NOTE

1. The word "racial" is put within quotes since the division of the human species into races is biologically incorrect. The genetic variation among humans is small and does not follow the dividing lines of the traditional races. There is no biologically defensible way to divide the human species into races or subspecies (contrary to many other species for which subspecies can be delineated) (Templeton 2013; Yudell et al. 2016).

REFERENCES

Baum, Robert J., James B. Weaver, Milton F. Lunch, and Paul T. Durbin (1985) "Access to Engineering Services: Rights and Responsibilities of Professionales and the Public," *Business and Professional Ethics Journal* 4:117–35.

Beitz, Charles R. (1979) *Political Theory and International Relations*. Princeton: Princeton University Press [Revised edition 1999].

Bonjour, Sophie, et al. (2013) "Solid Fuel Use for Household Cooking: Country and Regional Estimates for 1980–2010," *Environmental Health Perspectives* 121.7:784–90.

Brooks, David H. M. (1983) "Why discrimination is especially wrong," *Journal of Value Inquiry* 17:305–11.

Cumming, Oliver, Mark Elliott, Alycia Overbo, and Jamie Bartram (2014) "Does Global Progress on Sanitation Really Lag Behind Water? An Analysis of Global Progress on Community-and Household-level Access to Safe Water and Sanitation," *PloS one* 9.12:e114699.

Dees, Richard H. (2007) "Better Brains, Better Selves? The Ethics of Neuroenhancements," *Kennedy Institute of Ethics Journal* 17:371–95.

Dworkin, Ronald (1981) "What is Equality? Part 2: Equality of Resources," *Philosophy and Public Affairs* 10:283–345.

Fein, Rashi (1969) "Medical Care Needs in the Coming Decade," *Bulletin of the New York Academy of Medicine* 45.3:255–70.

Goldin, Claudia (1990) *The Gender Gap: An Economic History of American Women*. New York: Cambridge University Press.

Goldin, Claudia, and Lawrence F. Katz (2002) "The Power of the Pill: Oral Contraceptives and Women's Career and Marriage Decisions," *Journal of Political Economy* 110:730–70.

Hansson, Sven Ove (2004) "What are Opportunities and Why Should They Be Equal?" *Social Choice and Welfare* 22:305–16.

Hansson, Sven Ove (2007) "The Ethics of Enabling Technology," *Cambridge Quarterly of Healthcare Ethics* 16:257–67.

Hansson, Sven Ove (2016) "The Ethics of Making Patients Responsible," *Cambridge Quarterly of Healthcare Ethics*, in press.

Hunter, David (2013) "How to Object to Radically New Technologies on the Basis of Justice: The Case of Synthetic Biology," *Bioethics* 27:426–34.

Jacobson, Nora (1998) "The Socially Constructed Breast: Breast Implants and the Medical Construction of Need," *American Journal of Public Health* 88:1254–61.

Lamkin, Matt (2011) "Racist Appearance Standards and the Enhancements that Love Them: Norman Daniels and Skin-Lightening Cosmetics," *Bioethics* 25:185–91.

Lim, Stephen S., et al. (2012) "A Comparative Risk Assessment of Burden of Disease and Injury Attributable to 67 Risk Factors and Risk Factor Clusters in 21 Regions, 1990–2010: A Systematic Analysis for the Global Burden of Disease Study 2010," *Lancet* 380:2224–60.

Lippert-Rasmussen, Kasper, "Justice and Bad Luck," *The Stanford Encyclopedia of Philosophy* (Summer 2014 Edition), Edward N. Zalta (ed.), URL: https://plato.stanford.edu/archives/sum2014/entries/justice-bad-luck/.

Michelfelder, Diane, Galit Wellner, and Heather Wiltse (2016) "Designing Differently: Toward a Methodology for an Ethics of Feminist Technology Design," this volume.

Moore, Fiona N. (2002) "Implications of Nanotechnology Applications: Using Genetics as a Lesson," *Health Law Review* 10:9–15.

Murphy, Timothy F. (2007) "Access and Equity: International Standards and Assisted Reproductive Technologies," *Ethics, Law and Moral Philosophy of Reproductive Biomedicine* 2.1:12–18.

Nagel, Thomas (2005) "The Problem of Global Justice," *Philosophy and Public Affairs* 33:113–47.

Nesher, Lior, and Alan Jotkowitz (2011) "Ethical Issues in the Development of Tele-ICUs," *Journal of Medical Ethics* 37:655–57.

Newell, Christopher (1999) "The Social Nature of Disability, Disease and Genetics: A Response to Gillam, Persson, Holtug, Draper and Chadwick," *Journal of Medical Ethics* 25:172–75.

Nozick, Robert (1974) *Anarchy, State, and Utopia*. New York: Basic Books.

Nussbaum, Martha (2003) "Capabilities as Fundamental Entitlements: Sen and Social Justice," *Feminist Economics* 9.2-3:33–59.

Obasogie, Osagie (2007) "Racial Alchemy," *New Scientist* 195.2617:17.

Parfit, Derek (1997) "Equality and Priority," *Ratio* 10(3): 202–21.

Pogge, Thomas (2002) *World Poverty and Human Rights*. Cambridge: Polity Press.

Prüss-Ustün, Annette, et al. (2014) "Burden of Disease from Inadequate Water, Sanitation and Hygiene in Low- and Middle-Income Settings: A Retrospective Analysis of Data from 145 Countries," *Tropical Medicine & International Health* 19:894–905.

Rawls, John (1972) *A Theory of Justice*. Oxford: Oxford University Press.

Rösch, Christine (2016) *Ethics of Sustainability—An Analytical Approach*, this volume.

Sen, Amartya (1985a) *The Standard of Living*. Cambridge: Cambridge University Press.

Sen, Amartya (1985b) "Well-being, Agency and Freedom: The Dewey Lectures 1984," *Journal of Philosophy* 82:169–221.

Slemrod, Joel, and Caroline Weber (2012) "Evidence of the Invisible: Toward a Credibility Revolution in the Empirical Analysis of Tax Evasion and the Informal Economy," *International Tax and Public Finance* 19:25–53.

Templeton, Alan R. (2013) "Biological Races in Humans," *Studies in History and Philosophy of Biological and Biomedical Sciences* 44:262–71.

Walzer, Michael (1983) *Spheres of Justice: A Defense of Pluralism and Equality*. New York: Basic Books.

Woodruff, Paul (1976) "What's Wrong with Discrimination?" *Analysis* 36:158–60.

Yudell, Michael, Dorothy Roberts, Rob DeSalle, and Sarah Tishkoff (2016) "Taking Race Out of Human Genetics," *Science* 351.6273:564–65.

Chapter 5

Phenomenological Approaches to Technological Ethics

Robert Rosenberger

The philosophical tradition of phenomenology approaches philosophical problems by first attempting to deeply describe human experience in depth. The idea is that our commonplace, philosophical, and scientific understandings of the world are preloaded with deeply seated assumptions. A phenomenological approach attempts to "bracket" those assumptions and describe the "phenomenon" itself, that is, the experience itself as it is lived. Even our most basic conceptual distinctions between subjects and objects, mind and body, and users and technologies can be set aside, and it is not necessarily the case that they will be discovered to hold true to experience. A cannon of thinkers in this tradition, including Edmund Husserl, Martin Heidegger, Maurice Merleau-Ponty, Emmanuel Levinas, and Iris Young, among others, have made fundamental contributions to our understanding of epistemology, ontology, and ethics.

In what follows, I review some of the central insights of two contemporary lines of thought from the field of philosophy of technology that develop phenomenological accounts of technological ethics. The first account is called "postphenomenology," which combines insights from phenomenology and American pragmatism to describe our bodily relationships with technology. Postphenomenological insights build on Don Ihde's philosophical corpus, and analyze the always multiple ways that technologies mediate human bodily experience. The second account is Albert Borgmann's ethical assessment of our contemporary technological situation. Borgmann's phenomenologically inspired perspective warns of a large-scale unethical pattern in our relationships with technology, and it provides advice about how to break that pattern.

POSTPHENOMENOLOGICAL ETHICS

The postphenomenological school of thought represents an international and interdisciplinary group of researchers that develop and apply a framework of ideas for describing and analyzing user experience (e.g., Ihde, 2009; Verbeek, 2011; Hasse, 2015; Rosenberger & Verbeek, 2015). This perspective combines ideas about bodily experience and perception from the tradition of classical phenomenology with postmodern commitments to nonfoundationalism and antiessentialism from the American pragmatist tradition. This means that this account attempts to describe the user experience of technology without appealing to a transcendental conception of technology's "essence," or to a foundational understanding of "truth." Instead, this perspective seeks to describe the multiple ways that technologies can be understood to mediate user relations to the world, and the ways that technological practices become differently embedded in different cultural contexts. How does a technology change, shape, enhance, and limit a user's experience? And how is the world shaped, changed, and made what it is through a user's technological experience?

It is in the work of Peter-Paul Verbeek that postphenomenology is most throroughly developed into an ethical perspective (esp. 2011). According to Verbeek, if we understand technologies to mediate human experience of the world, then this mediation should be understood to shape both the users and the world through the mediation process. He writes that "human-world relationships should not be seen as relations between preexisting subjects who perceive and act upon a preexisting world of objects, but rather as sites where both the objectivity of the world and the subjectivity of those who are experiencing it and existing in it are *constituted*" (Verbeek, 2011, 15, emphasis in original). The humans who experience the world through their technologies, and the world which is experienced by those users, are altogether shaped into what they are by that technological mediation.

Since technologies mediate the relationships between humanity and the world, and give shape to both in the process, technological mediation also shapes our ethical situation. Verbeek writes: "By mediating human experiences and practices . . . technologies mediate moral decisions and actions. Technologies help us to phrase moral questions and find answers to them, and they guide our actions in certain directions" (2011, 52). In this view, the framing of an ethical decision is set by our relationships to technology. Thus, no matter which ethical approach you bring to whatever ethical question, it will be important to take careful account of how those questions have been made possible and made particular by the relevant mediating technologies, and to also explore the ways that things could be otherwise. If technologies help to phrase our moral questions, then we must spell out how they are doing so in particular cases. And if they guide our moral actions, then we must dig out and evaluate the ways they do so.

Case #1: Sonography

Verbeek's guiding example is the sonogram, and in particular its use in monitoring pregnancy. He claims that the mediation of the sonogram is what makes contemporary pregnancy into the particular ethical and medically guided decision-making process that it is today (Verbeek, 2008; Verbeek, 2011).

The sonogram transforms the various actors of the pregnancy into what they are, and does so in an ethically non-innocent manner. The fetus is separated and enlarged by the sonographic imaging, and is thus presented as if it is an independent being. The mother herself is correspondingly transformed into the environment within which that independent fetus resides, an environment that can more or less be healthy and hospitable. The entire pregnancy is reshaped into a medical situation, one which falls under the auspices of doctors and their expertise, one which is handled within hospitals at critical junctures, and one in which the fetus is approached as a patient. And the parents are transformed into decision makers. Unavoidable ethical decisions are introduced by this form of mediation concerning whether certain sonographic findings should prompt medical intervention or even termination of the pregnancy.

Verbeek notes that even those who choose to forego sonography are still shaped by the existence of this technology: opting out is itself already shaped as a moral choice. We should add that these dynamics also take on a political dimension, as when antiabortion activists distort fetuses and present them as independent entities, and as already roughly baby-sized, in their rhetorical arguments.

Human-Technology Relations

To further articulate technological mediation on a case by case basis, postphenomenology can be helpful for spelling out the kinds of bodily relationships users develop with their devices. Ihde has formulated an influential quartet of concepts for describing the different relationships that are developed between a technology and a user's bodily experience: embodiment relations; hermeneutic relations; alterity relations; and background relations. These concepts help to articulate how our devices are taken up. Do we operate a device by holding it in our hands? Do we look at the device and read information off it? Do we speak to it and listen for a response? Verbeek has recently provided insightful and provocative additions to this list, expanding it on either end in an attempt to account for proactive technological environments, and for bodily implants.

Embodiment Relations

The theme of "embodiment" has been a central focus of phenomenological thought since the work of Maurice Merleau-Ponty. Ihde builds on Merleau-Ponty's ideas, as well as Martin Heidegger's, to describe the ways that users take up technologies as a part of bodily and perceptual actions. He uses the term "embodiment relations" to refer to "material technologies or artifacts that we *experience as taken into our very bodily experience*" (2009, 42). When a technology is "embodied," the user's bodily awareness is transformed and extended through the device itself. A pair of glasses, to take the default example, mediates a user's experience by transforming her or his entire field of vision; a user does not look directly at the glasses, she or he experiences a transformed world through them.

For one accustomed to wearing the glasses, they become less and less aware of the device itself. The glasses come to take up less and less of a presence within one's awareness. In Ihde's language, the glasses take on a degree of "transparency" (2009, 42). Consider the experience of driving a car. A driver thinks more about the road ahead, and less about the car's interface; more about turning the car, and less about turning the wheel; more about stopping, and less about stomping on the brake. We could also say that the user's overall "field of awareness" is transformed by a device like the glasses, for example setting a boarder of blurriness around the user's entire field of vision, which is soon forgotten about. And in addition, for the accustomed user, glasses usage is deeply "sedimented," fixed within long-developed habits, for example enabling a user to ignore a smudge on the lens (Rosenberger, 2012; Rosenberger, 2014b).

Case #2: Cell Phones and Driver Distraction

Like driving, the act of talking on the phone is another rich example of a human-technology relation that involves well-developed bodily habituation and perceptual training. When the acts of driving and phone usage are performed together, that is, when someone uses the phone while driving, ethical and policy issues arise regarding traffic safety.

Cognitive science has found a preponderance of evidence showing that drivers are significantly impaired by cell phone usage (for a review, see Rosenberger, 2012). A dangerous level of driver distraction is associated with the act of talking on the phone, with texting proving to be the most distracting option. And perhaps most surprising is the reliable finding that handheld and hands-free phone use is associated with the same dangerous level of distraction. I take this to be a paradigmatic example of a complex ethical situation emerging from contemporary advances in interface design.

The phenomenology comes in on the question of explanation: why does phone conversation—handheld and hands-free—cause driving impairment? The vast experimental literature is lush with data, but thin on theory; the scientists are busy with the heroic work of proving the existence of these dangers. But it is possible to infer a general explanation from the language used in many of the articles: cell phone usage requires additional cognitive workload, too much for a driver to safely perform the already demanding task of driving. To put it differently, driver distraction results from our brains' inherently limited abilities to multitask.

I have developed a different interpretation of these data based on the postphenomenological framework reviewed above (Rosenberger, 2012; Rosenberger, 2014b). My suggestion is that cell phone—induced driving impairment is due to the particularities of the user experience of the phone. For one well accustomed to the phone, the device itself may be embodied with a high degree of transparency. But even more, for someone engrossed in conversation (be it verbal or text-based), I suggest that a specific field of awareness develops: the user's field of awareness can become almost entirely occupied by the conversation content and the presence of the interlocutor. For example, we can imagine a person talking on the phone alone in a room who is so engrossed in conversation that they do not even perceive the objects in the room in front of them. The same thing can happen in the car. Despite looking forward at the road, as the driver becomes engrossed in phone conversation, and as their field of awareness becomes mainly composed of that conversation, that driver can come to dangerously fail to perceive the road ahead.

Importantly, this relation to the phone can be deeply sedimented through a lifetime of usage. As such, this field of awareness composed mainly of the conversation (and not of the user's immediate surroundings) can come about in part through a strong force of habit. So despite what may be a driver's strong effort to focus on the road while talking on the phone, she or he can be pulled by habit into distraction, especially when the driving becomes uninteresting or the conversation becomes intense.

This line of theory has lead me, and many of the empirical researchers, to advocate for stricter regulations on using the phone while driving.

Hermeneutic Relations

The term "hermeneutics" refers to the philosophy of language translation and interpretation. Ihde uses the term "hermeneutic relations" to refer to technologies that are used by looking at or otherwise directly perceiving them, and then interpreting their readout. He writes that in the case of hermeneutic relations, "while the engagement remains *active*, the process is more analogous to our *reading and interpreting* actions than to our bodily action" (Ihde, 2009, 43). If a user already knows how to "read" a particular device, then the meaning of that readout may appear all at once to the user in the form of a perceptual gestalt. Such readouts can take any variety of forms, from the material composition of a mercury thermometer, to the audio clicks of a Geiger counter, to the imaged display of a sonogram.

Alterity Relations

The term "alterity" refers to the special experience of Otherness that characterizes our encounters with other people. Ihde uses the term "alterity relations" to refer to technologies with an interface similar to how we interact with another person, or a device that takes on a kind of "quasi-other" presence (Ihde, 2009, 43). With increasingly sophisticated computer interfaces, today we are seeing a proliferation of alterity-style devices, from voice-interactive dashboard GPS systems, to increasingly lifelike customer service answering machines.

Background Relations

With the term "background relations," Ihde describes our relationship to those devices that make up our "unattended-to background." Devices such as the gently humming refrigerator or the automatically adjusting climate control system remain "unthematized and taken for granted" (Ihde, 2009, 43).

Case #3: Computer Interface and Educational Frog Dissection

One topic wide open to phenomenological analysis is the experience of computer interface (e.g., Dreyfus, 2001; Suchman, 2007; Rosenberger, 2009; Wiltse, 2015). What is it like to sit in front of a desktop or laptop computer, or to hold and operate a smartphone or tablet? How can we best characterize the embodiment relations that are established with the keyboard, touchscreen, or mouse? How should we describe the hermeneutic relations that are established with screens, icons, and website interface? We could even ask how we should best interpret the alterity relations established with voice-interactive personal assistant smartphone applications.

Norm Friesen uses phenomenology to analyze computers in the classroom, highlighting their specific advantages and disadvantages, disadvantages in his view often obscured by hype (2011). Of course, educational policy itself is already morally loaded, but there is a specific ethical dimension to Friesen's main example: frog dissection. When compared to the "visceral assault" of the in-class vivisection of an actual frog body, with its smells and spurts and physical resistance, Friesen finds computer-simulated alternatives wanting. He writes, "The manifold sense impressions that assaulted the body in the description of the in-school dissection are either absent or very much muted in this virtual activity" (Friesen, 2011, 91f). And where in-class dissection involves actual cutting and pinning and manipulating, simulated dissection involves the same keystrokes, mouse clicks, and touchscreen swipes as all other computer usage. And he claims that where in-class dissection includes variability and unpredictability, simulated dissection involves only exactly what is prepreprogrammed in.

While Friesen claims to want to avoid coming down for or against frog dissection, his work comes across as an indictment of simulation. This has lead the two of us into debate (Rosenberger, 2011). Although I appreciate Friesen's general critique of classroom computing, I take issue with his preference of the dissection of frog corpses over simulated dissection (and I take his position to be the common one in the United States and Canada). First, while I quite agree with his assessment that computer simulation cannot now, and perhaps cannot ever, reproduce anything like the visceral quality of actually dissecting a dead animal, I challenge the assumption that this is the only or main way that we should evaluate simulation. If we can get past the idea that dissection simulation must mimic corpse dissection, then we may be able to unlock its distinct potential as an educational technology, exploring things impossible with an inert corpse, such as bodily movement, evolution, habitat, cell development, and the animal's distinct tadpole-to-frog life cycle. Second, we should not hold up corpse dissection as if it is an educational ideal, but analyze it as a concrete technology. This helps us to draw out (rather than conceal, I claim, as usual) its ethically fraught status, with samples often captured from the wild, and with disconcerting lessons about the disposability of animal life implied by the procedure. (See the 2011, 15(3) issue of the journal *Techné* for more on this debate.)

Cyborg Relations

In what I see as a sort of testing of the boundaries of Ihde's set of human-technology relations, Verbeek has developed the notion of "cyborg relations" (see Rosenberger and Verbeek, 2015; and his discussion of "cyborg relations" in Verbeek, 2011). It is possible that the notion of embodiment relations cannot fully capture the experience of devices that are implanted into the human body, in what could be called a "fusion relation." It is also possible that the notion of background relations cannot fully capture the experience of technological environments that automatically and actively adjust to their users, in what could be called "immersive relations." In these cases, the very notions of "users" and "technologies" and "the world" and even "usage" are put into question.

Variational Analysis and Cross-Examination

In the postphenomenological perspective, technological mediation is always context dependent and changeable depending on the situation. Don Ihde uses the term "multistability" to refer to the various ways that the same technology can have different meanings in different contexts, and can be taken up by different users for different purposes (2009, 12). But this notion at the same time notes that, due to the concrete material specificity of the device itself, a technology cannot be used to do simply anything. The relations between a user and a given technology will be limited to only some "stabilities" or "variations." (The terms "stabilities" and "variations" are roughly interchangeable in this literature.)

Variational Analysis

Ihde uses the term "variational analysis" to refer to the process of uncovering various stabilities for a multistable technology. A number of things must be taken into consideration, from "the materiality of technology, the bodily techniques of use, and the cultural context of the practice," to "the role of embodiment, now in trained practice, and the appearance of differently structured lifeworlds relative to historical cultures and environments" (2009, 18–19). Through both armchair brainstorming and empirical exploration, postphenomenologists search for the multiple stabilities available for any device, and hold this multistability up against "totalizing" accounts that conceive of technology in only one way. Ihde even portrays his commitment to the multistability of technology as itself an empirical result; through a career of performing variational analysis on many technologies, he claims that "what emerged or 'showed itself' was the complicated structure of multistability" (2009, 12).

Case #4: Driver Distraction Continued

Galit Wellner investigates the history of cell phones, conceiving of each time period of phone development as a different stability of a multistable line of historical advance (2015). With this attunement to the multistability of phones in mind, she has challenged my account of cell phone—induced driver distraction (*Case #2* above). Wellner contends that since technologies always remain multistable, it should be possible to develop a non-distracting stable relation to the phone and the car, perhaps one that involves divided attention. That is, according to Wellner, users can learn to safely use the phone while driving since we are never determined to have only one possible relation to technology. She writes, "Ordinary people regularly split their attention. Pilots do it. Parents do it. Even philosophers do it" (Wellner, 2014, 57). With this possible alternative relation to the phone considered, in which a user becomes trained to effectively divide attention between the phone and the driving, Wellner advocates against laws that restrict phone usage on the road.

We can first note that the cognitive science theory, which understands cell phone driving impairment to result from the brain's inherently limited abilities to multitask, appears to have no room for this sort of new learned stability for which Wellner urges. But as a postphenomenologist myself, I am also committed to the multistability of technology, including the phone and the car. So my account remains open to the possibility that users can develop this alternative divided-attention relationship to these devices. But, in my view, it is essential to remember just how deeply sedimented our normal relationship to the phone can be, set within the context our own individual histories of usage. So I contend that one should not simply decide one day to take up the divided attention relation to the car and assume it will be safe; this process would at least additionally entail unlearning our preexisting relationship with the phone. Considering the subtle yet strong nature of habituation, considering the ways that in-cab infotainment systems and smartphone apps often encourage dangerous hands-free communication, and considering the empirical findings that show us to be unreliable judges of our own level of distraction, I have argued against Wellner's recommendation, and for greater regulation of phone use while driving (Rosenberger, 2014b.) (For more on this debate see the 2014, 18(1–2) issue of *Techné*; and also Aagaard forthcoming.)

Variational Cross-Examination

If variational analysis is the name for the process of brainstorming and otherwise seeking out the various stabilities of a multistable technology, then we can consider what next steps can be followed in postphenomenological methodology. Sometimes we will be satisfied to simply have spelled out a technology's various stabilities—for example, if we are attempting to counter someone's claim that a technology only has one usage or meaning. But when we are engaged in concrete studies of particular cases, we may need something more.

After variational analysis has been performed and a variety of stabilities has been identified, I suggest that we should next cross-analyze those stabilities against one another. It can be productive to see what is revealed about each individual stability in light of its contrasts with others. For example, stabilities can be compared in terms of what usages they afford, and what different ways they might reshape our ethical decision making. They can be contrasted in terms of the different ways they inform experience—for example, what relations they consist of (embodied, hermeneutic, etc.), what aspects grow transparent, and how each composes a user's field of awareness, etc. Stabilities can be contrasted in terms of their particular material configurations, that is, what particular material modifications to the device are necessary to enable each stability. I use the term "variational cross-examination" to refer to this second step of postphenomenological methodology.

These kinds of cross comparisons can be especially useful when there is a "dominant" stability established in practice. If there is a mainstream, entrenched, "normal" stability, then we can learn things about that dominant stability by comparing it with the details of imagined alternatives, or against actual alternative stabilities taken up in practice by marginalized groups.

Peter-Paul Verbeek's analysis of sonography can be reinterpreted in these terms as a description of the dominant stability entrenched within mainstream Western culture (although certainly with differences across countries in the West). Perhaps if the sonographic device itself were to be modified in different ways, or if parents and doctors understood the practice in different ways, then moral decision-making processes would refract differently. If frog dissection computer simulations were differently designed, or if wet lab dissection classroom procedures were conducted differently, then different implicit lessons would be taught in each case about the value of animal life.

It is important to note an epistemological point: when engaging in variational analysis and cross-examination, an appeal is never made to a transcendental essence. That would be inconsistent with postphenomenology's commitments to pragmatic antiessentialism and nonfoundationalism. The basis for discovery about new information about these stabilities is the cross-comparison of these stabilities themselves. This means that, methodologically, as investigators, postphenomenologists must always keep in mind that their studies are performed from a particular subject position; what stabilities you happen to discover and contrast is relevant to what you learn (Rosenberger, 2014a; Rosenberger, forthcoming).

Kyle Powys Whyte develops a related line of thinking (2015). He recommends that postphenomenological investigations should be clear about exactly what kind of object is being analyzed as multistable, or as he calls it, the investigation's "pivot." This kind of reflexivity, in his view, also requires that the postphenomenological investigators must be clear about what sort of expertise they possess, and what sort of interactional expertise must be developed in order to effectively communicate with the relevant user communities.

Case #5: Anti-Homeless Design

One of the ways that phenomenological analysis can contribute to ethical inquiry is by simply drawing out into the open things otherwise obscured by the everydayness of the world. Because so much of perception and action is based in habit, and because so much of our daily lives are couched in "normality," phenomenological insights can be useful for theorizing those normal moments, and exposing the ethical issues obscured within them.

One example is the redesign of our public spaces to systematically push away the homeless. A variety of designs serve this function, including benches set with dividers to deter sleeping, ledges set with spikes to deter sitting, and garbage cans affixed with lids constructed to deter picking. To this list we can add the fences that close spaces to most users. And we can also add the purposeful removal of normal services from entire zones of cities, such as areas absent of seating, or shade, or publicly accessible restrooms. I have argued that it can be productive to conceive of these devices and spaces as multistable. For example, a typical bench is multistable in that it affords both sitting and sleeping stabilities. A bench that has been fit with seat dividers (sometimes in the form of "armrests") can then be understood as one that has been redesigned to close off the sleeping stability.

But since most of these designs do not interrupt the normal everyday usage of the non-homeless, these designs can be difficult to even notice. The phenomenology can thus be helpful for drawing out these ethically and politically fraught issues. This phenomenological contribution is important to the larger argument that can be made that, when combined with the panoply of anti-homeless laws (against camping, loitering, panhandling, etc.), these anti-homeless designs are an unjust and immoral way to approach the problem of homelessness (e.g., Rosenberger, 2014a; Rosenberger in process).

BORGMANN'S DEVICE PARADIGM AND FOCAL THINGS

Albert Borgmann builds on a variety of sources, including phenomenology, to create a distinct ethical perspective on technology, with implications for both design and also our own individual life choices (e.g., Borgmann, 1984; Borgmann, 2000; Borgmann, 2004). He has crafted a perspective that first identifies a large-scale ethical problem that pervades our relationships with technology, our strategies for technology design, and even the basic way we live our lives in the contemporary world. This perspective also provides advice about how to address this problem.

The Device Paradigm

Borgmann's central claim is that today we live our lives within a particular configuration of technology design and life arrangement, a pervasive one, and one with deep ethical implications. In a somewhat Aristotelian vein (and in a line of thought that historically runs through Heidegger), the target of Borgmann's ethical evaluation is not our individual ethical choices; he's not offering an alternative to utilitarianism or deontology or any theory of what makes a given choice good or evil, morally right or wrong. The target of this ethical perspective is our lives overall. What do we each individually want for ourselves? And do our contemporary relationships with technologies help us to live those desired lives, or do they lead us astray? Borgmann's central claim is that the contemporary pattern in our relationships to technology pulls us away from whatever lives we hope for ourselves.

His name for this pattern is the *device paradigm*. Borgmann's claim is that the tendency in both the ways we design and use technologies is to separate two things: what he calls a technology's "commodity," and its "machinery." In this terminology, the "commodity" is the thing that the technology provides to us, and the "machinery" is the mechanism by which that commodity is provided. The trend of the device paradigm is that our devices have made the commodity more and more readily available, and the machinery simultaneously more and more hidden. He writes, "There is a pattern to the abstraction of some valued function or object from its tangible circumstances and to the concealment of the machinery that provides for the free-floating availability of the valued item" (Borgmann, 2000, 420). For example, where a fireplace requires wood to be procured and chopped and for the fire to be tended and stoked, today's central heating unit is hidden from view and requires only a push of a button.

So far, this may sound okay. The ethical problem is that the availability and appeal of the commodities all around us can incline us to lead our lives largely in terms of the consumption of readily available commodities, and not in terms of our larger values. I like to think of it this way: ask yourself what you want for your life for a given day. Keep it abstract. Perhaps you want to be fulfilled, or to have a sense of accomplishment, or adventure. Maybe you want to enjoy good food or contemplate high art. Maybe you want to spend meaningful time with loved ones. Then ask yourself what things your technologies will incline you toward in an actual day. Borgmann's claim is that they tend to lead us away from our values, and instead toward frivolous entertainment (e.g., shallow and passive TV entertainment or wasted time surfing the Internet), context-free experience (riding in place on an Exercycle, rather than through the community or through nature), or reduced interaction with others (mass posts on social media or truncated text messages, instead of genuine communication).

Case #6: The Big Mac

Fast food is a representative example of the device paradigm. Setting aside issues of healthiness, or the wages of workers, Borgmann's point is that fast food is ubiquitous, readily available, convenient, and cheap. So much so that you can pull up to the building in your car and they will hand the already cooked food to you out through a tiny window. The Big Mac is emblematic in it includes the different courses of a traditional meal literally stacked on top of one another and eaten together all at once.

Is it ever morally acceptable, in these particular terms, to eat a Big Mac? Borgmann clarifies, "there are always occasions where a Big Mac, an exercycle, or a television program are unobjectionable and truly helpful answers to human needs . . . it is when we attempt to take the measure of technological life in its normal totality that we are distressed by its shallowness" (1984, 208). Insofar as fast food does not fit the larger values we may want to live our lives by (say, spending time with loved ones, sharing good and meaningful meals), it presents us with a case-in-point example of the logic of the device paradigm; with its ease, its ubiquity, and its ready availability, fast food draws us away from the more complex, more difficult, more inconvenient things that we simultaneously care more deeply about.

Focal Things and Practices

Borgmann's proposed solution to the device paradigm is that we should each decide for ourselves what objects and practices we want in the center of our lives, and then orient the rest of our lives around those things as much as possible. He writes that "such a practice is required to counter technology in its patterned pervasiveness and to guard focal things in their depth and integrity"

(Borgmann, 1984, 210). We must recognize the pattern of the device paradigm, and break it. That is, Borgmann's solution is not to abandon technology, but to make sure our technologies are working toward the practices we
set for ourselves.

Borgmann uses the term "focal things and practices" to refer to those
things we place into the center of our lives to counter the device paradigm.
Such focal things and practices "lead us to say: 'There is no place I would
rather be. There is nothing I would rather do. There is no one I would rather
be with'" (Borgmann, 2000, 421). A key example for Borgmann is the festive
meal. Such an event requires all kinds of related activities: cooking, planning,
coordinating with others, purchasing ingredients, travel, etc. These activities
may not be the easiest things, but they become meaningful in the service of
the meal. In this way the meal, as a focal practice, orients much of the rest
of our life, providing direction, and spreading meaning across those related
practices.

Case #7: Social Media and Online Multiplayer Gaming

Critics of Borgmann often consider whether there are any particular technologies that do not fit into the pattern of the device paradigm. His writing
is often dismissive of commonplace pastimes, like watching TV or talking
on the phone. So his work sometimes elicits rejoinders that this or that
technology can be engaging or fulfilling. In a careful contribution to this
vein of criticism, Diane Michelfelder offers a surprising and instructive
contrast between the examples of social media and Massive Multiplayer
Online Games (MMOGs).

Social media websites like Twitter and Facebook purport to bring
people together, enabling them to connect and communicate in a variety
of ways. But, building on Borgmann's own assessment of community on
the Internet (Borgmann, 2004), Michelfelder sees social media as easily
offering the commodity of sharing immediate and shallow bits of oneself.
She writes, "to join Facebook is arguably to enter into a process of self-
commodification distinguished by features such as the continuous availability of information about oneself" (Michelfelder, 2012, 211). So despite
what seems on the surface to be a community building technology, social
media tends to afford a reduced and hollow version, and thus instantiates
the logic of the device paradigm.

But Michelfelder sees hope when she turns to MMOGs. In her view,
in role-playing games like *World of Warcraft* (*WoW*), the players interact within a community, and they engage with one another in ways that
demand reflection on what type of person one should be (even if it is the

type of player that is consciously flouting conventions). She writes, "In offering affordances that relate positively to the development of one's own character, *WoW* and its affiliated discussion forums can be seen as lending themselves more to the formation of community than commodity" (Michelfelder, 2012, 211). Thus, according to Michelfelder, MMOGs serve as an example of a technology that, at least in general, positively affords a break with the device paradigm.

REFERENCES

Aagaard, J. (forthcoming). "Entering the Portal: Media Technologies and Experiential Transportation." In C. Hasse, J. K. B. O. Friis, O. Tafdrup, & J. Aagaard (eds.), *Postphenomenological Methodologies: New Ways in Studying Mediated Techno-Human Relationships*. Lexington Books.

Borgmann, A. (1984). *Technology and the Character of Contemporary Life*. Chicago: Chicago University Press.

Borgmann, A. (2000). "The Moral Complexion of Consumption." *The Journal of Consumer Research* 26(4): 418–22.

Borgmann, A. (2004). "Is the Internet the Solution to the Problem of Community?" In A. Feenberg & D. Barney (eds.), *Community in the Digital Age: Philosophy and Practice*: 53–67. Lanham: Roman and Littlefield.

Dreyfus, H. (2001). *On the Internet*. London: Routledge.

Friesen, N. (2011). *The Place of the Classroom and the Space of the Screen: Relational Pedagogy and Internet Technology*. Peter Lang.

Hasse, C. (2015). *An Anthropology of Learning: On Nested Frictions in Cultural Ecologies*. Dordrecht: Springer.

Ihde, D. (2009). *Postphenomenology & Technoscience: The Peking University Lectures*. New York: SUNY Press.

Michelfelder, D. P. (2012). "Web 2.0 as Community or Commodity?" In P. Brey, A. Briggle, & E. Spence (eds.), *The Good Life in a Technological age*: 203–14. Florence: Rutledge.

Rosenberger, R. (2009). "The Sudden Experience of the Computer." *AI & Society* 24: 173–80.

Rosenberger, R. (2011). "A Phenomenological Defense of Computer-Simulated Frog Dissection." *Techné* 15(3): 307–13.

Rosenberger, R. (2012). "Embodied Technology and the Dangers of Using the Phone While Driving." *Phenomenology & the Cognitive Sciences* 11: 79–94.

Rosenberger, R. (2014a). "Multistability and the Agency of Mundane Artifacts: From Speed Bumps to Subway Benches." *Human Studies* 37: 369–92.

Rosenberger, R. (2014b). "The Phenomenological Case for Stricter Regulation of Cell Phones and Driving." *Techné* 18(1–2): 20–47.

Rosenberger, R. (2015). "Driver Distraction from Dashboard and Wearable Interfaces." *IEEE Technology & Society Magazine* 34(4): 88–99.

Rosenberger, R. (forthcoming). "Notes on a Nonfoundational Phenomenology of Technology." *Foundations of Science*. DOI 10.1007/s10699-015-9480-5.

Rosenberger, R. (in process). *Guilty Technologies*.

Rosenberger, R., & P. P. Verbeek. (2015). "A Field Guide to Postphenomenology." In R. Rosenberger & P. P. Verbeek (eds.), *Postphenomenological Investigations: Essays on Human-Technology Relations*: 9–41. Lanham: Lexington Books.

Suchman, L. (2007). *Human-Machine Reconfigurations: Plans and Situated Actions, 2nd edition*. New York: Cambridge.

Verbeek, P. P. (2008). "Obstetric Ultrasound and the Technological Mediation of Morality: A Postphenomenological Analysis." *Human Studies* 31: 11–26.

Verbeek, P. P. (2011). *Moralizing Technology*. Chicago: Chicago University Press.

Wellner, G. (2014). "Multi-Attention and the Horcrux Logic: Justifications for Talking on the Phone While Driving." *Techné* 18(1–2): 48–73.

Wellner, G. (2015). *A Postphenomenological Inquiry of Cell Phones*. Lexington Books.

Whyte, K. P. (2015). "What is Multistability? A Theory of the Keystone Concept of Postphenomenological Research." In J. K. B. O. Friis & R. P. Crease (eds.), *Technoscience and Postphenomenology: The Manhattan Papers*: 69–81. New York: Lexington Books.

Wiltse, H. (2015). "Unpacking Digital Material Mediation." *Techné* 18(3): 154–82.

Chapter 6

Profession as a Lens for Studying Technology

Michael Davis

Engineering ethics is a subfield of both the ethics of technology and the ethics of professions. It is a subfield focusing on certain people (engineers) who help to shape technology in certain ways (by engineering) rather than on the processes, products, or systems they help to shape ("technology" in one everyday sense). Engineering ethics provides a means of distinguishing engineers from other technologists, such as geneticists, industrial designers, mechanics, nurses, and statisticians. It also suggests questions the answers to which should help researchers better understand not only the place of engineering in technology but also the place of other professions there, especially their distinctive contributions to the ethics of technology.

This chapter has three parts: first, a brief introduction to key concepts related to profession; second, a sketch of some advantages that studying technology through the lens of profession can have; and, third, advice concerning how a researcher should set about using that lens to study technology.

Though there are many technological professions, some of which I shall discuss in passing, I shall concentrate on engineering for two reasons. First, engineering is the technological profession I know best. Second, and more important, engineering seems to be the technological profession par excellence. Not only is it among the oldest and largest of technological professions; it is also the one that seems to come first to mind when someone says "technologist." Those who know nothing of engineering can know little of technology.

PROFESSION AND SOME RELATED CONCEPTS

By "profession," I mean *a number of individuals in the same occupation voluntarily organized to earn a living by openly serving a moral ideal in a morally permissible way beyond what law, market, morality, and public opin-ion would otherwise require*. This definition differs in an important way from definitions of "profession" that social scientists typically use. Unlike those, this one is not a mere list of facts that *often* go together (high income, advanced education, licensure, and so on). It is not the result of mere observation of people called "professionals" (everything from athletes to physicians). This definition is, rather, the result of discussions with self-described professionals in which I tried to state, in a way satisfactory to them, what they meant when describing themselves as members of a profession (especially when intend-ing to claim more than that they earn a living by some art, calling, or trade). The definition is meant to be true of *all* professions (strictly so called)—and immune to clear counter-example—not true simply of "most professions," "the most developed professions," or "the ideal type of profession." Since I have defended this definition at length elsewhere (e.g., Davis, 2009a), this chapter will simply point out six features especially relevant to the study of technology's ethics.

First, the definition distinguishes the professional from the mere expert. A professional is a member of a profession (or, by analogy, someone resem-bling a member of a profession in good standing, for example, when we describe someone without a profession as "a real pro"). While there can be just one expert in a field (though, generally, there are more), there can no more be a profession having only one member than there can be an army having only one soldier.

Second, the definition distinguishes profession from mere occupation. An occupation is just a number of individuals who earn a living by some typically full-time activity. An occupation is a mere aggregate of individuals. A profes-sion, in contrast, is *organized*. Its members seek to earn their living by maintaining *shared* standards of competence and conduct, standards beyond what law, market, morality, and public opinion would otherwise impose. To claim to be a member of a certain profession is to claim to adhere to those standards. Being a member of a profession is, therefore, always more than having a certain social function (such as designing or building) or practicing a certain discipline (such as calculus or carpentry). A profession is a *shared* discipline, shared not simply in the sense in which independent activities can share features because they are similar but in the sense in which participants in a cooperative practice share the practice. Members of a profession rely on one another to work in ways they approve and to avoid working in ways they disapprove.

One important question for those studying a profession is how this cooperation is achieved. Plainly, much of what is necessary for such cooperation must go on in the appropriate professional schools, but almost as plainly much seems to go on after the student leaves school and "enters the profession." Many professions, including engineering, seem to think that members are unlikely to know enough of the profession to count as full members until they have practiced for several years after graduation from an appropriate professional school. Until then, they are still "in training." We can therefore learn much about a profession from its curriculum (both formal and informal), but much too from what typically goes on in the early years of a professional's career.

Third, the discipline of each profession is inherently value-bearing. Whether technology as such is value-neutral may be an open question, but a technological *profession* cannot view the technology it works on as a matter of indifference. For example, an engineer who doubts that the product she is working on will improve the material condition of human beings has a reason, as an engineer, to consider ceasing to work on that product. Like other professions, engineering has a moral ideal it seeks to serve. A moral ideal is an outcome that all rational persons, at their rational best, recognize as an objective the pursuit of which deserves assistance, all else equal, or at least noninterference. Public health is such an ideal; so are justice, beauty, and knowledge. Engineering's moral ideal is (roughly) improving the material condition of human beings. What does not promise such improvement is, strictly speaking, not engineering (or, what comes to the same thing, not "good engineering").

The reverse, however, is not true. That an activity serves a profession's moral ideal does not guarantee that the activity belongs to the profession. For example, that a certain invention will improve the material condition of human beings does not mean that the invention is engineering, much less good engineering. The invention must also be designed, tested, and so on in the way engineers are supposed to do such things (i.e., according to engineering's professional standards). A profession is a discipline designed to achieve a certain objective *in a certain way*, not simply any activity serving that objective.

Fourth, the definition makes ethics an essential feature of profession. Of course, by "ethics" I do not merely mean ordinary morality (general standards of conduct), much less philosophical ethics (the attempt to understand morality as a reasonable undertaking). Instead, by "ethics" I mean morally permissible standards of conduct that apply to members of a group simply because they are members of that group. Architecture ethics applies to architects and no one else; computer ethics, to people when using computers and no one else; and so on. A profession's ethics (in this sense) consists of morally permissible standards (rules, principles, or ideals) that everyone in the group (at the rational best of each) wants everyone else in the group to follow even if their following the standards would mean having to do the same. (How these standards become morally binding, if they do, is an important question in the philosophy of professions. My own view is that the standards are morally binding because a professional is, as such, a participant in a voluntary, morally permissible cooperative practice.)

Given this definition of "ethics," a profession's *technical* standards are part of its ethics—at least those technical standards (typically, the vast majority) that members of the profession, at their rational best, want all other members to follow, even if their following them means having to do the same. What those shared standards actually are is, of course, an empirical question (but one the answer to which depends on both an analysis of "rational best" and an operationalization of it).

Fifth, while a professional may be in business, no profession is a business and no professional is, as such, simply in business. By "business," I understand any effort, whether individual, collective, or corporate, to make a "profit" (i.e., to take wealth from an enterprise beyond what one put t The profits of business come mainly from buying, selling, or exchanging goods or services (rather than from gift, taxation, theft, or other noncommercial activity). (For a fuller exposition of this definition and a defense of the distinction between business and profession, see Davis, 1994.) Though professionals typically practice their profession to make a living, their membership in their profession means (or, at least, should mean) that they always have the purpose of serving the profession's moral ideal (in addition or instead). Professionals may seek to serve that ideal even when such service seems unlikely to be profitable; hence, the explicit endorsement in many professions of work pro bono publico.

Sixth, the definition does not require that a profession call itself "a profession" to be a profession (in this sense). It only requires that the occupation in question (or some part of it) be organized in a certain way. That is important because this sense of "profession" seems to be both relatively new (maybe less than a century old) and still largely confined to English-speaking countries. In many languages, "profession" (or its nearest equivalent) is still little more than a synonym for "occupation."

The literature on professions outside the English-speaking world and, indeed, even in it, seems to suffer from confusion concerning the difference between having a word for a certain concept and having the concept. But, just as it is possible to recognize the difference between blue and cyan even if one does not have a word for cyan, so it is possible to organize an occupation in a certain way without having a term for that sort of organization. So, for example, whether engineering is a profession in France (in the relevant sense) cannot be answered by simply asking engineers in France, "Is engineering a profession?" Instead, a researcher must ask a series of questions such as the following:

- Why do you call yourself "an engineer"?
- Why do you follow these technical standards (the ones engineers share) rather than others?

- Do you care whether other engineers follow these technical standards? Why?
- Do you think other engineers would care whether you follow these standards? Why?
- What, if anything, do you expect of an engineer that you do not expect of a non-engineer?

What then is the connection between profession so defined and the ethics of technology? By "technology," I mean any (more or less) systematic arrangement by which people conceive, develop, manufacture, maintain, use, or dispose of artifacts (where "artifact" refers to any physical thing made for use, anything from artillery shells to biscuits, from circuits to software). I take this to be the common understanding of "technology" among philosophers and social scientists now studying technology (though perhaps not an "everyday sense").

Many of the people who conceive, develop, manufacture, maintain, use, or dispose of artifacts belong to one profession or another. They are accountants, biologists, computer scientists, dentists, or the like. Working according to their respective disciplines, they typically give the technology they work on a character that it would not otherwise have. So, for example, engineers will typically insist on a specific "safety factor" for any artifact that they design, a safety factor different from that which actuaries, botanists, chiropractors, or the like would use (if they would use any). The reason engineers have for their safety factor will typically come neither directly from chemistry, physics, or any other natural science, nor from law, market, morality, or public opinion, but from the experience of other engineers with the artifact in question (or ones that seem similar enough). (For examples of how standards actually come into being, see Vincenti, 1990 or Wells, Jones, and Davis, 1986.)

Since professional standards are largely a product of history, not natural or social science, the history of a profession is largely the history of its discipline, that is, a description of how its standards changed, including the failures that particular standards led to and the refinements such failures provoked. Professions are no more timeless abstractions than an individual human is. Every profession has its own biography. The standardization of its curriculum is an important part of that biography, indeed, it is often a defining moment in that biography.

Given these definitions, we can see that the term "ethics of technology" is ambiguous. While it can (among other things) simply mean: (1) the application of ordinary moral standards to what people involved with the artifacts of technology are doing, the term can also mean—in addition or instead; (2) the special standards members of a group, such as a profession, bring to what they do with the artifacts of technology; or (3) the attempt to understand how technology can be a morally good or, at least, a morally permissible undertaking (when it is). Insofar as technology is an activity involving people (rather than a mere collection of artifacts), the study of technology is always, at least implicitly, the study of ethics in at least one of these senses and, often, in two or even all three of them.

ADVANTAGES FOR STUDY OF TECHNOLOGY

We may distinguish at least four advantages that studying technology through the lens of profession can have. The first is opening a range of questions about what individual professions might bring to technology that others do not—not only what values they might bring but also what special knowledge, methods, or skills. For example, Benjamin Wright, "Chief Engineer of the Erie Canal" from 1817 to1828, was a self-taught surveyor with only a primary school education. He learned surveying to aid his speculation in undeveloped land. Though he certainly *functioned* as an engineer when directing the building of the canal (so much so that civil engineers have long claimed him as the "father of American civil engineering"), he is in fact proof that one could then still be a great builder without being an engineer (Weingardt, 2005, 5–9). The nineteenth century had many other important non-engineer builders. Only in the late nineteenth century did engineers (strictly so called) come to dominate large building projects. Today, a large project like the Erie Canal could not be built without engineers being involved at almost every stage.

Why do I deny that Wright was an engineer (strictly speaking)? First, his education. Not only did he not have the technical education a modern engineer would have, he did not even have the postsecondary technical education engineers in his time would have received at, say, the École Polytechnique or the military academy at West Point. Second, we can explain how he could have functioned as chief engineer of the Erie Canal without being an engineer (or working much as engineers would then have worked). Building canals, even canals as large as the Erie, required only relatively simple technology, simple enough that similar canals had been built in many earlier civilizations. Anyone who can survey can lay out a canal. If the canal requires locks (as the Erie did), their design and placement is still relatively simple, something an intelligent person can puzzle out from an old book and a little experience. The hard part of building the Erie was political (maintaining funding over more than a decade) and logistical (feeding, housing, and productively employing a great number of workers in the north of New York State, what was then still largely a forested wilderness).

Once we see that not all builders, not even all successful builders of great works, are engineers, we can ask what engineers—their distinctive ways of planning, testing, documenting, and so on—might have brought to building a canal that other technologists (such as surveyors) did not. We might then want to study what engineers did for railroads, since railroads seem to be the first civilian technology that absorbed many American engineers who were trained much as engineers are trained today. If, instead of focusing on the profession of engineering (especially, its discipline), we were to focus on the function of engineers (designing, building, and so on), we could not even distinguish between the history of technology (which includes the building of the Erie Canal) and the history of engineering (strictly speaking). Every technologist, or at least every successful technologist, would be an engineer (because he *functioned* as engineers now function), whatever his discipline and however far back in time we go. Even the builders of the Ring of Brodgar or the passage tomb at Newgrange would be engineers. Many interesting research questions, such as those about differences among technological professions, would be defined away.

A second, but related, advantage of studying technology through the lens of profession is that studying technology that way invites inquiry into the naming of certain technological activities, for example, the many activities now called "architecture" (computer architecture, virtual architecture, landscape architecture, and so on) or "surgery" (tree surgery, surgical strikes, pet surgery, and so on). Which of these activities actually belong to the profession its name implies? Which are similar enough for a strong analogy? And which are merely connected metaphorically? What purpose, if any, is an analogical or metaphorical naming intended to serve? Is the purpose legitimate? Such questions are open only if a researcher can distinguish between the profession strictly speaking (even when called something else, for example, "naval architecture" instead of "naval engineering") and activities called by the profession's name (though not belonging to that profession strictly speaking).

I note the possibility of such inquiry because engineering seems especially subject to having its name taken for activities that are not engineering strictly speaking. Some of the taking is historical accident. For example, the drivers of railroad trains today take the name "engineer" simply because long ago, before there were any engineers strictly speaking, anyone in charge of an "engine" (such as a catapult or winch) might be called an "enginer" or "engineer." (Perhaps Benjamin Wright's title, "Chief Engineer," carried that old sense when he assumed it in 1817, since he might as informatively have been called "Master of Works" or "Chief Builder.") Some taking, though deliberate, may nonetheless be justified. For example, "software engineers," though not engineers strictly speaking, intended their new profession to resemble engineering closely. The taking of the name was a commitment to that resemblance (for more on this, see Davis, 2009b). But, often, the taking of the name seems to be no more than an attempt to appropriate the reputation of engineering for an activity not deserving it: "social engineering" (for large-scale social experimentation), "re-engineering" (for a certain fad in organizational restructuring), "financial engineering" (for risky investment strategies), "genetic engineering" (for biologists' tinkering with genes), and so on (compare Hansson, 2006). These are all activities from which both engineers and their typical methods are (largely or altogether) absent. Much might be learned about the ethics of technology from inquiring into such rhetorical misappropriation. But such inquiry is open only if researchers have a way to distinguish legitimate uses of a profession's name from illegitimate. The lens of profession can provide that.

Third, once we begin looking at organizations through the lens of profession, we can see that most large organizations—and, indeed, many smaller ones—include several professions (not only accountants, engineers, and lawyers, but also botanists, chemists, computer scientists, librarians, mathematicians, technical writers, and so on). We can ask what each of these professions contributes to the overall work of the organization. The answer is not always obvious. For example, when I visited Argonne National Laboratory, I found that about half the "scientists" I talked with were engineers (i.e., identified themselves as engineers even when their job title identified them as something else). What they reported doing varied considerably, too much for me to see a pattern. So, I was left asking what engineering's distinctive contribution to science is, if there is a distinctive contribution. That is a question that can only be intelligibly asked if a researcher can distinguish (independent of job title) engineers in a science lab from others in the same lab. Much the same question can be asked about other engineers (and other professionals) in other organizations—from Boeing to the Environmental Protection Agency.

Indeed, I would suggest that much may be learned about the ethics of technology from studying the distinctive role of each of the professions involved in an artifact's conception, development, manufacture, maintenance, use, and disposal, especially when the professions seem to have inconsistent commitments and must nonetheless work together. The positive role of conflict among professions seems to be a subject of study that, though inviting, remains largely unexplored.

Fourth, the teaching of engineering ethics has recently been criticized for being too individualistic (too concerned with "micro-ethics") and failing to pay enough attention to social ethics ("macro-ethics") (e.g., Herkert, 2005 or Son, 2008). That criticism rests not only on a mistake about professional ethics but also on a long-standing tendency of those who study "STS" (science, technology, and society) to divide the world into *individuals* (the appropriate subject of psychology, biography, and so on) and *society at large* (their subject). What this division overlooks is what is now often called "civil society," the domain of voluntary associations that exists between the individual and society at large. Civil society includes business corporations, clubs, trade associations, nongovernmental organizations like Greenpeace or IEEE, religions, and—most important for our purposes—professions. There is, I believe, nothing (or, at least, nothing but prejudice) to stop those studying STS from studying civil society's role in technology. After all, civil society has long been a subject of study for social scientists not interested in technology.

One disadvantage of micro-ethics, insofar as it focuses on the individual rather than on the relevant profession, is (as everyone seems to agree) that it turns professional ethics into the individual application of morality to problems arising out of one's work. But macro-ethics has a corresponding disadvantage for the study of technology. Insofar as it focuses on "society" (society at large) rather than on the relevant profession, it turns every question concerning the ethics of technology into a question of political philosophy, a question of what society at large should do (e.g., what regulations government should adopt). The members of the relevant profession are reduced to lobbyists (interest groups) or mere informed citizens (individual experts).

Both micro-ethics and macro-ethics miss the special dimension that profession introduces into the ethics of technology. A member of a profession never practices her profession as a mere individual (as in micro-ethics). In a professional context, a professional always acts (or, at least, always should act) as a member of her profession, having not only commitments as a member that she does not have as a mere individual (her professional standards) but also special powers. Among those special powers is the ability to help develop new professional standards, standard that will be a matter neither of individual choice nor of social policy. Some of these new standards may appear in a profession's formal code of ethics (if there is one). Consider, for example, recent changes in codes of engineering ethics that have added "sustainable development" to the factors relevant to making good engineering decisions. But most of the new standards may be hidden in thousands of detailed changes in "technical standards," such as those ASME or IEEE adopt each year.[1] A profession need not wait for society at large to act to change the way it practices. It can itself change the way it practices. We can see that clearly once we start looking beyond micro- and macro-ethics, focusing instead on profession as making possible a sort of "meso-ethics" (Davis, 2010).

Of course, it may be argued that it is undemocratic for professions, or any other element of civil society, to set standards that operate much as social policy would (because those private standards in effect usurp the people's power). I need not refute that argument here. My point now is simply that the lens of profession allows us to see the important role a profession as such can have in (what amounts to) setting social policy, something that the argument from democracy must assume. I cannot, however, resist adding that the

argument from democracy, insofar as it is offered as an objection to professional self-regulation, seems to assume as well a "totalitarian" conception of
democracy, one in which "the people" or "society" (and they alone) have the
right to regulate everything and self-regulating associations must have the
right to self-regulation granted if they are to have that right at all. That is an
assumption not easily defended. While a profession's special standards may
have large-scale effects (and therefore count as social policy), those standards
in fact govern only the members of the profession. So long as a professional
standard benefits society or, at least, does it no harm, what right has society
to object? The totalitarian conception of democracy simply overlooks the
human right of voluntary association.

ADVICE ON USING THE LENS OF PROFESSION

By now, it should be clear what the lens of profession is and why those
engaged in the study of technology, especially, the study of its ethics, should
find the lens useful. If so, then it is time to offer some advice concerning how
to study the ethics of technology through that lens. The advice offered does
not constitute a handbook but merely some "helpful hints" developed by considering mistakes I have seen researchers make. While I have the impression
that researchers today are less likely to make such mistakes than researchers
even a decade ago were, I think it is still too soon for even one of these hints
to be omitted because it is "too obvious to be worth mention."

Each hint is stated as a way to avoid a certain kind of mistake in the study
of *engineering*. While I doubt the analogy with the study of other technological professions will always be clear, I shall say nothing about such analogies
here. Because of limitations of space, I must leave it to those who know the
other professions to work out the analogies (and disanalogies) themselves.

1. *One cannot learn the role of engineers in technology simply by observing
   them*, that is, by studying them the way we study bees or frogs. Engineering has an "inside" as well as an "outside." Much of what is distinctive
   in engineering goes on "inside" individual engineers. Interviewing engineers, asking them for their reasons as well as for what they did, should be
   a part of every research plan for a study of engineering. The reasons that
   engineers offer for what they did can change our interpretation of what
   they did. For example, though one might initially interpret the silence of
   engineers at a certain meeting as evidence that they approved the decision
   made at that meeting, interviewing them might reveal that they remained
   silent because they had already made their objections and been overruled.
   They were silent only because they believed that repeating their objections

would have been a waste of everyone's time. The decision taken at that meeting would then not count as an expression of the engineers' values.

2. *One cannot learn the role of engineers in technology merely by studying artifacts.* Different disciplines may produce similar artifacts. The values seemingly encoded in an artifact may, or may not, be the values that the engineers brought to the artifact's conception, design, development, or the like. Sometimes engineers fail to encode their values because they make a mistake. Sometimes they fail because the decision is taken out of their hands, for example, by "management" or the legislature. Most often, perhaps, they fail because they must compromise with others, some in other professions, or because the decision had to be postponed owing to an inability among engineers to agree on a change (even though all agree some change is needed). To learn the role of engineers in a technology, one must study in detail the engineers involved, not only their acts and the arguments they made but the thinking behind those acts and arguments. (For examples of how this might be done, see the substantial literature on the *Challenger* disaster, which includes Vaughan, 1996.)

3. *One should not rely on institutional title or apparent function to identify engineers.* In general, engineers can be identified by their education and experience (whatever their institutional title). If they were trained as engineers and have long worked as engineers typically work, they are (all else equal) engineers (strictly speaking). There are exceptions, however, and these should not be overlooked. First, there may be "engineers" who did not receive an engineering degree but instead one in chemistry, mathematics, physics, technical management, or the like, but who claim to be engineers because they have worked beside engineers long enough to have learned the discipline. If the engineers they work with agree that they are effectively engineers, they are "engineers by adoption" and should be so counted. Second, there may be "engineers" who, though educated as engineers and working as engineers typically do, do not consider themselves to be members of the profession but instead mere employees with certain skills or members of another profession. My impression (derived from interviews in the United States) is that such "engineers" are extremely rare. Indeed, I can recall meeting only one, a member of a department of electrical engineering who considered himself "more a physicist than an engineer." But some researchers, especially those studying engineers in France or Japan, have a different impression (see, e.g., Didier, 1999). For that reason, I think it always worth asking early in an interview of someone whom one supposes to be an engineer both "Are you an engineer?" and "Why did you answer as you did?" (Davis, 1997). The existence in a country of large numbers of "engineers" who deny that "engineer" is anything more than a job description is evidence that engineering is not

a profession there. It is, however, not decisive evidence. The engineers in question would also have to be indifferent concerning, for example, whether other "engineers" maintain engineering standards. If they understand themselves as working in cooperation with other engineers, not only others in their employer's organization but engineers outside of it, they may still understand themselves in a way consistent with being members of a profession.

4. *One should not only interview engineers about what they do but also ask them to evaluate each other and members of other professions they work with.* Part of being a member of a profession is expecting certain others, those one counts as members of one's own profession, to have certain abilities and to act in certain ways. Also part of being a member of a profession is being aware that others (those one counts as not belonging) will typically lack some of those abilities and act in ways different from one's own. So, for example, an engineer might say that "any engineer worth his salt" would use such-and-such a safety factor in a certain design while doubting that a chemist or manager would do the same.

5. *One should not limit research into engineering ethics to what is in a code of engineering ethics.* A profession need not have a formal code of ethics to be a profession. It merely needs technical standards that satisfy the definition of ethics (morally permissible standards of conduct every member of the profession, at his rational best, wants every other member to follow even if that means having to follow them too). The formal code of ethics may best be thought of as the most general part of the profession's ethical standards, a convenience it can do without and still be a profession. Even if there is a code of ethics, it may be that, as in engineering, few members of the profession actually consult it (or have even seen it). A crucial question for engineering to be a profession is whether engineers nonetheless rely on each other to act in accordance with the standards in the code—or, at least, when shown the code, can agree that it contains standards they want other engineers to follow even if the others following them would mean having to do the same.

6. *One should not assume that just any difference between engineering practice in one country and another (say, that engineers in one country present discoveries in tables while engineers in another country do it in equations) shows that the engineers lack a common profession.* Nor is it enough that philosophers or social scientists find a difference significant. The difference should be one the engineers themselves regard as significant enough to divide them (e.g., because it makes the work of the other engineers unreliable). To know that, a researcher must ask engineers. (See hint 1 above.)

7. *Any social scientist organizing a research group to study a question concerning engineering ethics (or the ethics of technology) should consider including both at least one philosopher and at least one engineer.* It is good to have a philosopher in a research group from the beginning to help researchers define their terms, make sure they end up studying what they set out to study (or something at least equally worthwhile), and otherwise help researchers do something useful. (For examples of what can go wrong in research not philosophically informed, see Davis, 1996.) It is also good to have an engineer participate not only to help the social scientists understand the engineering in question, when engineering is in question, but also to point out that engineering is not in question, when it is not. An engineer may also have important insights relevant to interpreting interviews both of engineers and of those who work with engineers.

NOTE

1. The organizations ASME and IEEE were formerly known (respectively) as the American Association of Mechanical Engineers and the Institute of Electrical and Electronic Engineers.

REFERENCES

Davis, M. "Is Engineering Ethics Just Business Ethics?" *International Journal of Applied Philosophy* 8 (Winter/Spring 1994): 1–7.

Davis, M. "Professional Autonomy: A Framework for Empirical Research," *Business Ethics Quarterly* 6 (October 1996): 441–60.

Davis, M. "Better Communications Between Engineers and Managers: Some Ways to Prevent Ethically Hard Choices," *Science and Engineering Ethics* 3 (April 1997): 171–213.

Davis, M. "Is Engineering a Profession Everywhere?" *Philosophia* 37 (June 2009a): 211–25.

Davis, M. *Code Writing: How Software Engineering Became a Profession*, Center for the Study of Ethics in the Professions: Chicago, 2009b (http://ethics.iit.edu/sea/sea.php/9).

Davis, M. "Engineers and Sustainability: An Inquiry into the Elusive Distinction between Macro-, Micro-, and Meso-Ethics," *Journal of Applied Ethics and Philosophy* 2 (2010): 12–20.

Didier, C. "Engineering Ethics in France: A Historical Perspective," *Technology in Society* 21 (1999): 471–86.

Hansson, Sven Ove. "A Note on Social Engineering and the Public Perception of Technology," *Technology in Society* 28 (2006): 389–92.

Herkert, J. R. "Ways of Thinking about and Teaching Ethical Problem Solving: Microethics and Macroethics in Engineering," *Science and Engineering Ethics* 11 (2005): 373–85.

Son, W.-C. "Philosophy of Technology and Macro-ethics in Engineering," *Science and Engineering Ethics* 14 (2008): 405–15.

Vaughan, D. *The Challenger Launch Decision* (University of Chicago Press: Chicago, 1996).

Vincenti, W. G. *What Engineers Know and How They Know It: Analytical Studies from Aeronautical History* (Johns Hopkins University Press: Baltimore, Maryland, 1990).

Weingardt, Richard. *Engineering Legends: Great American Civil Engineers* (Reston, VA: ASCE, 2005).

Wells, P., H. Jones, and M. Davis. *Conflict of Interest in Engineering* (Kendall/Hunt: Dubuque, 1986).

Part II

TOOLS

Chapter 7

Case Study Methodologies

Gertrude Hirsch Hadorn

Examining case studies is a common practice in fields such as ethics, philosophy, technology, history, education, anthropology, psychology, medicine, sociology, and political science. What is taken as a case, that is, the unit to be spatially and temporally delineated and investigated, differs according to the field and question to be answered: an episode, a person or group, an institution, a geographic region, the implementation of a program or technology, etc. The *Oxford English Dictionary* (*OED*) distinguishes between a case study for purposes of research, that is, "a process or record of research into the development of a particular person, group, or situation over a period of time; this as a method" and a case study for a heuristic or educational purpose, that is, "a particular instance or case that may be analysed or used as an example to illustrate a thesis or principle" (*OED* 2015a).

In *case studies for professional education*, students learn to relate a situation that is empirically described to a concept in order to understand this situation as a *case of a certain kind*. The Harvard Business School offers case descriptions of about three pages of real management situations for training students' competences to judge on a complex management problem. Basically, students learn to grasp real-world issues as a type of management problem (see https://cb.hbsp.harvard.edu/cbmp/pages/content/cases). In Problem-Based Learning, the cases are complex problems that cannot be solved by applying concepts that students already know. They have to acquire additional knowledge in a self-directed way and apply this to the case (Barrows and Tamblyn 1980). Developed at the McMaster University Medical School in Canada, Problem Based Learning is also used in technology education (Uden and Beaumont 2006). For Problem-Based Learning in the ethics of engineering see the Illinois Institute of Technology [http://ethics.iit.edu/eelibrary/case-study-collection].

Case study research includes two major tasks: to describe a case such as a complex situation in the real-world in the relevant aspects and to analyze this case in order to answer questions, which constitute the reasons for doing research on this case. For example, to conduct an ethical case study on a particular emission test for petrol motors, one has to empirically show whether this test has been intentionally manipulated to falsely pretend that emission standards are met, in order to ethically judge whether this is a case of moral corruption.[1] In the ethics of technology, case study research is done ex post and ex ante: studying cases of technologies that have been applied and cases of emerging technologies (Brey, 2017).

Despite being widely used, the practice of case study research faces criticism as summarized in the following quote:

> Case studies have become in many cases a synonym for free-form research where everything goes and the author does not feel compelled to spell out how he or she intends to do the research, why a specific case or set of cases has been selected, which data are used and which are omitted, how data are processed and analyzed, and how inferences were derived from the story presented. Yet, at the end of the story, we often find sweeping generalizations and "lessons" derived from this case. (Maoz 2002, 164–65)

This quote indicates that understanding what case study research is about, as well as using systematic procedures in doing this type of research, are important. In this primer to case study methods,[2] I distinguish case studies from other forms of research and specify four different types of case study research. Furthermore, I describe methods for selecting and delineating cases, for collecting and documenting data, and methods for content analysis. The ethical analysis of cases is the subject of other chapters in this book. However, in doing case study research collecting data, and considering concepts for structuring, and analyzing the material need to be developed hand in hand to ensure that the empirical description covers what is relevant for the ethical analysis.

WHAT IS CASE STUDY RESEARCH?

Typically, case study research is distinguished from other forms of research such as surveys or controlled experiments that I call "standardized research" for short. The criteria for this distinction relate to the sample, the methods, the research design, and the purpose or the intended results, but they don't hold for all types of case study research, and they are met in degrees.

All empirical research can be said to investigate cases in some way, but not every research on cases is case study research. In a survey, for instance, we infer from the investigation of a representative sample of cases whether a general empirical hypothesis holds. Surveys are not case studies, since they refer to cases only to measure how each case performs on the variables in question in order to describe how performances on variables are distributed among the population and influenced by each other. Case study research, on the contrary, investigates one or several cases that are of interest as particular cases by means of an intensive within-case analysis, while exploring those cases also from a cross-case perspective. It would be a serious methodological mistake to take evidence from a cross-case analysis of case studies to confirm a general hypothesis, since this requires statistical analysis of responses from a representative sample, measured on predefined scales. However, cross-case analysis may provide evidence concerning the transferability of results to other cases, given that cases are similar in the relevant aspects. Furthermore, a case study could be used for testing the validity of results from standardized research for a particular context.

Case study research typically uses qualitative methods in order to distinguish between the many aspects of a particular case and to conceptually describe and classify this case in the relevant aspects for answering questions on the case. Depending on the type of case study research, the framing and design of the research may not be decided definitively in advance. The freedom to take some decisions later on, or to adapt those in the course of doing case study research provides the opportunity to account for what has been learned about the case so far, in the course of doing this research. However, case study research should not be practiced as an arbitrary process that lacks systematic considerations. Therefore, decisions on the subject, concepts, hypotheses, methods, data, and so on, taken in the course of doing the research need to be documented in a case study protocol and justified, since these decisions bear on what may result from the case study. While qualitative methods can be adapted in the course of research, the application of quantitative methods requires that the decisions on sample, concepts, and methods have been taken definitively and in accordance with the preconditions for the application of these methods. Any adaptation of, for example, certain methodological decisions in the course of doing the research would be a fundamental mistake, since this would disqualify the reliability of results. Some basic differences between qualitative case study research and standardized quantitative research are visualized in figure 7.1.

While quantitative and qualitative methods answer different sorts of questions and require different preconditions, this doesn't exclude combining them. For instance, quantitative methods may be used in a later stage of a case study on multiple cases, when all decisions have been taken. Such combinations of methods are known as mixed methods (Tashakkori and Teddlie 2010). A mixed methods approach requires that qualitative and quantitative research

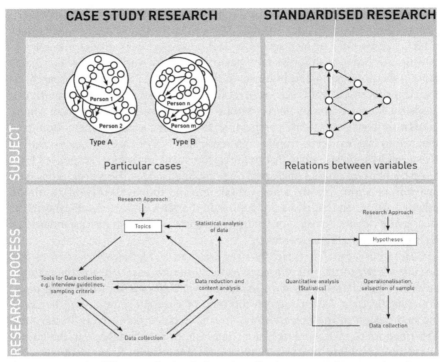

Figure 7.1   Basic differences in the design of qualitative case study research and standardized quantitative research. *Source*: Translated and adapted from Gutscher, Hirsch, and Werner 1996.

questions and methods are specified and applied in such a way that they relate to and complement each other (for examples see Gerring [2007], Cresswell [2014], and Miles, Huberman and Saldana [2014]). Criteria to decide whether a given problem is best addressed by a standardized research approach or by case study research include the state of knowledge on the topic; the complexity of the problem; available resources such as time, money, and know-how; the general purpose and the specific questions of this research; the available information on a given case (e.g., written or oral sources); and how the case is accessible for generating additional data (e.g., whether there are people who could be interviewed for additional information).

TYPES OF CASE STUDY RESEARCH

There is a multitude of purposes to look at cases qua particular ones that come with specific ways to design and conduct a case study (see Patton [2015] for an introduction into various designs and methods). The four volumes on case studies edited by Tight (2015) include canonical papers as well as recent articles on contexts, design, methodological issues and the use in different disciplines. I focus on four types of case study research that are useful in the ethics of technology: narrative case studies, case studies in applied research, in grounded theory, and in transdisciplinary research.

Narrative case study research[3] produces a story about a single case or a few cases, which is also called a "narrative." The information for a narrative case study could be elicited using interviews, via document analysis, by combing both, and by further methods. This type of case study research is often used to learn about the conditions that have brought about a particular event, process, or situation, about its consequences and what those mean to the people involved. A narrative case study in the ethics of technology starts by introducing possibly relevant ethical concepts in order to determine the various elements that are relevant for the ethical analysis such as the events, people involved, their beliefs, attitudes, values, norms, and the measures taken or not. These elements are then described and sequentially arranged in a story (narrative) to indicate how they seem to be connected. So the analysis of the case is often embedded in how the story is constructed and presented. Simons (2009) provides an introduction into narrative case study research with examples from education. She describes specific methods and discusses issues related to the whole research process: from designing the research and getting access to the field, to formulating questions, documenting, analyzing, and interpreting data as well as telling the story in the end.

The DC-10 case study (Fielder and Birsch 1992) is an example from the ethics of technology for this type of case study research. Here, several authors investigated different aspects of the history that has led to three major airplane accidents: the 1974 Paris crash, the 1979 Chicago crash, and the 1989 Sioux City crash. The guiding question is about who is responsible for the faults in the aviation safety system, and how the company handled these issues. Material, analysis, and comments are then presented in a story that is structured in a set of chapters in order to distinguish the different aspects and their contribution to these accidents.

In *applied research* case studies are used to exemplify a general topic, to specify general concepts or hypotheses for concrete cases, or to describe and explain particular cases also from a cross-case perspective. Understanding a certain case also requires the comparison with other cases in order to check hypotheses against further cases. Yin's (2014) seminal "Case Study Research: Design and Methods," first published in 1984, is an introduction to this type of case study research. It provides useful information on determining a study's question, the specific hypotheses, and the cases of analysis. Yin also gives an overview on methods for data collection, including the training of the investigator and writing a protocol, and on strategies for data analysis. This type of case study research is often used for the evaluation of programs after their implementation, where standardized methods are not appropriate to describe and analyze the diverse impacts from real-world interventions and their complexity.

A detailed introduction into the methods for case analysis in applied research is given by Miles, Huberman, and Saldana (2014). To illustrate how methods can be specified for application, they use the implementation of programs for the improvement of teaching and learning in several schools with each school, class, or teacher as one case. A special focus is on techniques to display the data for single-case analysis and methods for cross-case analysis such as matrix and network displays through different levels of coding. These displays provide a systematically structured basis for drawing and verifying conclusions from case study research. Gerring (2007) has a focus on the design of case study research for comparison across cases. He discusses various strategies for choosing cases and designing studies with multiple cases in order to analyze the causal complexity of cases. He combines qualitative and quantitative methods for sampling, research design, and analysis as an approach of mixed methods.

Grounded theory has been a milestone in the development of case study research as a systematic approach for investigating the problems in society for theoretical purpose. Grounded theory has been developed by the Chicago School of Sociology since the 1920s, including scholars such as Ernest Burgess, George Herbert Mead, Florian Znaniecki, and many others. They investigated how immigrants and outsiders in urban areas, as individuals, perceive and deal with their problems in order to learn about and understand problems that were new for sociology at that time. Several of their seminal papers are reprinted in Tight (2015). Their work has given rise to methods for developing what is now called "grounded theory" (for a more recent introduction see, e.g., Corbin and Strauss [2008]). Basically, the purpose is to learn from the analysis of contrasting cases about theoretical ideas for constructing distinctive conceptual types.[4] Consequently, grounded theory is closely linked with the development of qualitative methods and mixed methods approaches.

Case studies in *transdisciplinary research* use participatory and integrative approaches in order to investigate a real-world problem in a regional context.[5] A real-world problem is "a matter or situation regarded as unwelcome, harmful, or wrong and needing to be overcome" (*OED* 2015b). Real-world problems develop as a conflict between an empirical situation and the practices and values that are held in civil society, the public, and the private sectors. Due to these multiple, heterogeneous but relevant dimensions, real-world problems are of a different complexity than scientific problems. Although they include scientific problems—for example, a conflict between a hypothesis and the evidence from the case, or difficulties with how to apply a method or how to conceptually structure a situation—issues with diverse and contended values and the consequences for how a real-world problem is perceived and managed need to be addressed as well.

Transdisciplinary case studies investigate real-world problems while they try to

a. grasp the complexity of problems,
b. take into account the diversity of lifeworld and scientific perceptions of problems,
c. link abstract and case-specific knowledge, and
d. develop knowledge and practices that promote what is perceived to be the common good. (Pohl and Hirsch Hadorn 2007, 20)

This case study research is done jointly with representatives from the public and private sectors as well as from civil society. Their perspectives on the problem need to be considered in identifying and structuring a real-world problem for investigation, but also in taking decisions later on in the research process. The reason for integrating the broad range of all sorts of relevant information in a transdisciplinary case study is to come up with results that will work in practice. Integration, first of all, is about exploring the potential for agreement among the heterogeneous goals and values of stakeholders by referring to the common good ("target knowledge"). Secondly, integration is about comparing and relating heterogeneous perspectives and information about how the empirical situation works ("systems knowledge"). Thirdly, integration of information on the target and the system is needed for shaping the technical, economic, regulatory or additional means to improve the existing practices ("transformation knowledge"). Pohl and Hirsch Hadorn (2007) provide guidelines for doing this kind of participatory and integrative case studies, which typically proceed iteratively.

An instructive example is the transdisciplinary case study on green hydropower in Switzerland (Truffer et al. 2003). This project has led to a science-based and broadly accepted standard for green hydropower, which has been adopted, and adapted in other countries as well. Transdisciplinary case studies are often used in research for sustainable development and in sustainability assessments (Rösch, 2017).

The different types of case study research share some features, and they can be combined. For instance, the investigation of several contrasting real-world cases with the purpose of differentiating and elaborating concepts and theoretical ideas, as in grounded theory, can be combined with a narrative part. Furthermore, some methods for collecting, documenting, analyzing, and integrating information can be used in several types of case study research.

SELECTING AND DELINEATING CASES

Selecting cases for case study research is based on conceptual criteria, not on a random procedure. Basically, a case is selected because it is considered informative for the purpose of this case study. If the purpose is to develop a typology in a cross-case analysis, selecting diverse, extreme, and deviant cases is recommended (see Gerring 2007, 86–150). Or, if a real-world problem has become pressing, this is a reason to start a transdisciplinary case study. In the ethics of technology, the implementation of a particular technology might be chosen for a case study because this case was influential on how security standards have been fixed, or a regulation has been specified, or because it is unclear whether the harm brought about by the use of a technology is due to ethical misconduct, as in the DC-10 example.

Delineating the case, that is, deciding on which aspects of the case should be explored, requires a conceptual basis. For instance, if the purpose is to clarify who is responsible for damages that have resulted from the use of a technology, the concept of responsibility provides a heuristic to decide which aspects need exploration (Fahlquist, 2017). In this example, information on the following aspects would be required: Who is responsible, is this as an individual or a collective? Could the consequences of applying the technology be somehow foreseen? Which moral norms and regulations are applicable to the case? Is the authority entitled to take enforcing measures? A heuristic of explicit criteria for selecting and delineating the case enables a transparent and systematic research process. This also holds, if the decisions on selecting and delineating cases are taken stepwise or need refinement in the course of collecting and analyzing the material. (For a general discussion of conceptual criteria for selecting cases and material, see Miles, Huberman and Saldana [2014].)

COLLECTING AND DOCUMENTING DATA

Data collected in case study research are from existing documents or specifically generated for the purpose, using the various methods for data collection in social research, which can be applied in a qualitative or a quantitative format (see table 7.1 for an overview).

Case study research typically applies qualitative methods for the reasons mentioned above. To explain the characteristics of qualitative methods, I refer to the example of a qualitative interview on the topic of "best years as a teacher." In order to provide information about how a certain teacher thinks of what has been his or her best times, that is, this person's conception of the given topic, the range of possible answers must not be predetermined. To elicit a narration on the topic and get specific information so-called

Table 7.1   Qualitative and Quantitative Formats of Methods for Data Collection
Source: Translated and adapted from Gutscher, Hirsch and Werner 1996.

Methods for Data Collection	
Open, qualitative	*Standardized, quantitative*
Participatory / non-participatory observation, non-standardized observation	**Non-participatory, standardized observation**
Applied in observational studies or qualitative experiments using open observation or guidelines	Applied in observational studies, experiments or as part of a survey using a standardized observation scheme
Qualitative oral interview techniques	**Standardized oral or written questionnaire techniques**
Guidelines to be applied in e.g., expert interviews, semi-structured interviews, problem-focused interviews, narrative interviews; also as part of a qualitative experiment	Instruments for use in a survey or within an experiment
Open protocol or diary techniques	**Standardized protocol or diary techniques**
Applied in open settings using a barely structured recording scheme	Applied within an experiment or on the basis of surveys using a standardized recording scheme
Group discussion / focus groups	**Sociometric techniques**
Moderated interview and discussion of a small group of participants on a given topic	Quantitative reconstruction of relationship networks within families, groups, organizations based on oral or written surveys
Qualitative recording and processing of existing material	**Standardized recording and quantitative processing of existing material**
Text-, audio-, visual documents as well as further evidence (also physical) of human activities	Text and audio documents as well as further evidence (also physical) of human activities
Qualitative simulation	**Computer simulation**
Qualitative model of a problem to reason about possible consequences, e.g., qualitative scenarios, thought experiments	Mathematical model of a problem to calculate possible consequences, e.g., quantitative scenarios

W-questions are used, since those cannot be answered be "yes" or "no" but require a sentence. Examples of W-questions are: When did X occur? Why did X occur? Where did X occur? Who else was involved in X? What did X mean to you at that time? Responding in the interview by further W-questions to what the informant is telling is a semi-structured interview technique to elicit additional information for a structured analysis, while putting minimal restrictions on what the person might answer.

Quality criteria for the information that has been collected include range (Was it easy for the informant to bring up unforeseen aspects?); specificity (How does the informant articulate his or her opinion, decision, etc.?);

depth (Does the informant describe cognitive, emotional, and evaluative aspects?); and personal context (Does the informant describe her situation in relation to the topic?) of information (see Hopf 1978). W-questions are a means to account for these criteria when constructing the instrument and when doing the interview. However, a person who gives information of this quality is in a vulnerable position. Therefore, the researcher has to inform the person about the subject and take measures to reduce possible harm to her or him, to protect her information and not to exploit her or him (see DiCicco-Bloom and Crabtree [2006, 319], also for a short introduction into qualitative interviews).

Collecting data by using focus groups, that is, interviews or discussions with a group that are focused on a certain topic, is suitable if there are several perhaps conflicting perspectives on the case. Case studies in the ethics of technology often deal with contested issues. The participants of a focus group are selected for their different perspectives on or relations with the topic in question and are able to engage in an in-depth discussion. There are some rules for moderating a focus group, for the size of the group (typically 6–10 people) and the time that participants have to commit (e.g., about 1–2 hours) (see Liamputtong [2011] for an introduction to focus groups). For application in a case study, these rules need to be adapted to the topic and overall purpose of the focus group. For instance, the transdisciplinary case study on developing a standard for green hydropower in Switzerland used larger focus groups that met several times in order to learn about the perspectives of the various stakeholders, to initiate a dialogue, and to explore the potential for agreement on a standard later on, when decisions are taken in the democratic institutions.

Taking short handwritten notes during data collection is helpful to guide the process, since those notes can be used as an overview in the course of data collection, when there is still opportunity to ask for further information to improve for instance, range, specificity, depth and personal context of the information. For documenting the information from interviews, observational studies, or group discussions, digital, audio, or video recording is used. Depending on the purpose of the case study and the methods for analysis, the data are transcribed so that they can be processed later on by means of a text analysis program (for guidelines, see Bazeley 2013), or they are summarized in some kind of prestructured protocol sheet that displays the data according to a certain structure for analysis (for examples, see Miles, Huberman, and Saldana 2014).

CONTENT ANALYSIS

The data collected in a case study are typically verbal data in everyday language. The task of qualitative content analysis is to understand and interpret what people have said. This cognitive activity of the researcher consists in grasping the meaning of a phrase and judging, whether several phrases are about the same or different points, and selecting those that are relevant for answering the question of the case study. Qualitative content analysis selects and rephrases the relevant information in a way that reduces and structures the information given in everyday language, which is a way to generate new information or insights. Bazeley (2013) and Mayring (2015) provide broadly used introductions to qualitative content analysis. They explain the theoretical background, the basic principles and procedures as well as detailed techniques for transcribing the material, developing a conceptual structure for analysis, and applying the concepts to the material.

Mayring (2015) distinguishes between qualitative techniques for summarizing, for explicating and for structuring the material. The purpose of doing a summary is to reduce the material to the core points, and to provide an overview by rephrasing these points using more abstract categories. An explication clarifies ambiguous, vague, or otherwise unclear material by referring to additional material that helps to understand what is unclear.[6] Structuring consists in selecting those parts from the material that relate to the guiding concepts of the analysis, and to assess and order the extracted material accordingly. Each form of analysis proceeds in steps that may be taken iteratively. A summary, for instance, starts with determining the units of analysis and proceeds by various steps of reducing and abstracting from the material to then retest the summarizing statements. All three forms of content analysis are useful in case studies in the ethics of technology. For instance, structural analysis based on ethical concepts is useful to select and classify the relevant material. Explication is needed, if it is unclear how to understand and classify the material. The methods for developing a summary are helpful for presenting the results.

While generating categories and applying them to the material is a cognitive activity of the researcher, using software for the handling and display of the material is recommended. (For an overview on software packages see CAQDAS [http://www.surrey.ac.uk/sociology/research/research-centres/caqdas/support/choosing/], for the application of the broadly used NVivo software see Bazeley and Jackson [2013]). For handling the material with computer software a specific code is assigned to each of the categories that are used in the qualitative analysis. These codes are then assigned to the passages selected from the material. The display of the analyzed material operates on the codes. Using computer software for handling the material has important advantages. Material from several documents that are available electronically can be integrated into one dataset. Display of the coded material enables to easily check whether categories are applied consistently. Also, not much of an effort is required to adapt the categories or add new ones in the course of analyzing the material by revising of the code system and correcting the coding of passages, while saving former records allows for tracking the changes. Also, the coded material allows for certain statistical analyses such as frequency analysis.

SUMMARY AND CONCLUSION

In summary, a case study relates a complex empirical episode to particular concepts in order to conceive this episode as a case of a certain kind. In the ethics of technology, the general task is to find out and specify the ethical concepts and aspects needed to understand the case in question. The various types of case study research serve different purposes.

Narrative case studies are recommended for investigating cases that are of societal significance qua particular cases. For instance, if the moral and professional responsibility for major harms is unclear, this requires an analysis of the conditions that have brought about those harms, their long-term consequences, and what all this mean to the people involved. Telling the story about the case is a way to integrate the various elements into a coherent picture.

In the evaluation of risks related to regulations, a case study design of applied research for cross-case analyses is useful to learn about conditions that support or prevent the occurrence of certain effects. Cross-case analyses also serve learning about the transferability of policy measures, that is, whether a measure may be effective if applied to another case.

Case study research using grounded theory is appropriate to investigate problems of emerging technologies that require new or differently specified ethical concepts. Grounded theory applies a design for cross-case analysis and consecutive sampling in order to learn about new problems and develop a typology for characterizing and differentiating problems.

Transdisciplinary case studies are recommended for investigating real-world problems, where the framing of the problem, the goals to be reached and the means to be established are contended in society—not least for disagreement on ethical issues. Participation of representatives from the public and private sector as well as the civil society is a means to integrate their perspectives in taking decisions on structuring the problem, setting goals, and developing measures in a case study.

In performing the research, one has to make sure that the empirical description of the case in question includes those aspects that are relevant for the ethical analysis. Equally importantly, the ethical concepts used should be relevant for the case in question. This puts demands on how we select and delineate cases, how we collect data, and how we select and apply concepts for structuring and analyzing the material. Qualitative methods of empirical research can be applied with some degree of flexibility. But, to achieve systematicity, decisions taken on methods in the course of doing the research must be documented, justified, and kept transparent for those who use the results from a case study. Case studies may be less expensive and take less time than standardized research. While case study research and standardized research cannot answer the same sorts of questions, due to their different conditions for proper application, they may be combined in a mixed methods approach that can answer more questions than what each of the methods can do.

NOTES

1. "Moral corruption" is a concept used by Gardiner (2011), if decision makers intentionally obscure that the measures they take to address reducing greenhouse gas emissions in fact facilitate intergenerational buck-passing.

2. I would like to thank Eva Lieberherr, Carolina Adler, and Marie-Christin Weber for valuable comments and editorial help.

3. Other terms for this type of case study research are "ethnographic," "idiographic," or "ideographic," which are popular in history and cultural anthropology.

4. A kindred approach is Max Weber's procedure to construct ideal types, for an introduction see Hirsch Hadorn (1997). While Weber's approach is based on his theory of social action, the background of grounded theory is in symbolic interaction theory.

5. Case studies in post-normal science (De Marchi and Ravetz 1999) and in policy sciences (Brunner 2010) are of the same type.

6. Difficulties for interpretation that need to be explicitly mentioned if they occur are: Can we infer from someone saying, for example, "I'm fine" that this person really has this property, that is, feels well? Is the frequency of a certain phrase a reliable indicator for how important this is for him or her? Should qualitative data analysis be restricted to what is explicitly stated or should the latent meaning also be considered?

REFERENCES

Barrows, Howard S., and Robin M. Tamblyn. 1980. *Problem-Based Learning: An Approach to Medical Education.* New York: Springer.

Bazeley, Patricia. 2013. *Qualitative Data Analysis: Practical Strategies.* London: Sage.

Bazeley, Patricia, and Kristi Jackson. 2013. *Qualitative Data Analysis with NVivo, 2nd edition.* London: Sage.

Brey, Philip. 2017. "Ethics of Emerging technologies." In *Methods for the Ethics of Technology*, edited by Sven Ove Hansson, pp. 175–91. London: Rowman and Littlefield.

Brunner, Ronald D. 2010. "Adaptive Governance as a Reform Strategy." *Policy Sciences* 43: 301–41.

Corbin, Juliet M., and Anselm L. Strauss. 2008. *Basics of Qualitative Research: Techniques and Procedures for Developing Grounded Theory, 3rd edition*. Thousand Oaks, London, New Delhi: Sage Publications.

Cresswell, John W. 2014. *Research Design: Qualitative, Quantitative, and Mixed Methods Approaches, 4th editon*. Thousand Oaks: Sage.

De Marchi, Bruna, and Jerome R. Ravetz. 1999. "Risk Management and Governance: A Post-normal Science Approach." *Futures* 31: 743–57.

DiCicco-Bloom, Barbara, and Benjamin F. Crabtree. 2006. "The Qualitative Research Interview." *Medical Education* 40: 314–21. Accessed March 3, 2016. doi: 10.1111/j.1365–2929.2006.02418.x.

Fahlquist, Jessica N. 2017. "Responsibility Analysis." In *Methods for the Ethics of Technology*, edited by Sven Ove Hansson, pp. 129–42. London: Rowman and Littlefield.

Fielder, John H., and Douglas Biersch (eds.). 1992. *The DC-10 Case: A Study in Applied Ethics, Technology, and Society*. Albany: State University of New York Press.

Gardiner, Steven M. 2011. "A Perfect Moral Storm." In *A Perfect Moral Storm: The Ethical Tragedy of Climate Change*, edited by Stephen M. Gardiner, 19–48. University Press Scholarship Online. Accessed March 3, 2016. doi: 10.1093/acpro f:oso/9780195379440.001.0001.

Gerring, John. 2007. *Case Study Research: Principles and Practices*. Cambridge: Cambridge University Press.

Gutscher, Heinz, Gertrude Hirsch, and Karin Werner. 1996. "Vom Sinn der Methodenvielfalt in den Sozial- und Humanwissenschaften." In *Umweltproblem Mensch. Humanwissenschaftliche Zugänge zu umweltverantwortlichem Handeln*, edited by Ruth Kaufmann-Hayoz, and Antonietta Di Giulio, 43–78. Bern: Haupt.

Hirsch Hadorn, Gertrude. 1997. "Webers Idealtypus als Methode zur Bestimmung des Begriffsinhaltes theoretischer Begriffe in den Kulturwissenschaften." *Journal for General Philosophy of Science* 28: 275–96.

Hopf, Christel. 1978. "Die Pseudo-Exploration—Ueberlegungen zur Technik qualitativer Interviews in der Sozialforschung / Pseudo-exploration—Thoughts on the techniques of qualitative interviews in social research." *Zeitschrift für Soziologie* 7: 97–115.

Liamputtong, Pranee. 2011. *Focus Group Methodology: Principles and Practice*. London: Sage.

Mayring, Philipp. 2015. *Qualitative Inhaltsanalyse: Grundlagen und Techniken, 15th editon*. Weinheim: SAGE.

Maoz, Zeev. 2002. "Case Study Methodology in International Studies: From Storytelling to Hypothesis Testing." In *Evaluating Methodologiy in International Studies: Millenial Reflections on International Studies*, edited by Frank P. Harvey, and Michael Brecher, 455–75. Ann Arbor: University of Michigan Press.

Miles, Matthew B, A. Michael Huberman, and Johnny Saldana. 2014. *Qualitative Data Analysis: A Methods Sourcebook, 3rd edition*. Los Angeles, et al.: Sage.

Oxford English Dictionary (OED). 2015a. "Case Study, n." Oxford University Press. Accessed November 6. http://www.oed.com/.

Oxford English Dictionary (OED). 2015b. "Problem, n." Oxford University Press. Accessed November 6. http://www.oed.com/.

Patton, Michael Quinn. 2015. *Qualitative Research and Evaluation Methods: Integrating Theory and Practice, 4th edition*. Thousand Oakes: Sage.

Pohl, Christian, and Gertude Hirsch Hadorn. 2007. *Principles for Designing Transdisciplinary Research: A Proposition by the Swiss Academies of Arts and Sciences*. Oekom: München.

Rösch, Christine. 2017. "Ethics of Sustainability." In *Methods for the Ethics of Technology*, edited by Sven Ove Hansson, pp. 17–34. London: Rowman and Littlefield.

Simons, Helen. 2009. *Case Study Research in Practice*. Thousand Oaks: Sage.

Tashakkori, Abbas, and Charles Teddlie (eds.). 2010. *Mixed Methods in Social & Behavioral Research, 2nd edition*. Thousand Oakes: Sage.

Tight, Malcolm (ed.). 2015. *Case Studies: Vol. I–IV*. Thousand Oakes: Sage.

Truffer, Bernhard, Christine Bratrich, Jochen Markard, Armin Peter, Alfred Wüest, and Bernhard Wehrli. 2003. "Green Hydropower: The contribution of Aquatic Science Research to the Promotion of Sustainable Electricity." *Aquatic Sciences* 65: 99–110. Accessed March 3, 2016. doi: 10.1007/s00027-003-0643-z.

Uden, Lorna, and Chris Beaumont. 2006. *Technology and Problem-based Learning*. Hershey, PA: Information Science Publishing.

Yin, Robert K. 2014 [1984]. *Case Study Research: Design and Methods, 5th edition*. Thousand Oakes: Sage.

Chapter 8

Ethical Tools

Payam Moula and Per Sandin

There are some tasks which can only be performed with a certain tool. In order to remove a particular part from a certain brand of car without damaging the car, you might need a special type of wrench. Other tasks can be performed without a particular tool, but are greatly facilitated by a tool. You can often remove a bike tire using only your fingers or perhaps a short wooden stick, but it is much easier, less uncomfortable, and there is less risk of damaging the tube if you use a couple of tire levers designed for the purpose—in particular if you do not have vast experience of changing bike tires.

So-called *ethical tools* are typically tools in this second sense. The usual understanding is that experts in ethics (typically moral philosophers) have acquired an ability to perform ethical analyses. However, laypersons who have not acquired this ability can take a shortcut by using some sort of tool—like a checklist, a code of conduct, a flowchart, or perhaps even a decision support system. A typical example of this attitude is the one expressed by Ben Mepham who in presenting his "ethical matrix" argues that its "principal aim is to *assist non-philosophers* to appreciate the value of ethical insights in arriving at well-considered ethical judgments" (Mepham 2010, p. 18, our emphasis).

In this chapter, we will describe what ethical tools are and give some examples of their use in technology assessment. We will highlight some benefits and problems with the use of ethical tools, discuss some criteria for evaluating such tools, and suggest directions for future research.

WHAT ARE ETHICAL TOOLS?

In the discussion about ethical tools, there are several terms used to refer to more or less the same thing: "ethical tool," "framework," "method," "methodology," or "instrument" (Moula and Sandin 2015).

In the outcome of an ambitious research program on tools for assessment of new biotechnology, Beekman et al. (2006, p. 14) define ethical tools as "practical methods designed to improve ethical deliberations by broadening the values considered and/or stakeholder involvement." Expanding this definition, Moula and Sandin (2015, p. 264) state that "an ethical tool is a practical method and/or conceptual framework with the main purpose of helping the user(s) improve their ethical deliberations in order to reach an ethically informed judgment or decision." Against the particular background of biotechnology assessment, Beekman et al. also categorize ethical tools based on domain of application: policy-making, public engagement, and agri-food markets (Beekman et al. 2006, p. 16).

At a more theoretical level, many ethical tools try to ensure that the most common ethical theories are incorporated in the tool. But what does this amount to in practice? Very roughly, it can be said that most ethical tools work like more or less sophisticated checklists to ensure that the user(s) consider the *right aspects* in the *right order*. Sometimes, they offer guidelines for *weighing* the aspects against one another. Another way of putting this is that the most important constituent parts of an ethical tool usually are inclusion,[1] order, and (occasionally) weighing.[2]

Perhaps the most common ethical tools are various codes of conduct. These may be very simple, like Rotary's "Four Way Test":[3]

Of the things we think, say or do:

1. Is it the TRUTH?
2. Is it FAIR to all concerned?
3. Will it build GOODWILL and BETTER FRIENDSHIPS?
4. Will it be BENEFICIAL to all concerned?

At the other end of the spectrum, a code of conduct or code of ethics might contain hundreds of pages. Some of them are also available as applications for smartphones and similar devices for easy access and navigation. Within professional ethics having ethical codes is fairly common. Many professions have their own ethical guidelines or code of ethics.

Other examples of ethical tools include more or less complex flowcharts (a good example is the CoMoRe "toolkit" presented by Deblonde, De Graaf and Brom, 2007), scoring sheets and "computer games" intending to elicit the users' moral intuitions and aid in categorizing them as leaning to some degree toward a particular position in normative ethics (an example is Animal Ethics Dilemma).[4]

The concept of corporate social responsibility (CSR) is today widely known and used in the world of business and politics as well as in academic research. CSR is in itself not an ethical tool. It is not a method built to help with ethical decision making or deliberation in specific cases, but rather a model for incorporating social responsibility into corporate business models. Since having emerged in the 1940s there are today a wide range of CSR models (Claydon 2011), with many attempts being made to measure CSR (Gallardo-Vázquez and Sanchez-Hernandez 2014).

TOOLS IN TECHNOLOGY ASSESSMENT

The use of ethical tools has been proposed and tried in various instances of assessment of new technologies. For example, the area of medicine and health care has a wide variety of tools. Health technology assessment (HTA) has developed into its own field with its own proposed ethical tools (Burls et al. 2011), and adaptations of existing tools to fit HTA (Bombard et al. 2011). Below we present examples of two types of ethical tools and give examples of where they have been used. First, we present the ethical matrix and then a couple of different meeting formats.

The Ethical Matrix

The ethical matrix was created by Ben Mepham in the 1990s with the aim "to assist non-philosophers to appreciate the value of ethical insights in arriving at well-considered ethical judgements" and especially in issues regarding the introduction and application of technology in society (Mepham 2010, p. 18). It is one of the most well-known ethical tools and it has been used in areas such as food production and commerce (Mepham 2000); genetic modification of farmed fish (Kaiser et al. 2007); carbon capture and storage technologies (Boucher and Gough 2012); transgenic animal farming (Small and Fisher 2005); and environmental remediation, restoration of radioactively contaminated areas, and long-term management of radioactive waste (Oughton et al. 2004, Cotton 2009).

The ethical matrix is a tool in which a set of ethical principles are applied to a number of stakeholders or affected groups with regard to a specific issue. The theoretical inspiration behind the ethical matrix comes from the work of John Rawls but mainly from Beauchamp and Childress' (2013) *Principles of Biomedical Ethics*. Rawls emphasizes that ethical principles ought to be embodied in common sense morality, while Beauchamp and Childress provide the principlist approach which the matrix adopts. It provides four principles which prima facie have a strong standing in medical ethics: nonmaleficence, beneficence, autonomy and justice. Usually the ethical matrix combines nonmaleficence and beneficence into "well-being." These three principles are intended to represent Kantian deontology, Benthamite utilitarianism, and

Rawlsian social contract theory (Mepham 2010). These three can however be swapped for other principles or additions can be made. Schroeder and Palmer (2003) suggest that within the context of technology assessment and specifically food ethics the principle of justice should be replaced by a principle of solidarity. The reason for this substitution is to add "an element of obligations rather than rights to the matrix," while also introducing virtue theory in addition to principles (Schroeder and Palmer 2003, p. 306).

In the matrix itself the principles are tabulated against relevant groups of stakeholders. Included stakeholders vary, depending on the technology and area of concern. The ethical matrix creates a grid where each principle applied to each stakeholder creates a cell which can be filled with morally relevant considerations. The result is a mapping of how particular stakeholders are affected with respect to each principle.

The ethical matrix has been highlighted for its ability to aid its user in *identifying* ethically relevant considerations. By including different stakeholders and major ethical theories (in the pluralistic spirit of principlism), the likelihood of identifying the relevant considerations is increased. It has the benefits of simplicity and user-friendliness.

The ethical matrix has been criticized for its lack of ability to aid its user in actually reaching a decision (Forsberg 2007; Schroeder and Palmer 2003; Cotton 2014). This criticism revolves around the fact that the matrix does not aid in weighing the different considerations against each other; the tool does not have any built-in mechanism for closing down decision making. Attempts have been made to improve the matrix with regard to this criticism. In a revised version of the ethical matrix, Mepham includes a scoring system in order to help with weighing the different considerations. Mepham proposes a Likert-type scale ranging from −2 (strongly infringe a principle) to +2 (strongly respect a principle). While claiming that this helps with establishing relative perceptions, it should nevertheless not be viewed as a decision model (Cotton 2014).

Another point of criticism relates to the top-down approach of the matrix, where the principles and stakeholders are largely decided beforehand by the facilitators. What if the most important stakeholders are not included in the matrix in the first place? Biases of the facilitators might be reproduced and reinforced. For instance, consider a group of traffic planners performing an ethical technology assessment of some inventions in traffic technology using an ethical matrix. If, for some reason, cyclists or people using wheelchairs are left out of the process and overlooked in the matrix at the outset, there is no guarantee that their interests will be taken into consideration. Focus might be in the wrong place. This criticism can be met by allowing the users to choose principles and stakeholders to a higher degree. This, however, involves a risk of some relevant principles and stakeholders being overlooked, if the users are not given enough to start with. A reasonable middle ground might be providing the users with the principles and the main stakeholders, while also encouraging them to add additional stakeholders if they think it necessary.

Meeting Formats

Tools like the ethical matrix can in principle be used by a single individual. Other tools are designed to involve several participants.

The ethical Delphi is a tool for exchanging views and arguments between experts (Millar et al. 2007). The tool is inspired by the Delphi method developed by the RAND Corporation in the 1950s. It has been used to elicit expert opinion on matters such as ethical issues in counseling (Herlihy and Dufrene 2011), developing ethical rules for boundaries of touch in complementary medicine (Schiff et al. 2010), and different questions within research ethics (Reynolds et al. 2008; van der Vorm et al. 2010; Downing et al. 2015). The tool consists of a virtual committee where the experts anonymously in a series of rounds exchange ideas, thoughts, and values. After each round, an administrator makes a summary of the ideas and arguments expressed. A second round is instigated after the first round, where the participants are asked to comment on matters expressed in the previous round. This process allows for an expert panel to elicit and discuss the ideas, arguments, and values they find most important. The process might stop after two rounds or go on until all the participants feel that the subject is sufficiently discussed and the summary after the rounds no longer adds to the discussion. Unlike the original Delphi method developed by RAND, the ethical Delphi is not focused on reaching consensus but rather highlights where consensus and disagreement exist.

The ethical Delphi method is perhaps appropriate when investigations of expert knowledge and opinions are desired. The tool allows for a more bottom-up approach than, for example, the ethical matrix. This gives the users more influence over what topics are discussed. The ethical Delphi can also be used regardless of the distance between contributors. The anonymity of the users is supposed to lower the risks of bias affecting their judgment of the input. In two different case studies where the ethical Delphi was used to assess genetically modified (GM) salmon in fish farming, several advantages and disadvantages of the tool were identified (Millar et al. 2007). The advantages with the tool were that it allows the group to set the agenda, anonymity prevents peer domination, the written dialogue enables equality of advocacy opportunity, and experts are exposed to new perspectives from experts in other fields. Among the disadvantages were the risk of bias in the selection of experts, that some ethical concerns may go unnoticed if not raised and also that it might be difficult to decide what conclusions can be drawn at the end. Another disadvantage pointed out by Cotton (2015) is that the use of the ethical Delphi does not allow for transparency. If, as is often the case in ethical technological assessment, transparency and public legitimacy are of importance, then the ethical Delphi looks like a black box that cannot be opened.

The *consensus conference* is an ethical tool, developed by the Danish Board of Technology in the late 1980s, which focuses on public participation and deliberation (Sclove 2000). As demand for public participation in technology assessment has grown, the number of consensus conferences in different countries has also grown (Nielsen et al. 2007). Examples where consensus conferences have been used are in assessing regulation of clinical research in children (Levine et al. 2011), developing a code of ethics for nurses (Lin et al. 2007), constructing guidelines for ethical use of neuroimages in medical testimony (Meltzer et al. 2014), and issues of human biomonitoring (Nelson et al. 2009).

The main aims of a consensus conference are to involve the public in trying to reach consensus and allowing for public involvement in an issue, typically a controversial one. Additional aims for using a consensus conference might be added: educating the public on an issue, or making the public's opinion known to experts, for example.

Public "involvement" or "participation" can however be ambiguous concepts associated with differing values, assumptions, and goals (Nielsen et al. 2007). Rowe and Frewer (2000) make a point by showing that involving the public in science and technology policy can be done in several ways and on different levels. At the lowest levels, involving the public can mean one-way communication, while higher levels are characterized by dialogue and two-way information exchange. Participation can have instrumental value in the sense of improving a technological assessment or making it more legitimate to the public. Arguably, participation can also be intrinsically valuable in the sense of being an inherent feature of democracy and transparent decision making.

The consensus conference, which usually takes place over several days, involves lay people and assigns them to panels that deliberate on a selected topic with the help of experts. Even though the design of the conferences might vary they have certain features in common: (1) The layperson goes through a learning process on the selected topic. This can be done with lectures or with assigned readings. (2) The panel of laypersons selects questions that the members feel they need to get answered in order to form a justified opinion. (3) A panel of experts answers these questions to the laypersons at the public conference. (4) The panel of laypersons considers the issue and presents their conclusions in a document at the end of the conference.

Consensus conferences have the benefit of including the public. However, some features could be problematized. Nielsen et al. (2007) compared three consensus conferences on GMOs and GM foods carried out in France,

Norway, and Denmark. One of their results is that the consensus conference cannot always be used as a tool in different national and political settings and still produce comparable results. Democratic ideals, conceptions of the value of public participation and ideas about legitimacy differ, and therefore the aims and conditions of fulfillment of a consensus conference will differ with regard to the democratic culture.

Other worries and points of criticism have been raised with regard to the conferences. One is that attendance might be low and the laypersons are self-selected, which might create a bias of people who are different from those who do not attend. Another is that while consensus might be positive to strive for, and in the final document achieved, it is not always clear whether it is genuinely achieved for all participants or if difference of opinion is less outspoken from minority views or from individuals who are less dominant in social groups.

Convergence seminar is a rather novel ethical tool designed to include the public and to ethically evaluate emerging technologies and deal with their future uncertainty and risk (Godman and Hansson 2009). Examples of where the tool has been used are to evaluate brain machine interface technology (Jebari and Hansson 2013) and nanobiotechnology (Godman and Hansson 2009). The seminars build on a model of decision making called *hypothetical retrospection* (Hansson 2007). The idea is that when evaluating future possibilities, the reaction "Don't do that, you may come to regret it!" is usually a sound type of argument. Hypothetical retrospection is used to achieve more stability under future uncertainty.

The seminars include three phases. In the first, the participants are divided into three groups that discuss different future scenarios. The three different groups share the first part of the scenario describing the current state of affairs, but from there the groups have different continuations of their scenarios. The scenarios are concrete and describe in outline the future branch including the process from which some decision has been made until the final point where the hypothetical retrospection is enacted. Each group now discusses what happens in their scenario and what they can learn from it. In the second phase, the participants are regrouped into three new groups with each group containing members from each of the groups from the first phase. One person from each group in phase one recapitulates their scenario and their discussion about it. The groups then discuss and compare the different scenarios. In the third and final phase, all participants meet. Here the groups from phase two recap their discussions and possible conclusions. After the groups' presentations a shared discussion takes place between all the participants and is led by the moderator.

A positive feature of the seminars is that they can be performed in a few hours which in comparison to some other ethical tools makes them user-friendly. A potential limitation with this method, and similar ones, is that the participants in the seminars are to a too large extent steered by the content of the given scenarios (Godman and Hansson 2009).

EVALUATING ETHICAL TOOLS

An interesting and perhaps overlooked question is how we ought to evaluate tools; especially given the wide range of ethical tools that exist.[5] Much energy has been put into developing ethical tools, and while some attempts have been made at discussing evaluation of tools (Wilding 2012; Rowe and Frewer 2004), many of these focus on one ethical tool, namely, the ethical matrix (Forsberg 2007; Cotton 2009). What is a good ethical tool, and how should we decide which tool to use? These questions are surprisingly scantily treated in the literature.

Forsberg proposed that ethical tools should show *intramethodological* and *intermethodological* stability. Intramethodological stability means that the same user(s) in similar situations should reach the same conclusions. Intermethodological stability means that different user(s) should reach the same conclusion.

Intramethodological stability appears to be unproblematic: if a tool does not show this kind of stability, there seems to be an element of chance or randomness with regard to what conclusion the users draw. However, intermethodological stability is a more problematic notion (Moula and Sandin 2015). If a tool turns out to be too intermethodologically stable, that is, if different groups were to reach the same conclusions, this might be a result of the tool's being biased. Ethical tools are supposed to help their users identify relevant considerations, and sometimes offer help with weighing them, but tools are not supposed to provide final answers that are independent of its users. The judgment and ethical reasoning of the users have to play a part and should allow for different users with different values or priorities to reach different conclusions.

Kaiser et al. (2007) develop general criteria for evaluating ethical tools. They introduce the concept of *ethical soundness* for tools which is supposed to provide more structured evaluations of ethical tools. They propose the following definition of ethical soundness:

> An ethical framework is ethically sound, if and only if, its application produces understanding of ethically relevant considerations in such a way that within a given body of knowledge and on condition of its competent use no further considerations would decisively alter the normative conclusions drawn from the framework by the users. (Kaiser et al. 2007, p. 68; passage italicized in original)

A problem with the proposed definition is its binary nature—it does not allow degrees. With this definition ethical tools come in two categories; ethically sound tools and ethically unsound tools. This is arguably unintuitive: usually it makes good sense to talk about tools as being more or less good. Kaiser et al. (2007) are probably aware of this difficulty and provide five indicators which they think could aid us in knowing whether a tool meets the demand of ethical soundness or not. The criteria are

1. Inclusion of values at stake;
2. Transparency;
3. Multiplicity of viewpoints, that is, different ethical viewpoints that exist in a pluralist society are taken into account;
4. Exposition of case-specific ethically relevant aspects, including factual information;
5. Inclusion of ethical arguments.

Arguably these could be reduced to two: comprehensiveness (of values, facts, principles, and arguments) and transparency.

Another attempt at a structured way of evaluating ethical tools is provided in Moula and Sandin (2015). As the fundamental principle for how to evaluate tools, they propose *purposiveness*; that is, how well a tool achieves its designed purposes. This seems to be in line with how we evaluate tools in general. As the general purpose of an ethical tool they propose "the aim to help their users improve deliberations in order to reach ethically informed judgments or decisions." Tools can then be divided and evaluated according to their additional purposes; for example, some tools are more specifically designed to reach a decision or to facilitate public engagement.

Specific properties of different tools that affect their quality (purposiveness) can then be identified. For all ethical tools comprehensiveness and user-friendliness is proposed. For decision-making tools the *ability to guide users to a decision according to ambition*, and *theoretical justification of decision supporting mechanism* are proposed. If the tool is used in a context where the result of its use is likely to be scrutinized by others, then *transparency* is of importance. For public engagement tools it is proposed that the tool should display *procedural fairness* which ensures fair treatment of the public and all individuals in the process of using the tool.

SUGGESTIONS FOR FURTHER RESEARCH

It is reasonable to assume that there will be a demand for ethical tools also in the future. At the very least, they can contribute to the legitimacy of decisions with ethical import. This means challenges both from an academic and a more practical point of view.

First, the use of information and communication technologies. There are indeed a number of "ethics apps," computer games, etc., of varying degrees of complexity: two examples are the *Decision* app from the Markkula Center for Applied Ethics,[6] and the Baker Ethics Training Game (the latter focuses on corporate ethics) from Tiny Universe.[7] However, the full potential of such technologies and applications is yet to be realized. In particular, this has implications for the increased use of technical systems with some degree of autonomy, such as self-driving cars and military applications.

Secondly, the development of ethical tools can conceivably change the role of professional ethicists. If decision makers use ethical tools to a greater extent, what, if any, will be the role of the ethicists? This relates to the question of elitism that sometimes lurks behind the idea of ethical tools—namely, that experts don't really need the tools; the tools are just aids for those who are not sufficiently versed in ethics. It is possible that developed ethical tools might make some expert judgment redundant, and this is something ethicists will have to relate to.

Third, a sometimes overlooked feature of ethical tools is that many of them are limited to being used among users who are part of the same moral community. (By a "moral community" we mean a group of people who share at least a significant portion of their ethical values, norms, etc.) Users typically have to share enough of ethical values for the use of the tools to work. This is most salient in tools that strive for a consensus or are used by a group of people instead of an individual.

CONCLUSION

Ethical tools are instruments designed to help the users improve their ethical deliberations. Within technology assessment many ethical tools are used to help with the assessment or to include different views and stakeholders into the assessment. Different tools however are suitable for different situations and purposes. Some are designed to elicit expert opinion, some to include laypersons, some can be used by individuals while others cannot, some are designed to reach a consensus while some are not, and some are more suited for being action guiding than others. While many tools exist, systematic evaluations of the tools are sparse and help with deciding which tool to use for different technological assessments might be developed.

NOTES

1. Emphasized by Kaiser et al. (2007).

2. Cf. Deblonde, De Graaf and Brom (2007). Some of the problems associated with weighing aspects of ethical tools are discussed in Forsberg (2006).

3. https://www.rotary.org/myrotary/en/learning-reference/about-rotary/guiding-principles (accessed December 18, 2015).

4. http://www.aedilemma.net/ (accessed December 18, 2015).

5. This section builds on Moula and Sandin (2015).

6. https://www.scu.edu/ethics/ethics-resources/ethical-decision-making/ (accessed March 3, 2016).

7. https://itunes.apple.com/gy/app/baker-ethics-training-game/id1081484174?mt=8 (accessed March 4, 2016).

REFERENCES

Beauchamp, Tom L., and James F. Childress. 2013. *Principles of Biomedical Ethics*, 7th ed. Oxford: Oxford University Press.

Beekman, Volkert, Erik de Bakker, Heike Baranzke, Oyvind Baune, Marian Deblonde, Ellen-Marie Forsberg, Ronald de Graaff, Hans-Werner Ingensiep, Jesper Lassen, Ben Mepham, Annika Porsborg Nielsen, Sandy Tomkins, Erik Thorstensen, Kate Millar, Barbara Skorupinski, Frans Brom, Matthias Kaiser, and Peter Sandøe. 2006. *Ethical Bio-technology Assessment Tools for Agriculture and Food Production*. Final Report Ethical Bio-TA Tools (QLG6-CT-2002-02594). LEI, The Hague.

Bombard, Yvonne, Julia Abelson, Dorina Simeonov, and Francois-Pierre Gauvin. 2011. "Eliciting Ethical and Social Values in Health Technology Assessment: A Participatory Approach." *Social Science & Medicine* 73:135–44.

Boucher, Philip, and Claire Gough. 2012. "Mapping the Ethical Landscape of Carbon Capture and Storage." *Poiesis & Praxis* 9:249–70.

Burls, Amanda, Lorraine Caron, Ghislaine Cleret de Langavant, Wybo Dondorp, Christa Harstall, Ela Pathak-Sen, and Bjørn Hofmann. 2011. "Tackling Ethical Issues in Health Technology Assessment: A Proposed Framework." *International Journal of Technology Assessment in Health Care* 27:230–37.

Claydon, Jane. 2011. "A New Direction for CSR: The Shortcomings of Previous CSR Models and the Rationale for a New Model." *Social Responsibility Journal* 7:405–20.

Cotton, Matthew. 2009. "Evaluating the 'Ethical Matrix' as a Radioactive Waste Management Deliberative Decision-support Tool." *Environmental Values* 18:153–76.

Cotton, Matthew. 2014. Ethics and Technology Assessment: A Participatory Approach. Berlin: Springer.

Deblonde, M., R. De Graaf, and F. Brom. 2007. "An Ethical Toolkit for Food Companies: Reflections on Its Use." *Journal of Agricultural and Environmental Ethics* 20:99–118.

Downing, Julia, Caprice Knapp, Mary Ann Muckaden, Susan Fowler-Kerry, and Joan Marston. 2015. "Priorities for Global Research Into Children's Palliative Care: Results of an International Delphi Study." *BMC Palliative Care* 14. Accessed March 31, 2016. DOI: 10.1186/s12904-015-0031-1.

Forsberg, Ellen-Marie. 2007. "A Deliberative Ethical Matrix Method–Justification of Moral Advice on Genetic Engineering in Food Production." *Dr. Art. Diss. Faculty of Humanities*. Oslo: University of Oslo.

Gallardo-Vázquez, Dolores, and M. Isabel Sanchez-Hernandez. 2014. "Measuring Corporate Social Responsibility for Competitive Success at a Regional Level." *Journal of Cleaner Production* 72:14–22.

Godman, Marion, and Sven Ove Hansson. 2009. "European Public Advice on Nano-biotechnology—Four Convergence Seminars." *Nanoethics* 3:43–59.

Hansson, S. O. 2007. "Hypothetical Retrospection." *Ethical Theory and Moral Practice* 10(2):145–57.

Herlihy, Barbara, and Roxane L. Dufrene. 2011. "Current and Emerging Ethical Issues in Counseling: A Delphi Study of Expert Opinions." *Counseling and Values* 56:10–24.

Jebari, Karim, and Sven Ove Hansson. 2013. "European Public Deliberation on Brain Machine Interface Technology: Five Convergence Seminars." *Science and Engineering Ethics* 19:1071–86.

Kaiser, Matthias, Kate Millar, Erik Thorstensen, and Sandy Tomkins. 2007. "Developing the Ethical Matrix as a Decision Support Framework: GM Fish as a Case Study." *Journal of Agricultural and Environmental Ethics* 20:65–80.

Levine, Robert J., Myron Genel, Leona Cuttler, Dorothy J. Becker, Lynnette Nieman, and Robert L. Rosenfield. 2011. "Overcoming Burdens in the Regulation of Clinical Research in Children: Proceedings of a Consensus Conference, in Historical Context." *International Journal of Pediatric Endocrinology* 1: 19. Accessed March 31, 2016. DOI: 10.1186/1687-9856-2011-19.

Lin, Chiou-Fen, Meei-Shiow Lu, Hsien-Hsien Chiang, Chun-Chih Chung, Tze-Luen Lin, Teresa J. C. Yin, and Che-Ming Yang. 2007. "Using a Citizen Consensus Conference to Revise the Code of Ethics for Nurses in Taiwan." *Journal of Nursing Scholarship* 39:95–101.

Maon, François, Adam Lindgreen, and Valérie Swaen. 2009. "Designing and Implementing Corporate Social Responsibility: An Integrative Framework Grounded in Theory and Practice." *Journal of Business Ethics* 87:71–89.

Meltzer, C. C., G. Sze, Rommelfanger, K. Kinlaw, J. D. Banja, and P. R. Wolpe. 2014. "Guidelines for the Ethical Use of Neuroimages in Medical Testimony: Report of a Multidisciplinary Consensus Conference." *American Journal of Neuroradiology* 35:632–37.

Mepham, Ben. 2000. "A Framework for the Ethical Analysis of Novel Foods: The Ethical Matrix." *Journal of Agricultural and Environmental Ethics* 12:165–76.

Mepham, Ben. 2010. "The ethical matrix as a tool in policy interventions: The obesity crisis." In *Food Ethics*, edited by Franz-Theo Gottwald, Hans Werner. Ingensiep, and Marc Meinhardt, 17-30. New York: Springer.

Millar, Kate, Erik Thorstensen, Sandy Tomkins, Ben Mepham, and Matthias Kaiser. 2007. "Developing the Ethical Delphi." *Journal of Agricultural and Environmental Ethics* 20:53–63.

Moula, Payam, and Per Sandin. 2015. "Evaluating Ethical Tools." *Metaphilosophy* 46:263–79.

Nelson, Jessica W., Madeleine Kangsen Scammell, Rebecca Gasior Altman, Thomas F. Webster, and David M. Ozonoff. 2009. "A New Spin on Research Translation: The Boston Consensus Conference on Human Biomonitoring." *Environmental Health Perspectives* 117:495–99.

Nielsen, Annika Porsborg, Jesper Lassen and Peter Sandøe. 2007. "Democracy at Its Best? The Consensus Conference in a Cross-National Perspective." *Journal of Agricultural and Environmental Ethics* 20:13–35.

Oughton, Deborah, Ellen-Marie Forsberg, Ingrid Bay, Matthias Kaiser, and Brenda Howard. 2004. "An Ethical Dimension to Sustainable Restoration and Long-Term Management of Contaminated Areas." *Journal of Environmental Radioactivity* 74:171–83.

Reynolds, J., N. Crichton, W. Fisher, and S. Sacks. 2008. "Determining the Need for Ethical Review: A Three-Stage Delphi Study." *Journal of Medical Ethics* 34:889–94.

Rowe, Gene, and Lynn J. Frewer. 2000. "Public Participation Methods: A Framework for Evaluation." *Science, Technology & Human Values* 25:3–29.

Rowe, Gene, and Lynn J. Frewer. 2004. "Evaluating Public-Participation Exercises: A Research Agenda." *Science, Technology & Human Values* 29:512–56.

Schiff, Elad, Eran Ben-Arye, Margalit Shilo, Moti Levy, Leora Schachter, Na'ama Weitchner, Ofra Golan, and Julie Stone. 2010. "Development of Ethical Rules for Boundaries of Touch in Complementary Medicine—Outcomes of a Delphi Process." *Complementary Therapies in Clinical Practice* 16:194–97.

Sclove, R. E. (2000). "Town Meetings on Technology: Consensus Conferences as Democratic Participation." In *Science, Technology, and Democracy*, edited by Daniel Lee Kleinman, 33–48. Albany: State University of New York Press.

Schroeder, Doris, and Clare Palmer. 2003. "Technology Assessment and the 'Ethical Matrix'." Poiesis & Praxis 1:295-307.

Small, Bruce H., and Mark W. Fisher. 2005. "Measuring Biotechnology Employees' Ethical Attitudes towards a Controversial Transgenic Cattle Project: The Ethical Valence Matrix." *Journal of Agricultural and Environmental Ethics* 18:495–508.

van der Vorm, A., A. L. van der Laan, G. Borm, M. Vernooij-Dassen, M. Olde Rikkert, E. van Leeuwen, and W. Dekkers. 2010. "'Experts' Opinions on Ethical Issues of Genetic Research into Alzheimer's Disease: Results of a Delphi Study in the Netherlands." *Clinical Genetics* 77:382–88.

Wilding, Ethan T. 2012. "Framing Ethical Acceptability: A Problem with Nuclear Waste in Canada." *Science and Engineering Ethics* 18:301–13.

Chapter 9

Responsibility Analysis

Jessica Nihlén Fahlquist

When analyzing responsibility in the context of technology, conceptual as well as normative questions arise. In order to discuss the normative issues, several conceptual distinctions should be made. First, we have to distinguish between legal and moral responsibility. The two are related, but not identical. Legal responsibility is analyzed, decided, and implemented by legislators and lawyers. It is possible that an agent, for example, an engineer or a manager, is legally responsible without being morally responsible or the other way around. In this chapter, the focus is on moral responsibility. Technology raises a number of questions concerning moral responsibility. The two most important questions are the following. First, do engineers have a special moral responsibility? Second, does technology affect responsibility? In the following sections, these two questions guide the discussion, which intro- duces conceptual and normative questions relating to responsibility, but also provides examples of how these questions are relevant to the responsibility of engineers and the way that technology affects responsibility. The chapter begins with a brief introduction to the philosophical discussion of moral responsibility. Subsequently, it introduces the distinction between backward- looking and forward-looking responsibility and the discussion on individual and collective responsibility. Finally, two notions of *taking* responsibility are introduced, that is, responsibility as task and virtue.

DETERMINISM, FREE WILL, AND MORAL RESPONSIBILITY AS BLAMEWORTHINESS

Interestingly, the word "responsibility" is fairly new, that is, new in the history of philosophy. The oldest confirmed use of the term in English is from 1642, but it existed in French in the fifteenth century (*Oxford English Dictionary* 2010). Responsibility became an important concept in a political context, when representative governments emerged in Europe toward the end of the eighteenth century (McKeon 1957, Williams 2008).

The novelty of the term does not mean that we did not hold each other accountable prior to modern society. Aristotle is often mentioned in philosophical texts about responsibility, and he wrote primarily about responsibility as blameworthiness. Aristotle argues that if an agent did something wrong voluntarily, that is, freely and knowingly, he is blameworthy (Aristotle's *Nicomachean Ethics*).

In the philosophical literature, the most contested question concerning responsibility is whether an agent can reasonably be held responsible for her actions even if there is no free will. If it turns out that human beings are predetermined to act in certain ways, that is, that we have no choice, are we morally responsible? In essence, is moral responsibility compatible with determinism? This debate on moral responsibility is carried out within the frameworks of compatibilism and incompatibilism, the former arguing that responsibility is compatible with determinism and the latter denying this (e.g., Fischer and Ravizza 1993).

The concept of responsibility in this discussion focuses on moral agency, capacity and their relation to responsibility as blameworthiness. It is a largely backward-looking concept. In a sense, the participants in this debate are interested in reasonable conditions for holding someone responsible in the sense of blameworthiness. In ordinary language as well as in the philosophical debate, a basic notion is that a person is responsible if certain conditions are fulfilled. For example, if someone was forced to do something that we normally consider wrong, we are generally reluctant to hold her responsible, that is, we would excuse her for acting wrongfully. The following is a useful list of conditions that are often seen as prerequisites for holding an agent morally responsible in the sense of blameworthiness (Van de Poel et al. 2012):

1. Capacity
2. Causality
3. Knowledge
4. Freedom
5. Wrongdoing

The first condition requires that the potentially responsible agent is a moral agent who has a certain capacity for rational thinking and moral deliberation. It is common to exempt some groups of human beings from responsibility—for example, children and people with mental disorders—because they lack the capacity to act responsibly (e.g., Wallace 1994; Van de Poel et al. 2012). Causation is a complex notion, but unless the agent is causally linked, in some way, to the action or consequence for which she might be held responsible, she may not be held responsible. Causation is sometimes fairly straightforward. However, in some cases the causal links are less clear. For example, it has been argued that consumers in industrialized countries contribute to structural processes causing global injustice and that they are, therefore, responsible (Young 2006). The way that individuals contribute to climate change is another example of a relatively loose causal connection. However, it is clear that some, more or less tangible, causal connection is required for moral responsibility. As we saw above, the conditions of knowledge and freedom have been seen as prerequisites of moral responsibility as blameworthiness since Aristotle. The most common excuses that people offer when they think they are wrongfully held responsible are "I did not know" and "I was forced." The last condition requires that there has been some wrongdoing. What counts as wrongdoing differs depending on ethical theory, and possibly contextual considerations. However, we do not hold others responsible in the sense of blameworthiness unless there appears to have been some kind of wrongdoing (Van de Poel et al. 2012).

EMOTIONS AND REFLECTION

There is an emotional as well as a cognitive element involved in responsibility ascriptions. Let us imagine that an innocent person is stabbed to death.

A common first reaction for most people when someone is stabbed is to get emotional. We get angry and feel sympathy for the victim's family. Perhaps we think about what we would do if it happened to a family member or friend. With time, the emotional reaction is accompanied, and perhaps moderated, by reflection and analysis. We may find out that the perpetrator committed the crime after having been released from the psychiatric clinic, where he had spent most of his adult life due to regular psychoses. Some questions that may come to mind are the following. What caused the killer to stab an innocent person? What was the extent of the perpetrator's psychiatric problems? Could the social services, hospitals, or other institutions have acted differently to prevent the tragedy? These are merely a few of the questions that contribute to making our thinking about the event more complex and detached than the initial emotional reaction (Nihlén Fahlquist 2008).

According to an influential idea defended by Strawson, the reactive attitudes—for example, resentment and moral indignation—are all there is to moral responsibility. It is our expectations of our own and others' behavior that lead to feelings of guilt, remorse, and responsibility. When we have been injured or offended by someone else's actions, we are normally expected to feel resentment unless there are special considerations. These considerations are very similar to the conditions mentioned above and relate to for example, the status as moral agent or a lack of knowledge. When such special considerations are relevant, our reactive attitudes are modified (Strawson 1993).

However, the reactive attitudes do not to tell the whole story of what moral responsibility is. As members of the moral community we also have the capability to step back and analyze the situation from a more detached perspective.

It should be noted that it is not clear that the emotional reaction is less valid, from a normative perspective, than the detached view. There is research in psychology indicating that emotions are necessary for our thinking, possibly even for making rational decisions (e.g., Damasio 1994). It has been argued that emotions are also needed for ethical deliberation (Roeser 2012). Roeser discusses this idea in relation to technological risk, arguing that responsible engineers use their moral emotions in order to make good decisions concerning risk. Additionally, she argues that the moral emotions of laypeople should be taken seriously, when deliberating about the ethics of risk (Roeser 2006).

There is a difference between *being held* responsible and *being* responsible that is not captured by the notion of reactive attitudes (Fischer and Ravizza 1993). We are able to, and regularly do, criticize and question our own and others' reactive attitudes. Hence, to be morally responsible is not merely to be a target of reactive attitudes. According to Fischer's revised Strawsonian theory, "Agents are morally responsible if and only if they are *appropriate* recipients of reactive attitudes" (ibid.). Hence, whereas the first element of moral responsibility is the reactive attitudes toward the actions of co-agents in a moral community, the other element is critical reflection of these practices. It should be kept in mind that we are still merely talking about responsibility as blameworthiness. Although not the only notion of responsibility, it is an important one and it is applicable to engineering. When risks materialize or warning signs are ignored, the question arises about whether someone is to blame. If it turns out that an engineer, for example, did something wrong, she may be blamed. However, if we also get the information that she was not provided with the correct information or that her manager forced her to act wrongfully, our willingness to hold her responsible is probably modified. There are two important aspects of holding someone responsible in the sense of blaming. First, when other people have done something wrong, we blame them for reasons of fairness. Second, the practice of blaming ideally deters people from performing certain wrongful actions. It keeps people within the boundaries of moral community. These two aims of holding others responsible, that is, fairness and efficacy, bring us to an important distinction, that is, the one between backward-looking and forward-looking responsibility.

BACKWARD-LOOKING AND FORWARD-LOOKING RESPONSIBILITY

As we have seen, we appear to hold others responsible for undesired events, partly for reasons of fairness. When a moral agent has caused an undesired event or outcome, and when she does not have a valid excuse, it is reasonable to hold her responsible. Furthermore, holding someone responsible involves an emotional reaction, but also an element of reflection and deliberation. In addition, there is an underlying idea that if people are blamed when they do wrong, others will be deterred from repeating the wrongful actions. This is one of the expressions of what we could call the efficacy aim of responsibility ascriptions (Nihlén Fahlquist 2006b). We ascribe responsibility for undesired events in order to prevent similar things from happening in the future. Sometimes, the agent who did wrong is the one who should also do something about it. For example, if Anna throws a vase at Beth because she is mad at her, our holding Anna responsible (if we assume that we have all the information needed for a moral assessment) would include both aspects and we would blame her *and* expect her to apologize and clean up the mess. However, the two kinds, or aspects, of responsibility do not *necessarily* coincide. For this reason, a distinction should be made between backward-looking and forward-looking responsibility. This distinction has also been called passive versus active responsibility and retrospective versus prospective responsibility (e.g., Bovens 1998; Van de Poel and Royakkers 2011). The distinction is highly relevant to technological risks. Consider the oil spill caused by the Deepwater Horizon explosion in 2010 or the Fukushima nuclear accident in 2011. Following these events, discussions about responsibility arose and the focus of the public's concerns is twofold. First, what and who caused it to happen? Second, how can it be prevented in the future and whose task is it to do so? Sometimes, the two questions are conflated, but it is important to keep them separate since it is not always reasonable to ascribe backward-looking and forward-looking responsibility to the same agent.

In order to disentangle the notions of backward-looking and forward-looking responsibility, we need to distinguish between different questions that could be raised after an undesired event like the Fukushima nuclear accident. Although people often disagree, normatively, about who is responsible for what, some disagreements could sometimes simply be due to the ambiguity of "being responsible." Part of the confusion is the common propensity not to clearly separate the following questions:

- Who caused A?
- Who is to blame for A?
- Who should do something about A?

With the help of these questions, we should make use of the following distinction:

- Backward-looking responsibility ascriptions (consisting of backward-looking causal responsibility and blame);
- Forward-looking responsibility ascriptions (consisting of forward-looking causal responsibility, *potential* backward-looking causal responsibility and *potential* blame) (Nihlén Fahlquist 2006a).

In order to fully understand this distinction, we will now look at an example where the different notions of responsibility went from being ambiguous to becoming more explicit. In the area of road traffic, it is common to think about road users as responsible for accidents. One expression of this is the public demands for more severe punishments when the media reports about fatal instances of drunk driving. However, this is not the only way to think about responsibility and road traffic safety.

In 1997, the Swedish government adopted a new goal to guide traffic safety policy. It was called Vision Zero and the basic idea was that it is not ethically acceptable to have a numerical goal stating how many annual fatalities are acceptable in road traffic. For example, to state that "the goal for 2017 is that 300 people are killed in road traffic" could be interpreted as the acceptance of road fatalities or even fatalism, that is, an idea that fatalities are inevitable as long as we have road traffic. Instead, it was argued that the only ethically justified goal is that no one is killed in road traffic. The new goal also entailed a shift of focus from the backward-looking responsibility of the individual road users to the forward-looking responsibility of the system designers (Nihlén Fahlquist 2006a). The new framework acknowledges that a driver may be said to have causal responsibility for a collision, but the accident additionally entails a forward-looking responsibility for someone else, in this case the so-called system designers, that is, for example local government and car producers. An individual driver may have caused a collision through her inability to notice a pedestrian at a crossing. This inability could potentially be reduced, for example, by vehicle technology, road design, or street lighting. Consequently, the driver in this case could be causally responsible for it, but she is not necessarily blameworthy, and it may be someone else's forward-looking responsibility to prevent similar accidents in the future. In this case, the system designers did not cause the accident, but they are responsible to make sure that the systems are changed in a way that prevents similar collisions in the future.

INDIVIDUAL AND COLLECTIVE RESPONSIBILITY

The road traffic example is illustrative of the need to make another distinction, that is, the one between individual and collective responsibility. As we saw, it is often the case that individuals and collective entities, for example, a company or a local government, are responsible to differing degrees. In situations where there are several actors and/or institutions involved, responsibility can be shared between different agents, and these could be individuals or collective entities. In everyday language, it is common to talk about companies, nations, and governments as responsible. However, philosophically it is a contested question whether collectives can be morally responsible (May and Hoffman 1992). One question that arises in this situation is to what extent each individual agent is responsible in cases where, for example, a company is held responsible. When the Deepwater Horizon oil rig exploded, who was morally responsible—the CEO, the management team, or everyone working at Shell? One important question today is who is responsible for climate change. Individuals act in their everyday lives, but states and institutions like the United Nations negotiate what has to be done by whom. In addition, corporations act in ways that promote or impair the goals to mitigate and adapt to climate change. To what extent should individuals, as citizens and consumers, be seen as responsible for climate change and to what extent should states and corporations be held responsible?

There are different opinions on this. Some would argue that individuals contribute to climate change by their everyday actions, like driving their cars, and that they by virtue of this are morally responsible for climate change. Others would argue that governments have failed to introduce laws and a societal structure, for example, a sustainable infrastructure and that they, by virtue of this, are responsible. An alternative way of framing the issue is to say that the most important condition for responsibility in this case is the ability to do something about the immense problem instead of focusing on causation and blameworthiness. Evidently, the question of responsibility and climate change raises questions concerning backward-looking and forward-looking responsibility, but also individual versus collective responsibility (e.g., Sinnott-Armstrong 2005; Jamieson 2007; Jacobsen and Dulsrud 2007; Nihlén Fahlquist 2009).

Ideally, responsibility ascriptions should be: (a) fair; and (b) effective (Nihlén Fahlquist 2006b). The tension between fairness and efficacy is present in the debate on climate change too. Fairness, in this context, could mean that the responsibility ascriptions are normatively reasonable in some sense, for example, that the conditions concerning knowledge and freedom are fulfilled. However, in order to solve the problems of climate change adaptation and mitigation, the one we ascribe responsibility to should also be able to solve the problem, that is, be effective. For example, if we ascribe responsibility to children under the age of five, the problems associated with climate change would probably not be solved. Of course, this responsibility ascription would not be fair either. However, it is possible to imagine fair, but ineffective responsibility ascriptions. Similarly, it is also possible to imagine responsibility ascriptions that are effective, but unfair. These two aims correspond with consequentialist and deontological ethical theories. Consequentialists would emphasize the effects and effectiveness of responsibility ascriptions. Deontologists, on the other hand, would only be interested in the fairness of responsibility ascriptions (Nihlén Fahlquist 2006b). Most nonphilosophers are likely to be interested in both aims and most public debates on responsibility include both aspects. From this perspective, the question of who is responsible for climate change could focus on what would be the fair distribution of responsibility or what would be the most effective one. It could also focus on who caused climate change and is blameworthy, or whose forward-looking responsibility it is to solve the problems of mitigation and adaptation.

When a risk has materialized in the context of engineering, this aspect of responsibility ascriptions is relevant in the following sense. There are likely to be several agents involved, for example, engineers, managers, politicians, and customers. Consider the Deepwater Horizon oil spill again, or the Challenger accident in 1986. When distributing responsibility after an event like that, a combination of effectiveness and fairness aspects is relevant. Ideally, if a manager, politician, or engineer did something wrong she should be held responsible, that is, responsibility ascriptions should be fair. In addition, we also want to avoid similar events from happening in the future and should ascribe responsibility with this in mind too.

THE PROBLEM OF MANY HANDS

Arguably, collective responsibility is more important now than it has ever been. Human activities increasingly take place in collective contexts. Research, innovation, and technological development are often performed in large projects that involve many different actors. When a large number of agents are involved in causing a negative outcome, it may be problematic to identify who is responsible. This has been referred to as the "problem of many hands" (Thompson 1980; Van de Poel et al. 2012). It was first formulated in a political context, referring to the moral responsibility of public officials. Thompson argued that because there are so many different officials involved, contributing to policies in many different ways, it is difficult to ascribe moral responsibility for the organization's conduct. For the public, it is almost impossible to find someone who can be said to have independently taken some crucial decision leading up to the undesired situation, that is, who caused it knowingly and freely. The problem of many hands is now primarily discussed in engineering ethics and business ethics (Harris et al. 2005 [1995]; Nissenbaum 1996; Doorn and Van de Poel 2012; Nihlén Fahlquist et al. 2015).

The problem of many hands can be seen as an epistemic problem, a problem of how to identify the person was causally responsible. Insiders usually know more about the causal links, so this is mainly a problem for outsiders (Davis 2012). Construed in this way, the problem could be avoided by making each individual's causal contribution more transparent. In contrast, the problem is a moral problem if interpreted as a situation where none of the individuals is (or can be held) responsible but in which the collective of individuals is morally responsible (Van de Poel et al. 2012).

TAKING RESPONSIBILITY

One way to look at the problem of many hands is to view it as resulting from a lack of responsible behavior, and this brings us to yet another aspect of responsibility. Responsibility is not merely to be distributed after a negative outcome has occurred. In ordinary language, we often talk about taking, or failing to take, responsibility. The focus is then on the individual and whether she sees herself as responsible. This notion is forward-looking and not focused on blameworthiness.

There are primarily two ways of conceptualizing forward-looking responsibility as taking responsibility. First, distributing responsibility could be seen as distributing tasks or obligations (c.f. Goodin 1986). Second, responsibility could be seen as a character trait or virtue. Both of these concepts are relevant to technology. We will now take a closer look at these two concepts, starting with task responsibility.

According to Goodin, responsibilities are to utilitarianism what duties are to deontological ethics. The main difference, he argues, is that whereas duties dictate actions, responsibilities dictate results (Goodin 1986). Responsibilities require certain self-supervisory activities and it is the flexibility in the choice of actions that differentiates responsibilities from duties. For example, a duty may dictate that the agent ought to "give the dog food." In contrast, a (task) responsibility may state that the agent should see to it that "the dog is fed" or that "the dog is not hungry," which could include, for example, delegating the feeding of the dog to someone else. In addition, responsibilities are not binary in the same way as duties, but they can be discharged to varying degrees. Duties, according to this line of thought, are either discharged or not. Responsibilities, on the other hand, could be more or less discharged. The agent could have delegated the task to someone, but not properly made sure that the job was done, thereby taking responsibility to some extent, but not fully.

When ascribed responsibility in this sense, the agent ought to "see to it that X," that is, make sure that the expected state of affairs, the result X, occurs. It is not enough that X occurs, but the agent must have "seen to it" that it does (Goodin 1986). This concept of responsibility is not completely unrelated to backward-looking responsibility and blame. If someone fails to discharge their task responsibilities, they may be blamed for that. It is part of being responsible in the forward-looking sense of being assigned a task to achieve a certain result that one may also be blamed if one does not do that.

If we think about engineering, this kind of responsibility is highly relevant, as most engineers are expected to achieve certain results but less often have managers telling them exactly which actions need to be done in order to achieve those results. Most people would probably agree that it is part of the professional responsibility of engineers to judge and evaluate actions and to come up with a plan of actions in order to achieve a desired result. It is reasonable to argue that this professional responsibility entails a *moral* responsibility, and that engineers and researchers take moral responsibility to differing degrees.

Some people are more likely to take on responsibility. In this sense, the tendency to take on responsibility can also conceptualized as a virtue, that is, a character trait that some people cultivate through life experiences (Williams 2008). A "responsible" person or a person who is willing to "take responsibility" is someone who is more likely to take on and fulfil responsibilities ascribed to her, but the notion involves more than that. Virtue ethics focuses more on character than isolated actions, in contrast with consequentialism and deontological ethics. In consequence, when used in the virtue ethical sense, a person is responsible if she has certain character traits, attitudes, and emotions which make her behave in a certain way over time. Even if a responsible person is more likely to fulfil responsibilities ascribed to her, the underlying idea is that she also takes on more than what others dictate.

Arguably, responsibility as a virtue involves cognitive abilities, but also emotions. Unless someone cares about other people, it does not make sense to talk about *feeling* responsible and even *taking* responsibility for other people (Nihlén Fahlquist 2015). Let us apply this notion to engineering. If we consider what it means to take responsibility for safety, health, and the environment in a way that exceeds specified tasks, it presupposes having the ability to morally imagine how real people could be affected by failures and the materialization of risks. Some people have cultivated this character trait or disposition to act better than others. The extent to which a person is "responsible" in this sense could be a consequence of genes, upbringing, experiences, and other factors. Whereas we can all reflect on our own experiences and try to learn from them, it is obviously more difficult to affect our own genes and upbringing.

The idea of *taking* responsibility is highly relevant to technological design and the way users are affected by different design choices. It is imaginable that technologies affect the disposition of users to behave responsibly in different ways. There are many examples in the context of car design and infrastructure. Accidents are usually a combination of what the drivers do, what the vehicles do, and how the road infrastructure is designed. When some of the tasks previously performed by human drivers are delegated to technology, this shift affects the way we think about responsibility. For example, in the future, when cars are likely to be driverless human beings in the vehicle will all be passengers. It would not be surprising if such a situation will change our disposition to take responsibility for road traffic. Another example is the so-called alcohol interlock. This is a device measuring the driver's blood alcohol concentration (BAC) level through an exhalation sample required to start the engine. If the measured level is above the maximum level set, the car will not start. If this device was mandatory in all cars, drunk driving could be virtually eradicated. Alcohol interlocks are currently used differently in different countries, for example in public transport. It has been suggested that mandatory interlocks could be a way to solve the problem of drunk driving (Grill and Nihlén Fahlquist 2012). This could possibly affect drivers' disposition to take responsibility for safety. People may, for instance, come to view the interlock as a general test for being fit to drive, thereby ignoring other risks for example, fatigue or other drugs (Grill and Nihlén Fahlquist 2012). The alcohol interlock can be said to be a so-called behavior-steering technology or persuasive technologies, that is, technologies intentionally designed to change the user's behavior, attitude, or beliefs. This could be done by giving the user feedback of her actions or omissions and by trying to "suggest" a desired pattern of behavior (Fogg 2003; Spahn 2012; Nihlén Fahlquist et al. 2015). Whereas some of these technologies have been said to "manipulate" the user, others merely "convince" her. It appears reasonable to think that whereas some technologies enhance responsibility, others potentially hamper it. The alcohol interlock removes the possibility to drive under the influence of alcohol, thereby forcing drivers to be sober (at least when driving). This could be seen as a morally impermissible way of steering behavior and removing individual responsibility for sober driving (Nihlén Fahlquist et al. 2014). However, in the case of drunk driving, it clearly affects other people who risk becoming victims of the drunk driver's failure to take responsibility. For this reason, it may be more appropriate to focus on the potential victims in this case and to argue in accordance with the liberal principle stating that we are free to do what we want as long as we do not harm others, thereby stating that the interlock is morally permissible (Grill and Nihlén

Fahlquist 2012). On the other hand, if drunk driving were such that it only affected the drunk driver herself, it would be different. If that were the case, alcohol interlocks would be a paternalistic measure, which may or may not be morally permissible depending on our choice of normative perspective (Grill and Nihlén Fahlquist 2012).

Let us look at a second example of how technology may affect users' willingness or capacity to take responsibility. GPS is increasingly being used to track human beings and one of the applications is to use the technology to track children. There are several companies developing GPS applications for child protection and a number of products on the market. In Sweden, a number of preschools have started to use GPS as a means to keep track of children. If a child's parents use GPS and know all her whereabouts, this could be seen as sending the message that someone else is in control and presumably also takes responsibility. Youths, whose parents aim for a high degree of control, potentially experience this as a sign that their parents do not see them as competent (Pomerantz and Eaton 2000). If parents use technology to control and essentially take responsibility for children at all times, children may not develop into responsible adults. In order to become responsible they need to learn how to manage in different kinds of situations, learning through experience. GPS and other technologies which facilitate this tendency to overprotect children could then possibly hamper children from developing the virtue of responsibility (Nihlén Fahlquist 2015).

If technological design can affect people's tendency to take responsibility, it is the task of engineers to reflect on how best to include these considerations in engineering. There are no straightforward answers to the question how this should be done, but including a discussion on technology and responsibility as a virtue when it appears relevant is a first important step.

CONCLUSION

Questions of moral responsibility are primarily relevant to technology in two ways. First, engineers arguably have a moral responsibility for what they do as engineers, which goes beyond their work description. Second, the design of technology potentially affects responsibility in different ways. In this chapter, we have explored the following two questions. We have seen that there are different concepts and notions that are applicable to the context of engineering, and many different ways in which engineers can be said to have moral responsibility for what they do. The moral responsibility of engineers can be seen as a matter of task distribution, that is, a dictation of results that should be achieved, for example, "a safe and environmentally friendly car." Additionally, it could be construed as a virtue, that is, a character trait or a disposition to take responsibility for more than what the employment contract specifies. Additionally, technology can affect responsibility in different ways. First, technologies can affect the distribution and balance of responsibility between individuals. Second, they can alter the way responsibility is distributed between individuals in different roles, that is, parent and child. Third, technology can affect the way responsibility is distributed between the individual and collective agents—for example, the government and the industry. In addition to responsibility distributions, technology potentially affects our willingness to *take* responsibility, that is, our behavior over time.

REFERENCES

Aristotle. 2000. *Nicomachean Ethics* (Cambridge Texts in the History of Philosophy). Cambridge, UK; New York: Cambridge University Press.

Bovens, M. 1998. *The Quest for Responsibility: Accountability and Citizenship in Complex Organisations*. Cambridge: Cambridge University Press.

Damasio, A. 1994. *Descartes' Error: emotion, reason and the human brain*. New York: Putnam.

Davis, M. 2012. "Ain't No One Here But Us Social Forces": Constructing the Professional Responsibility of Engineers. *Science and Engineering Ethics* 18(1): 13–34.

Fischer, J. M., and Ravizza, M. (eds.). 1993. *Perspectives on Moral Responsibility*. Cornell University Press, Ithaca.

Fred, D., and Paul, Jeffrey (eds.). 1999. *Responsibility*: 218–49. Cambridge University Press, Cambridge.

Goodin, R. E. 1986. Responsibilities. *Philosophical Quarterly* 36: 50–56.

Grill, K., and Nihlén Fahlquist, J. 2012. Responsibility, Paternalism and Alcohol Interlocks. *Public Health Ethics* 5(2): 116–27.

Harris, C. E., Pritchard, M. S., and Rabins, M. J. 2005 [1995]. *Engineering Ethics: Concepts and Cases* (Third Edition). Belmont, CA: Wadsworth.

Jacobsen, E., & Dulsrud, A. 2007. Will Consumers Save the World? The Framing of Political Consumerism. *Journal of Agricultural and Environmental Ethics* 20: 469–82.

Jamieson, D. 2007. When Utilitarians should be Virtue Theorists. *Utilitas* 19(2): 160–83.

May, L., Hoffman, S. (eds.). 1992. *Collective Responsibility: Five Decades of Debate in Theoretical and Applied Ethics*. Lanham, MD: Rowman & Littlefield Publishers.

McKeon, R. 1957. The Development and the Significance of the Concept of Responsibility. *Revue Internationale de Philosophie* 11(39): 3–32.

Nihlén Fahlquist, J. 2015. Responsibility and Privacy—Ethical Aspects of Using GPS to Track Children. *Children & Society* 29(1): 38–47.

Nihlén Fahlquist, J. 2008. *Moral Responsibility and the Ethics of Traffic Safety*. PhD. Stockholm: Royal Institute of Technology.

Nihlén Fahlquist, J. 2009. Moral Responsibility for Environmental Problems—Individual or Institutional? *Journal of Agricultural and Environmental Ethics* 22(2): 109–24.

Nihlén Fahlquist, J. 2006a. Responsibility Ascriptions and Vision Zero. *Accident Analysis and Prevention* 38: 1113–18.

Nihlén Fahlquist, J. 2006b. Responsibility Ascriptions and Public Health Problems. Who is Responsible for Obesity and Lung Cancer?" *Journal of Public Health* 14(1): 15–19.

Nihlén Fahlquist, J. 2015. Responsibility as a Virtue and the Problem of Many Hands. Ibo van de Poel, Lambèr Royakkers, Sjoerd Zwart, Tiago di Lima, Jessica Nihlén Fahlquist, and Neelke Doorn (eds.), *Moral Responsibility in Innovation Networks.* Routledge.

Nihlén Fahlquist, J., Doorn, N., and Van de Poel, I. 2015. Design for Responsibility. In Jeroen van den Hoven, Ibo van de Poel, and Pieter Vermaas (eds.), *Ethics and Values in Technological Design.* Springer.

Nissenbaum, H. 1996. Accountability in a Computerized Society. *Science and Engineering Ethics* 2(1): 25–42.

Oxford English Dictionary. 2010. *Responsibility.* Accessed online on August 15, 2016, www.oed.com.

Pomerantz, E. M., and Eaton, M. M. 2000. Developmental Differences in Children's Conceptions of Parental Control: "They Love Me, But They Make Me Feel Incompetent". *Merrill-Palmer Quarterly* 46: 140–67.

Roeser, S. 2012. Emotional Engineers: Toward Morally Responsible Design. *Science and Engineering Ethics* 18(1): 103–15.

Roeser, S. 2006. The Role of Emotions in Judging the Moral Acceptability of Risk. *Safety Science* 44: 689–700.

Sinnott-Armstrong, W. 2005. It's Not My Fault. In W. Sinnott-Armstrong & R. B. Howarth (eds.), *Perspectives on Climate Change: Science, Economics, Politics, Ethics.* Amsterdam: Elsevier.

Smetana, J. G., Campione-Barr, N., and Daddis, C. 2004. Longitudinal Development of Family Decision Making: Defining Healthy Behavioral Autonomy for Middle-Class African American Adolescents. *Child Development* 75: 1418–34.

Strawson, P. 1993. Freedom and Resentment. *Proceedings of the British Academy* 48, 1962: 1–25, reprinted in John Martin Fischer and Mark Ravizza (eds.), *Perspectives on Moral Responsibility*: 50–52. Cornell University Press, Ithaca.

Van de Poel, I., and Royakkers, M. M. 2011. *Ethics, Technology and Engineering.* Wiley-Blackwell. Chichester, West Sussex.

Van de Poel, I., Nihlén Fahlquist, J., Doorn, N., Zwart, S., Royakkers L., and di Lima, T. 2012. The Problem of Many Hands: Climate Change as an Example. *Science and Engineering Ethics* 18(1): 49–67.

Wallace, R. J. 1994. *Responsibility and the Moral Sentiments.* Cambridge, MA: Harvard University Press.

Williams, G. 2008. Responsibility as a Virtue. *Ethical Theory and Moral Practice* 11(4): 455–70.

Young, I. M. 2006. Responsibility and Global Justice: A Social Connection Model. *Social Philosophy and Policy* 23(1): 102–30.

Chapter 10

Privacy Analysis—Privacy Impact Assessment

Stefan Strauß

Although everyone is directly or indirectly concerned with privacy, Gary Marx was right in pointing out that it is not like the weather. While we cannot control the weather, a lot can be done for privacy (Marx 2012). A certain need for action emerges from informatization, that is, the widespread pervasion of society with information and communication technologies (ICTs). Digital information increasingly becomes a major driving force in our informational ecosystem. We are now in a stage of convergence between analog and digital environments that affects the roles and meanings of privacy and data protection and reinforces the demand for new ways to deal with them. The problem is aggravated by the multidimensionality and the relatively abstract character of privacy. ICTs provide a broad scope of usage contexts and many new modes of interaction between personal and nonpersonal entities (e.g., information exchange, sharing and creating content, and virtual collaboration). While these interactions partially meet societal needs such as communication and exchange, they also create vast amounts of information that can infringe upon the privacy of the involved individuals. Depending on the technology design the boundaries between personal and nonpersonal information can become less distinct, leading to uncontrolled disclosure of personal information. This has strong impact on informational self-determination, which is a core concept of privacy protection. Informational self-determination and the distinction between different types of privacy (such as privacy of the person, behavior, communications, and data) are essential to comprehend (potential and real) threats to privacy caused by contemporary and emerging technologies in their different contexts of usage.

This chapter focuses on these issues and provides an overview of means to explore the privacy impacts of information technologies. After presenting some theoretical background on privacy and its roles and meanings the chapter discusses privacy impact assessment as a tool for analyzing and appraising the extent to which ICTs affect privacy and data protection.

ROLE AND MEANING OF PRIVACY

Before taking a closer look at privacy impact assessment this section presents basic issues of privacy and data protection. The most common notion of privacy is the classical definition as "the right to be let alone" (Warren/ Brandeis 1890). More clearly, Westin (1967) defined privacy as "the claim of individuals, groups or institutions to determine for themselves, when, how, and to what extent information is communicated to others." Privacy is a societal achievement and thus the right to privacy is recognized as a fundamental human right. Article 12[1] of the Universal Declaration of Human Rights (UDHR) states that "no one shall be subjected to arbitrary interference with his privacy, family, home or correspondence, nor to attacks upon his honour and reputation. Everyone has the right to the protection of the law against such interference or attacks." Similarly, in the European Convention on Human Rights (ECHR) Article 8 is dedicated to privacy:

> 1. Everyone has the right to respect for his private and family life, his home and his correspondence. 2. There shall be no interference by a public authority with the exercise of this right except such as is in accordance with the law and is necessary in a democratic society in the interests of national security, public safety or the economic well-being of the country, for the prevention of disorder or crime, for the protection of health or morals, or for the protection of the rights and freedoms of others.

Most national laws in democracies worldwide have incorporated these regulations, directly or indirectly. In brief, "privacy defines a state where an individual is free from interference" (Strauß, forthcoming). While interfering with privacy is overseen by the law, it is highly important that such interference is always an exception to the rule and by no means a permanent option. Consequently, interference is only allowed under certain conditions: that is, to fulfil public interest in accordance with the law and to protect the foundations of a democratic society (ibid.). In general, the right to privacy includes the freedom from interference to protect against infringement from individuals, public and private organizations, government, and other institutions. This is part of the predominant principle of liberty in democratic societies. However, privacy is not to be misunderstood as an individual's right to decouple from society. To the contrary, it provides relief from different kinds of social frictions and thereby "enables people to engage in worthwhile activities that they would otherwise find difficult or impossible" (Solove 2006, p. 484). It empowers other fundamental rights and freedoms such as those of expression, thought, movement, and association. Privacy is thus also a substantial enabler of individual involvement in society, and harms to privacy "affect the nature of society and impede individual activities that contribute to the greater social good" (ibid., p. 488). It is therefore essential for the well-being of the individual as well as of society to protect this fundamental right. In order to achieve an appropriate protection it is necessary to understand how technologies and practices affect privacy. This is a general aim of privacy impact assessment (PIA): to investigate to what extent a technology or application is compatible with the protection of privacy.

SCOPE AND APPROACH OF PRIVACY IMPACT ASSESSMENT

At a general level, intrusions into privacy are the consequence of surveillance activities whereby personal data is being collected and analyzed. Different actors, individuals, as well as institutions can intrude into one's privacy. However, threats to privacy do not merely occur when surveillance is actively conducted but already when personal information is being processed or stored. The European Court of Human Rights has declared that "mere storage of information about an individual's private life amounts to interference within the meaning of Article 8 (right to respect for private life) of the European Convention on Human Rights" (EUCHR 2014).

The technological processing of (personal) information is largely determined by how a technology is designed. Therefore, technological design can have impact on privacy. If a technology is not designed in a way that protects personal information from intrusion or infringement, then privacy is at risk. From the concerned individuals' perspective, this risk induces a certain (perceived or factual) loss of control over personal information. These control issues refer to the concept of informational self-determination (ISD).[2] The introduction of ISD had high impact on European data protection legislation and represents a major issue in contemporary privacy protection. ISD defines a state in which the individual affected by information processing is aware of this process (e.g., what personal information is stored for which purpose) and is also capable of controlling how it is processed. Hence, the main aspects of ISD are knowledge about the context of information processing and control over that context in terms of personal information flows (Strauß/Nentwich 2013). Privacy-intrusive technology constrains or removes one's capability to informational self-determination. To allow for ISD, central privacy principles such as commensurability, purpose limitation, data minimization, and transparency have to be fulfilled.

Understanding to what extent a technology or practice of information processing bears privacy risks is a core aspect of privacy impact assessment. Wright and De Hert (2012, p. 5) define PIA broadly as "a methodology for assessing the impacts on privacy of a project, policy, programme, service, product or other initiative which involves the processing of personal information and, in consultation with stakeholders, for taking remedial actions as necessary in order to avoid or minimize negative impacts." PIA is thus more than a tool; it is a systematic process for identifying and evaluating the potential privacy effects of the processing of personal information. Ideally, PIA should be applied already at early stages of technology development to ensure that privacy and data protection are respected. In this regard, PIA is a form of risk assessment that identifies and reduces vulnerabilities of technology in terms of privacy. Conducting a PIA can serve different objectives: above all, to identify privacy risks to individuals and to identify the extent to which an organization is in compliance with privacy and data protection regulations. Conducting a PIA can also contribute to the trustworthiness of the organization in which it is performed. In economic terms, a PIA can also help an organization to avoid or reduce costs of information processing. Furthermore, it is a means to improve transparency and accountability concerning how (personal) information is being processed.

De Hert (2012, p. 40) highlights that "three generic requirements have to be met for privacy limitations . . . : legality (Is there a legal basis in law for a technology that processes data?), legitimacy (Is the processing pursuing legitimate aims?) and necessity (Is the processing necessary in a democratic society?)." These basic requirements determine some common grounds (related to legal aspects) of privacy protection and represent core elements of PIA. While a PIA does not necessarily deal with legal issues in particular (which, as De Hert [2012] notes, itself can be complicated to grasp and interpret), it is important to keep these basic requirements in mind. Similarly important is the consideration of common privacy principles (as expressed, e.g., by the OECD) such as purpose und usage limitation of personal information collection, transparency and accountability, source and quality of the information, concepts for storage, access, and protection of personal information, etc. (OECD 2013). There are several approaches to PIA that differ in details and in the particular contexts they are applied to. However, regardless of the differences, conducting a PIA in general includes the following basic steps (cf. Bayley/Bennett 2012; Spiekermann 2012; Cavoukian 2010):

- Characterization/description of the application/technology
  - What personal information is processed and how is it processed?
  - Which entities are involved in the processing of this information? (third-party involvement in information processing)

○ What is the lifecycle of personal information? (from creation/collection to processing, use, storage, and deletion)
• Identification and assessment of privacy risks
  ○ What personal information is collected, and how is it used and protected?
  ○ What are the risks and their likelihood?
• Identification and recommendation of existing or new controls to protect against the risks (developing ways to avoid or reduce the identified privacy risks)
• Documentation of risk resolution and residual risks. (PIA report)

TYPES AND DIMENSIONS OF PRIVACY

The identification of privacy risks is a crucial part of PIA. The list of potential risks and threats to privacy can be quite long. Different kinds of technology entail several types of (potential and real) privacy infringements. With the rapid development of technologies and applied techniques it becomes further complicated to identify to what extent privacy is intruded upon by a particular technology. This is aggravated by the circumstance that the boundaries between the different technologies become less and less distinct. To come to a better conceptual understanding of privacy and the risks it is exposed to, a consideration of the different types and dimensions of privacy is important. This makes it possible to draw a more differentiated map of privacy risks which benefits a solid privacy impact assessment.

Clarke (2006) provides a valuable classification of four major types of privacy: privacy of the person; privacy of personal behavior; privacy of social communications; and privacy of personal data. The first type of privacy makes reference to what is also known as bodily privacy, and aims at protecting the physical space and the body of a person. The second type of privacy aims at safeguarding the personal behavior of individuals, such as for instance religious practices and sexual activities. The third type of privacy covers some of the relationships and social ties that any individual builds and operates in. Finally, the privacy of personal data refers to the integrity and protection of all the sensitive data about an individual. Finn et al. (2013, p. 6ff.) complement Clarke's approach with additional dimensions and provide a typology of seven types of privacy:

1. Privacy of the person: addresses issues of keeping body functions and body characteristics (such as biometrics or genetic information) private. This type also refers to the strong cultural meaning of the physical body.
2. Privacy of behavior and action: one's "ability to behave in public, semi-public or one's private space without having actions monitored or

controlled by others." This type includes "sensitive issues such as sexual preferences and habits, political activities and religious practices" (ibid., p. 6f.).

3. Privacy of communication: the ability to communicate freely via different media without fear of interception, wiretapping, or other forms of surveillance of communication.

4. Privacy of data and image: this type includes issues about protecting personal data so that it is not automatically available to other individuals and organizations. Individuals should have the right to substantially control that data and its use. An image represents a particular form of personal data that can be used to identify and observe persons based on their visual characteristics.

5. Privacy of thoughts and feelings: This type addresses one's freedom to think and feel whatever he or she likes without restriction. "Privacy of thought and feelings can be distinguished from privacy of the person, in the same way that the mind can be distinguished from the body. Similarly, we can (and do) distinguish between thought, feelings and behaviour. Thought does not automatically translate into behaviour" (ibid., p. 7).

6. Privacy of location and space: addresses an individuals' ability to move freely in public or semi-public space without being identified, tracked, or monitored. "This conception of privacy also includes a right to solitude and a right to privacy in spaces such as the home, the car or the office" (ibid., p. 7). Considering a growth in mobile computing devices such as smartphones and location data, the protection of locational privacy can be expected to increase in importance (cf. Blumberg/Eckersley 2009; Clarke 2012).

7. Privacy of association (including group privacy): affects one's right to associate with whomever one wishes without being monitored. Included are involvements or contributions in groups or profiles. This type of privacy is closely linked to other fundamental rights such as freedom of association, movement, and expression.

This typology allows reflecting on technologies or applications and their impact on privacy and how a particular technology may cross the boundaries between different privacy types. Table 10.1 exemplifies this for different technologies and demonstrates that technologies can have a variety of privacy impacts. A distinction between different privacy types provides a more detailed picture of how privacy is affected, thereby facilitating the selection of appropriate measures of protection. A very common technology that intrudes on privacy is the CCTV.[3] At first glance, CCTV mainly affects two types of privacy: those of the person and of location and space. Sometimes it also affects privacy of association, namely, if a group of persons is captured on CCTV. However, considering the combination of CCTV and a database for processing the images, this technology also touches privacy of data and image. When CCTV systems record activities, they also affect privacy of behavior and action. With new forms of "smart" CCTV that can recognize, for example, faces or patterns of behavior (such as how one moves), this type of privacy can be affected even deeper. CCTV equipped with a microphone could also intrude into privacy of communication.

Another example with increasing relevance is biometrics, that is, technological means of recognizing individuals based on the measurement of their physical characteristics (cf. ISO 2009). In its broadest sense, biometrics focuses on (physical) information about the human body, most commonly the term refers to technologies such as fingerprint and iris scanners and increasingly face and vein pattern recognition and even DNA profiling. A biometric system is basically an automated pattern recognition system that uses information about one's body for, for example, identification and access control.[4] (cf. Wilson 2010). Further processing of biometric information for profiling, pattern recognition, and other forms of data mining is becoming more and more common in the security domain. While these technologies have an obvious impact on privacy of the person or body, biometrics in a wider sense also affects other types of privacy such as privacy of data and image, as well as privacy of location and space.

This privacy typology is useful for analyzing the privacy impacts of a particular technology, for instance, social networking sites (SNS) as shown by Strauß and Nentwich (2013). The core aim of SNS and other social media is to communicate, share information, create different forms of content and interact with others. Thus, privacy of communication, data and image, and association are affected by this technology. Depending on what information a user reveals, social media can potentially reveal many details of a person's life and thus also provide insight into that person's behavior, shared thoughts, or locations and places.

The smartphone is another prominent technology that serves multiple purposes. It can be understood as a conglomerate of different intertwined technologies that entail a number of privacy impacts. The most obvious types are communication and association, as a phone primarily serves as a communication tool which then can also give insight into one's connections with other persons. But smartphones also serve many other purposes: they can reveal one's location and can be tracked, they can be equipped with a camera, used for online services to share information via, for example, social networks or apps, or can even be used to scan biometrics, etc. Hence, smartphone surveillance can give deep insights into the surveyed persons' behavior, thoughts, and feelings.

Table 10.1   Privacy Types Affected by Different Technologies. Own Presentation Based on the Typology of Finn et al. (2013). An "X" Indicates that the Privacy Type is Widely Affected; "(X)" means that this Privacy Type is Partially or Potentially Affected

Privacy of ... *Technology*	(Smart) CCTV	Biometrics	Social Media	Smart phones
Person	(X)	X	(X)	(X)
Behavior & action	(X)		(X)	(X)
Communication			X	X
Data & image	X	(X)	X	X
Thoughts & feelings			(X)	(X)
Location & space	X	(X)	(X)	X
Association	(X)	(X)	X	X

The extent to which a particular technology or application affects privacy is of course context-dependent, which Nissenbaum (2010) highlighted with the term "contextual integrity." Hence, the mapping presented in the table can only provide a general overview but not a strict assignment. For instance, while social media can potentially reveal many details of a person's life, what they can reveal depends on what information she shares and what information about her is automatically collected. It is also important to consider that contemporary and emerging technologies are increasingly interrelated and interoperable. The example of smartphones highlights that one device can include a number of different technologies with accordingly broad privacy impacts. This typology should therefore not be seen as a panacea but as a baseline to examine more in depth the extent to which a technology entails or reinforces privacy impacts. In the next step, measures to reduce privacy threats can then be developed. An umbrella term for such measures is privacy-by-design (PbD) which aims at reducing privacy risks by, for example, avoiding or limiting the disclosure or processing of personal information (cf. Cavoukian 2011; Strauß/Nentwich 2013). An example would be the use of obfuscating or pixelating techniques on images and photos to avoid unintended facial recognition—for example, via CCTV or photos shared on social media. Another example is user control mechanisms to prevent apps from collecting and processing personal information. Encryption of information can improve privacy protection and reduce the risk of unintended content disclosure (e.g., the instant messenger Cryptocat). Anonymization techniques are essential to reduce the availability of personal information. These are just some loose examples to point out that privacy protection is feasible in and with technologies. A generally crucial PbD requirement is data minimization, which means that the processing of personal data should be avoided and only those data that are inevitably necessary should be collected and processed; and this only as long as they are needed. The crux is of course that in many cases technologies lack PbD, and the increasing role of digital networks complicates data minimization approaches. Furthermore, organizations collecting personal information via technology often have little awareness about why and how to protect privacy. In this regard, PIA can serve as an important means to demonstrate flaws and highlight the relevance of privacy-friendly technologies. This underlines the necessity of performing privacy impact assessment in order to reduce risks and improve safeguards of this fundamental right.

THE CIRCLES OF PIA AND THE COSTS OF SURVEILLANCE

While the previous section presented an approach to elaborating how technologies can affect different privacy types, we will now turn to how privacy risks can be comprehended on a larger scale and with a stronger focus on societal impacts. Raab and Wright (2012) suggest a useful analytical lens with a model that brings forth the negative effects of insufficient respect for privacy. This model provides extended analytical dimensions to assess privacy impacts in a wider sense which can be useful in addition to the outlined privacy typology. It distinguishes between the four stages (or circles) of PIA which are interrelated. (See figure 10.1.)

The circles can be understood in analogy to a drop of water that triggers a wave-like effect. Hence, privacy intrusion can entail a wave of interrelated impacts at different levels. PIA_1 represents individual privacy. PIA_2 includes PIA_1 and, in addition, other impacts on the individual's relationships, positions, and freedoms. PIA_3 includes PIA_2 plus impacts on groups and categories and, finally, PIA_4 consists of PIA_3 plus impacts on the society

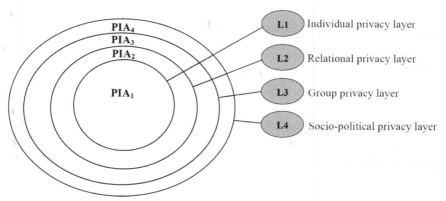

Figure 10.1　Circles of PIA and privacy layers. *Source*: Own representation, based on Raab and Wright (2012, 379).

and political system. This model can serve as a useful heuristic to develop a (layer-based) taxonomy of privacy risks and the costs of surveillance and privacy intrusion on four layers (Strauß 2015a): the individual (L1), relational (L2), group (L3), sociopolitical (L4) layers. L1 puts emphasis on the negative impacts on an individual whose privacy is intruded. Costs in this layer include effects of restrictions to individual behavior such as mainstreaming or normalizing behavior and conformity, inhibition of actions, self-censorship and, as a consequence, loss of informational self-determination, autonomy, and freedom. Social costs of avoidance (cf. Song 2003) can be used as an umbrella term for this kind of costs.

The relational layer (L2) is based on L1 and adds the costs of surveillance to the individual's social and political interactions and relationships with others. Costs in this layer include the so-called chilling effect, by which is meant the tendency of individuals to feel intimidated by surveillance and thus make less use of their fundamental rights (e.g., as they fear sanctions). This also includes fear of being associated with persons who are under suspicion. Costs at this layer include decrease in trust (between associated individuals), fear of sharing one's opinion (reduction in freedom of expression/speech), fear to meet and exchange views with others, and fear to participate and engage in public issues. This has negative effects on other fundamental rights such as freedom of expression, association, and movement and it can lead to a reduction in civic engagement and political participation.

While L1 and L2 focus on individual implications, the group layer (L3) includes the negative effects of surveillance on the groups that the individual is part of. Costs at this layer concern how individuals are treated as a consequence of surveillance or a privacy-intrusive action (and thus usually affect more than one person). Such costs include social sorting and classification for instance of customers or passengers in social or ethnic groups (e.g., travelers from countries classified as "rogue nations"). This kind of treatment can reinforce various forms of discrimination (racial, ethnic, or social exclusion) and aggravate social inequalities, mistrust among different social groups and racism (cf. Lyon 2003).

The sociopolitical layer (L4) is based on all the prior layers and addresses those costs of surveillance and privacy intrusion that concern the functioning of society and the political-administrative system. This includes a wider loss of privacy as a public good, loss of freedom of speech, the reversal of the presumption of innocence (as everyone can be under suspicion), and increasing mistrust in the political-administrative system that undermines social and democratic activities, and finally can lead to an erosion of democracy.

The outlined cost categories are mainly of a social nature and thus cannot be quantified as required in a cost-benefit analysis. Besides these social costs there are of course also economic costs caused, for example, by the implementation and operation of surveillance technology and practices (which are often passed on to citizens and customers who then indirectly pay for being monitored). Privacy intrusion and surveillance imply that personal information is collected and analyzed which also increases the complexity of the system. The trend of automated data analysis (e.g., in the field of big data) where data mining techniques and profiling are used to recognize behavioral patterns and identify suspicious behavior, further increases complexity. High complexity can lead to increasing proneness to errors, and the correction of errors again causes additional costs (cf. Strauß 2015b). An additional risk is given by a growth in the amount of information being processed, which can attract different kinds of intruders. In general, a lack of privacy protection can also entail a number of negative economic impacts and additional costs. Privacy intrusion and surveillance can also cause negative societal impacts in economic terms (externalities), such as a reduction of welfare because of limited solidarity fostered by discrimination, decrease in innovation entailed by increased conformity and normalized behavior, declining individual responsibility and civic engagement and courage, or increasing dependency of society on surveillance technology.

This cost-centered model serves as a general analytical lens to reveal that surveillance and privacy intrusion are costly issues that put nothing less than democratic core values at stake. The emphasis on costs intends to demonstrate that neglecting privacy is neither socially nor economically reasonable but can, on the contrary, bring negative impacts in every respect. This model also underlines the important role of privacy impact assessment in a wider societal context.

SUMMARY AND CONCLUSIONS

The approaches presented in this chapter provide useful means to analyze the privacy impacts of a technology or application. The processing of information widely decoupled from space and time that was enabled by ICTs has created a myriad of great applications. However, the flip side of the coin is that many contemporary and emerging technologies put high pressure on privacy protection. The permanent availability of (personal) information is a basic feature of current technologies and applications that are increasingly connected as parts of digital networks. Since most of these technologies do not contain adequate PbD features, personal information is often disclosed beyond the control of the concerned individuals. This situation reinforces a number of privacy challenges. Privacy impact assessment is an approach to tackle these challenges by exploring to what extent a technology or practice of information processing bears privacy risks and to improve protection mechanisms.

As technological development entails a wide array of potential privacy risks, awareness about these risks as well as a solid conceptual understanding of the different types of privacy is crucial. The outlined privacy typology contributes to that and allows the drawing a more differentiated picture of the extent to which a technology affects privacy. Exploring the different types of privacy affected can also facilitate the choice of protective measures such as PbD features to be implemented in technologies and practices.

The analysis of privacy impacts is often one-sidedly focused on technology at the expense of a wider societal perspective. Additional analytical lenses can be of avail to go beyond these limitations. The presented cost-centered approach is useful in this regard since it highlights the negative social consequences of privacy intrusions and surveillance. As privacy represents an enabler of other fundamental rights and freedoms (expression, movement, association, etc.) limitations of privacy also affect these other rights and have negative long-term effects on society as a whole. The outlined model to consider the costs of privacy intrusion and surveillance can contribute to grasping these societal impacts and their interplay on a larger scale. This is relevant not least in order to point out that privacy protection is not (as often framed) an inconvenience but, on the contrary, vital for the functioning of society and democracy.

NOTES

1. Similar is Art. 17 of the UN Covenant of Civil and Political Rights, http://www.hrweb.org/legal/cpr.html.

2. In Germany, ISD is a fundamental right (called "Recht auf informationelle Selbstbestimmung" in German) introduced by the German Federal Constitutional Court in 1983. Judgment of the First Senate from December 15, 1983, 1 BvR 209/83 et al.—Population Census, BVerfGE 65, 1.

3. Closed circuit television.

4. It has to be noted that the recognition process is mainly based on a calculated probability that a specific physiological or behavioral characteristic is valid.

REFERENCES

Blumberg, A. J., and Eckersley, P. (2009) "On Locational Privacy, and How to Avoid Losing it Forever," *Electronic Frontier Foundation*, August 2009, at https://www.eff.org/wp/locational-privacy.

Cavoukian, A. (2010) "Privacy Risk Management: Building Privacy Protection into a Risk Management Framework to Ensure that Privacy Risks are Managed, by

Default," *Information and Privacy Commissioner of Ontario, Canada.* https://www.ipc.on.ca/images/Resources/pbd-priv-risk-mgmt.pdf.

Cavoukian, A. (2011) "Privacy by Design: Strong Privacy Protection—Now and Well into the Future," A Report on the State of PbD to the 33rd International Conference of Data Protection and Privacy Commissioners. *Information and Privacy Commissioner of Ontario, Canada.* https://www.ipc.on.ca/english/Resources/Reports-and-Submissions/Reports-and-Submissions-Summary/?id=1125.

Clarke, R. (2006) "What's 'Privacy'?" http://www.rogerclarke.com/DV/Privacy.html.

Clarke, R. (2012) "Location Tracking of Mobile Devices: Ueberveillance Stalks the Streets." http://www.rogerclarke.com/DV/LTMD.html.

European Convention on Human Rights (ECHR) (EUCHR—European Court of Human Rights (2014) Factsheet—data protection http://www.echr.coe.int/Documents/FS_Data_ENG.pdf.

Finn, R. L., Wright, D., and Friedewald, M. (2013) "Seven Types of Privacy," pp. 3–32 in Gutwirth, S., R. Leenes, P. de Hert, and Y. Poullet (eds.), *European Data Protection: Coming of Age.* Dordrecht: Springer.

ISO—International Standards Organisation (2009) ISO/IEC JTC1 SC37 SD2 Harmonized Biometric Vocabulary.

Lyon, D., ed. (2003) *Surveillance as Social Sorting. Privacy, Risk and Automated Discrimination.* London: Routledge.

Marx, G. T. (2012) "Foreword by Gary T. Marx: Privacy is Not Quite Like the Weather," pp. v–vix in Wright, D., and P. de Hert (eds.), *Privacy Impact Assessment.* Law, Governance and Technology Series no. 6, Dordrecht: Springer.

Nissenbaum, H. (2010) *Privacy in Context—Technology, Policy, and the Integrity of Social Life.* Stanford: Stanford University Press.

OECD—Organization for Economic Co-operation and Development (2013) *The OECD Privacy Framework.* http://www.oecd.org/internet/ieconomy/privacy-guidelines.htm.

Raab, C. D. and D. Wright (2012) "Surveillance: Extending the Limits of Privacy Impact Assessment," pp. 363–83 in Wright, D., and P. de Hert (eds.), *Privacy Impact Assessment: Law, Governance and Technology Series no. 6.* Dordrecht: Springer.

Solove, D. (2006) "A Taxonomy of Privacy," in *University of Pennsylvania Law Review* 154(3): 477–560.

Song, A. (2003) "Technology, Terrorism, and the Fishbowl Effect: An Economic Analysis of Surveillance and Searches," *The Berkman Center for Internet & Society Research Publication* 5(September): 1–26.

Spiekermann, S. (2012) "The RFID PIA—Developed by Industry, Endorsed by Regulators," pp. 323–46 in Wright, D., and P. de Hert (eds.), *Privacy Impact Assessment.* Dordrecht: Springer.

Strauß, S., and Nentwich, M. (2013) "Social Network Sites, Privacy and the Blurring Boundary Between Public and Private Spaces," *Science and Public Policy* 40(6): 724–32.

Strauß, S. (2015a) "Towards a Taxonomy of Social and Economic Costs," pp. 212–18 in Wright, D., and R. Kreissl (eds.), *Surveillance in Europe*. London/New York: Routledge.

Strauß, S. (2015b) "Datafication and the Seductive Power of Uncertainty—A Critical Exploration of Big Data Enthusiasm," *Information* 6(4): 836–47. http://www.mdpi. com/2078-2489/6/4/836.

Strauß, S. (forthcoming) "A Game of Hide and Seek?—Unscrambling the Trade-off between Privacy and Security," in Friedewald, M. et al. (eds.), *Discourses of privacy and security*. London/New York: Roudledge.

Universal Declaration of Human Rights (UDHR). https://www.un.org/en/documents/ udhr/.

Warren, S. D., and Brandeis, L. D. (1890) "The Right to Privacy," *Harvard Law Review* 193 (1890) IV(December 15, 1890), No. 5. http://faculty.uml.edu/sgalla-gher/Brandeisprivacy.htm.

Westin, A. (1967) *Privacy and Freedom*. New York: Atheneum.

Wilson, C. (2010) *Vein Pattern Recognition: A Privacy-Enhancing Biometric*. London, New York: CRC Press.

Wright, D., and De Hert, P. (2012) "Introduction to Privacy Impact Assessment," pp. 3–32 in Wright, D., and P. de Hert (eds.), *Privacy Impact Assessment: Law, Governance and Technology Series no. 6*. Dordrecht: Springer.

Chapter 11

Ethical Risk Analysis

Sven Ove Hansson

Modern risk analysis is largely based on a quantitative methodology. The usual procedure is to measure risk as the product of the probability of an undesired event and some measure of its severity. For instance, if there is a probability of 1 in 1,000 that 5,000 persons will die, then this is treated as equivalent to $(1/1,000) \times 5,000 = 5$ deaths. Unfortunately, this simple measure does not provide all the information that is needed in risk management decisions. It leaves out important ethical aspects, such as who contributes to the risk and with what intentions, what role those exposed to the risk have in the decision to take the risk, how the risk and its associated benefits are distributed, etc. We need to deal systematically with the ethical issues of risk. This chapter proposes one way to do so.[1]

1. STAKEHOLDERS AND RISK ROLES

Ethical issues typically concern human relations. We will focus on the relationships among people who have different roles in relation to a risk. In discussions on risk the term "stakeholder" is often used to cover in principle any person or organization with some kind of concern or interest in the issue at hand. For the purpose of ethical analysis, it is useful to focus on three roles that stakeholders can have.

In every risk management problem, there are people who are potentially exposed to a risk. Sometimes there are several exposed groups that may have different interests in the matter. For instance, when a factory uses a dangerous chemical, this can lead to risk exposure of its workers, people living in the immediate vicinity, and people fishing in contaminated waters at considerable distance from the factory. These three groups are all exposed to risk, but they are so in different ways and to different degrees. In an ethical analysis it is essential to identify the *risk-exposed* and to clarify if there are several groups of such persons whose concerns and interests may differ.

Every risk management issue has *decision makers* with an influence on the risk exposure. Often, risk-exposed persons make important decisions themselves—examples of this are when skiers decide whether to go off-piste and cyclists whether to use a bicycle helmet. But the decision maker can also be someone else, such as a company deciding whether to use explosive chemicals in a process or a rescue leader deciding which buildings to evacuate. If there are several decision makers it is important to identify all of them and clarify what impact their respective decisions have on the risk.

Risks are seldom taken unless they are associated with some advantage. In other words there are *beneficiaries*, people benefiting from the risk being taken. Sometimes the beneficiaries and the risk-exposed are the same persons. The only benefit of going off-piste seems to be the risk-exposed skier's own exciting experience. But in other cases the risks and the benefits accrue to different persons. For instance, a company can sometimes cut costs by choosing dangerous work processes. The owners reap the economic benefits, but the risk of injury is run by the workers.

For risks with a dominant natural cause, there may be no beneficiary in the usual sense. Typically, no one gains from floods, landslides, or pandemics. But in most of these cases there is another role, namely that of carrying the costs of prevention, rescue, and mitigation. Such costs are often covered by others than those exposed to the risks. We therefore have, in these cases as well, a third role in addition to those of the risk-exposed and the decision makers, but the third role is not that of a beneficiary in the sense of someone who benefits from the risk itself. Instead, those who have this role face losses if actions are taken to prevent or mitigate the risk. We can use the term "counter-affected" for persons in this position. Much of what will be said below of beneficiaries applies as well to the counter-affected (Hansson 2016).

Each of these three positions can be occupied by several groups of affected or concerned people. It is often difficult to decide whether persons who gain or lose very little from a risk-inducing project should be included among the beneficiaries respectively the risk-exposed.[2] For instance, when a new railroad is built, there may be people whose travel time is reduced by just a minute or two. There may also be people living at some distance from the railroad who will experience a hardly noticeable increase in the ambient noise level. It is in most cases advisable to include people with such "marginal" risk roles in the analysis. Obviously, their interests will have less weight than those of people who are affected to a higher degree.

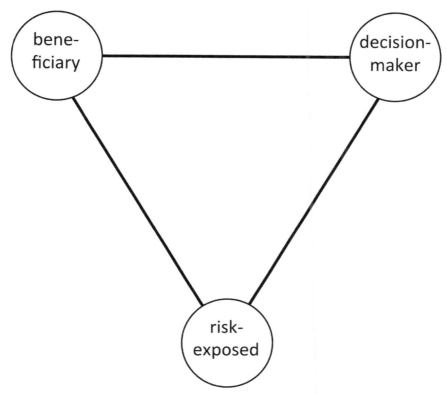

Figure 11.1   The three major roles involved in most risk decisions.

In addition to the three major risk roles there may also be others that need to be taken into account, such as experts and media. However, the most important ethical issues tend to concern these three roles and their interrelations. As figure 11.1 illustrates, the three risk roles give rise to three classes of binary relations. Along each of the three axes we should look for relations of (partial or complete) *overlap* and relations of *dependence*. By overlap it is meant that two, or perhaps all three, of these roles are filled (in part) by the same persons. Are the risk-exposed also beneficiaries, are the risk-exposed themselves decision makers, and are the decision makers also beneficiaries? By dependence is meant that one of these groups depends on one of the others, for instance in terms of employment, subsistence, or access to information. Are the risk-exposed economically dependent on the decision makers, or do they depend on the beneficiaries for information about the risks? In the next three sections, we will exemplify how each of the three binary relations can be investigated in these terms.

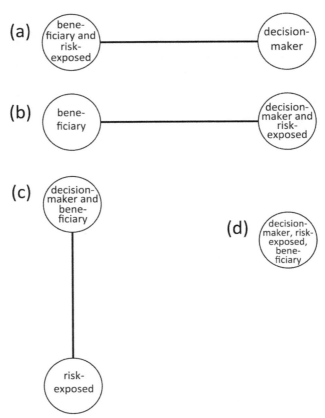

Figure 11.2 The four reduced situations in which two or more of the risk roles coin-cide. Jonathan Wolff (2010) has proposed names for these situations: (a) paternalism, (b) maternalism, (c) externalities, and (d) individualism.

2. THE RISK-EXPOSED AND THE BENEFICIARIES

In some cases, the risk-exposed and the beneficiaries are the same person(s). Then the triangle can be reduced to a diagram with only two types of agents, as in figure 11.2a. Important among such cases are those of medical treatment and diagnosis. The risks associated with a medical intervention concern the same person who will reap the potential benefits. Weighing the advantages and disadvantages of a treatment against each other can be difficult, but there is at least one type of difficulty that we do not have to worry about here: since the same person's interests are in both scales of the balance we do not have to deal with the issues of interpersonal comparisons that often make risk decisions ethically and socially controversial (Hansson 2003; 2013).

Other important cases when the risk-exposed and the beneficiary coincide are risks taken for one's own pleasure (such as bungee jumping) or when working for oneself (such as climbing without a lifeline when mending one's own roof).

Situations when the risk-exposed and the beneficiary coincide are usually perceived as comparatively unproblematic from an ethical point of view. This applies in particular if the third risk role, that of decision maker, is also played by the same person(s), as in figure 11.2d. If someone carries a risk herself and also receives all the benefits that it is associated with, what reasons can there be for others to prevent her from deciding to take the risk?

Although this is a convincing argument, it may not be applicable in all the cases when it is assumed to be so. Many risks that are described as only a single person's affair may in fact also affect others. For instance, a decision to ski in an area with an impending avalanche may in the end put a rescue team at great risk. Furthermore, all kinds of self-destructive behavior can have disastrous effects for the person's family and others who depend on her. This is something that John Stuart Mill returned to repeatedly. In *On Liberty* (1859) he maintained that "no person ought to be punished simply for being drunk" (Mill [1859] 1977, p. 282), but if a drunkard or gambler squanders the money needed to pay his debts or to support and educate his family, then "he is deservedly reprobated, and might be justly punished: but it is for the breach of duty to his family or creditors, not for the extravagance" (p. 281). In *Auguste Comte and Positivism* (1865) he went even further and advocated a duty to preserve one's own health in order to fulfill one's duties to others:

> We agree with [Comte] in the opinion, that the principal hygienic precepts should be inculcated, not solely or principally as maxims of prudence, but as a matter of duty to others, since by squandering our health we disable ourselves from rendering to our fellow-creatures the services to which they are entitled. As M. Comte truly says, the prudential motive is by no means fully sufficient for the purpose, even physicians often disregarding their own precepts. The personal penalties of neglect of health are commonly distant, as well as more or less uncertain, and require the additional and more immediate sanction of moral responsibility. (Mill [1865] 1969, p. 340)

Irrespectively of whether we agree with Mill on this, when a situation is presented in the way illustrated in figure 11.2a or 11.2d we have good reasons to critically consider whether the lists of beneficiaries and risk-exposed are complete or there are others—such as dependents of the risk-exposed—whose interests have moral relevance.

But let us now turn to the cases when the beneficiary and the risk-exposed are different persons. These cases are often problematic since they raise what is arguably the most difficult problem in the ethics of risk, namely, under what conditions it is justified that someone is exposed to a risk in order for someone else to receive an advantage (Hansson 2003; 2013). Many of the most contested risks in society have this structure. Indeed, empirical evidence shows that the distribution of risk exposures has an ethically problematic pattern: risks are unequally distributed, both between and within countries. It is usually the people who are disadvantaged in other respects who are also the most exposed to risks. The ambient environment tends to be worse in poor than in well-to-do neighborhoods. People with low incomes have more dangerous jobs than those who are better paid, and they eat less healthy food (Bryant and Mohai 1992; Ringquist 2000; Shrader-Frechette 2002; Hansson 2014). Ethnic minorities are often particularly affected by inequalities in risk exposure, a phenomenon that has been called "environmental racism" (Bullard 2001; Saha and Mohai 2005). The differences in risk exposure between rich and poor countries are dramatic:

> Children born in sub-Saharan Africa are 20 times more likely to die in the first 5 years of life than children born in Europe or North America. Childbearing women are nearly 140 times more likely to die in labor than women in high income countries. Overall, life expectancy in sub-Saharan Africa is 26 years shorter than in wealthy parts of the world. Collectively, health inequalities translate into nearly 20 million deaths every year—and have for at least the past 2 decades. This represents approximately one-third of global deaths, including millions of deaths related to inequalities within countries. (Gostin 2012)

To this should be added that the populations most at risk from anthropogenic climate change are low-income people in developing countries, who do not gain much from the activities that give rise to climate change (Okereke 2010). In the ethical analysis of risk, it is essential to find out how each risk exposure is distributed, how this distribution compares to the distribution of its associated advantages, and how it compares to the general distribution of social advantages and disadvantages.

An unequal distribution need not be morally wrong. Possible justifications of an unequal distribution should be identified and evaluated. Four important classes of such justifications are: self-interest, desert, compensation, and reciprocity. (Another such justification is voluntariness or consent, to which we will return in the next section.)

By *self-interest* is meant here that a risk is taken in order to gain advantages solely for the person who takes it. This is often a sensible justification for why no one else should take that risk. Arguably (but with the Millian reservations mentioned above) you should be allowed to save money by repairing your house with a dangerous, defective tool even if you could afford buying a new one. There is no injustice involved in the fact that this risk falls entirely on you and on no one else.

A claim that those who are more risk-exposed than others *deserve* to be so would typically have to refer to their own previous actions or behaviors that disqualify them from better treatment. Such arguments could potentially be invoked to defend risky experiments on prisoners, or dangerous prison work. However, that would be a form of stochastic punishment that could rightly be classified as cruel and against basic principles of human rights (Doughterty 2007). Generally speaking, arguments to the effect that certain persons deserve to be risk-exposed will have low plausibility.

The use of *compensation* for risk exposure is much more plausible. Compensation can be either risk-triggered or harm-triggered. A risk-triggered compensation is given for the risk exposure irrespective of whether any harm occurs, whereas a harm-triggered compensation is only given if the harm materializes. A higher wage for a dangerous work is an example of the former, and disability benefits paid for injuries at work an example of the latter.

Some types of damages can be fully compensated for. Losses of money can be compensated with the same amount of money. Similarly, if a person's car is wrecked, then she can, in general, be fully compensated by being given a new car, or money to buy one. However, if she loses her home in a fire, then compensation in the form of money or a new home can often only be partial, since objects with a sentimental value do not in general have a replacement. At the extreme end, death, severe bodily injury, the destruction of unique historical or artistic artifacts, and many types of environmental damage cannot be compensated for in the full sense of the word.

In some cases, compensation can even be counterproductive. If neighbors protest against the damage to the environment caused by an industrial activity, then offering them money will not solve their concerns but can instead be criticized as an attempt to buy them off. On the other hand, if their concern is that house values will go down, then monetary compensation may be appropriate (Fischer 2001). In some cases, nonmonetary compensation may be more propitious than paying out money. For instance, it may be more befitting to compensate damage to a park by developing another park in the vicinity than by paying money to the locals (O'Hare et al. 1983). In an ethical analysis of risk, we need to reflect on whether the risk or the potential harm is compensable from a moral point of view. If it is (fully or in part) compensable, then we also need to find out whether adequate compensation has been offered.

Finally, a risk imposition can be justified by *reciprocity*. By this is meant that is part of a social system of reciprocal exchanges of risks and benefits (Hansson 2003; 2013). For instance, if others are allowed to drive a car, exposing me to certain risks, then in exchange I am allowed to drive a car and expose them to the corresponding risks. This (we may suppose) is to the benefit of all of us. In order to deal with the complexities of modern society, we also need to apply this principle to exchanges of different types of risks and benefits. We can regard such risk exposures as acceptable that are part of a social system of risk exchanges that works to everyone's advantage. Ideally, a person who has a higher share of the risks than the benefits from some technology is in the reverse situation with respect to other technologies, and on the large social scale this will at least approximately even out. However, as already mentioned, actual distributions of risks and benefits do not usually follow such an ideal pattern.

3. THE RISK-EXPOSED AND THE DECISION MAKERS

Let us now turn to the relationship between the risk-exposed and the decision makers. The most crucial issue here is to what extent the risk-exposed themselves decide on the risk (as in figures 11.2b and 11.2d). When investigating this, it is essential to keep in mind that most risky situations result from a social process in which decisions by several agents have, directly or indirectly, contributed to the risk. When a worker is injured through a machine failure, the causal chain includes the worker's own decision to apply for a job with potentially dangerous machines, the employer's or his representative's decision to buy the machine in question, their further decisions about its use and maintenance, the machine manufacturer's decisions about its construction, etc. Similarly, behind a smoker's death from a smoking-related disease there is a complex combination of causes, including the smoker's decision (usually as a minor) to smoke her first cigarette, but also many decisions by cigarette manufacturers and others who contribute to the tobacco epidemic. It is in fact difficult to find a clear example of a risk exposure that does not have, among its causal factors, both actions by the risk-exposed and actions by others.

Unsurprisingly, those who contribute to the risk exposure of others tend to deemphasize their own causal role and instead emphasize that of the risk-exposed persons themselves. Hence, tobacco companies have sponsored anti-paternalist campaigns that focus on the right of smokers to smoke (Taylor 1984; Chapman 1992). The (implicit) inference seems to be that if the smoker has a moral right to risk harming herself, then the tobacco company has a moral right to encourage her to do so and to provide her with the requisite means. This, however, does not follow. A person's moral right to expose herself to a risk or a harm does not necessarily imply a right for others to facilitate or contribute to her doing so (Hansson 2005).

Generally speaking, a risk-exposed person's own contribution to a risk can diminish the moral blameworthiness of others who contribute to the same risk. However, it does not necessarily provide them with a moral carte blanche to do anything they can to facilitate or encourage her risk-taking. For instance, selling cyanide to an acutely depressed person who can be expected to use it for suicide is (ceteris paribus) not as blameworthy as sneaking it into her food, but it may nevertheless be blameworthy to a considerable degree.

A professional ethical analysis has to go beyond the misleading binary division of risk exposures into voluntary and nonvoluntary ones, with its implicit assumption that if a person takes a risk voluntarily, then nobody else is to blame. Instead an ethical analysis should include a nuanced discussion of the various decisions and actions that contribute to the risk. Each of these decisions and actions should be ethically appraised in relation to the alternatives available.

Attempts to prevent self-harming actions are often criticized for being paternalist. Paternalism consists in interfering with someone for her own good. Such interference is in principle always problematic since we assume for good reasons that each individual has a right to make decisions affecting only herself, based on whatever motives she may have. But it is also important to note that arguments against paternalism can only protect *self-harming* actions and activities, not activities that may potentially harm others. For instance, a company that sells and promotes tobacco does not thereby harm itself or its owners. It harms other people, namely, the smokers whom it recruits and sustains. Therefore, these activities are not protected by anti-paternalism. The same applies to actions such as driving with unbelted passengers, selling unsafe fireworks, and hiring people to work with dangerous machines. We may very well reach the conclusion that some of these contributory other-harming actions are morally unassailable, but that must be a conclusion from serious moral analysis, not just from a classification of certain other actions as voluntary. Too often, the entire blame for harmful social practices is placed on their victims, whereas others who contribute are exempted from blame. Such victim-blaming practices often avert attention from potential targets of social reform (Becker 1986; Burris 1997; Needleman 1998).

As an example of this, the conventional view on traffic accidents focuses on the responsibility of individual drivers. Suppose that a driver drives too fast, loses control over the vehicle and hits another vehicle so badly that several persons are killed. Obviously, the speeding driver was blameworthy, and this should be reflected in the legal aftermath of the accident. However, many other decisions have contributed to make this and other similar accidents possible. Government has decided to build roads that allow for high velocities. Automobile manufacturers have decided to sell cars that can be driven at much higher velocities than the maximum allowable speed, and governments have chosen to allow the sale of such cars. An ethical analysis of traffic accidents should highlight these decisions as well.

Voluntariness and related concepts such as consent and acceptance must always be related to the alternatives that are available to the person in question. People seldom choose or accept a risk per se. Instead, they choose or accept combinations or "packages" of risks and benefits. A person who consents to the risks of a surgical operation does in fact consent to the combination of these risks and the chances of improved health associated with the operation. She would not consent to the risks alone. Similarly, a person who chooses to jump bungee does not consent to the risk per se, but to a package consisting of the risk and its associated advantages, primarily the thrill. If she had the choice of an otherwise exactly similar jump but with a safer cord, then she would presumably choose the safer alternative. In the same way, a worker who accepts a job with a high risk of serious injury actually consents to a package consisting of these risks and the benefits associated with the job, primarily the pay. He has not consented to the risk per se, and would presumably not take the risks without the associated benefits. Importantly, he may be very dissatisfied with how the available packages (work offers) are constructed.

In an ethical risk analysis, it is not sufficient to study the choices that people make among the available packages of risks and benefits. We also need to investigate the decision-making processes through which these packages were constructed. Situations are common in which the risk-exposed can freely choose among the available packages but have little or no influence on how these packages are put together. Such situations should be carefully distinguished from those in which the risk-exposed are included in the decision-making process as a whole. If a person has made a choice under circumstances that she cannot influence then her choice constitutes consent *under* these circumstances, not *to* them.

In order to participate meaningfully in a decision, one must have sufficient capacity to make informed decisions. In medical ethics three important groups of persons have been identified who lack this capacity: minors, mentally handicapped, and temporarily unconscious persons. Special ethical principles have been developed for their protection; for instance, much stricter rules apply to medical research on these groups than on legally competent persons who can give informed consent. A strong case can be made that similar principles should be applied more generally in risk-related decision making. If members of these groups are exposed to risks, then this must always be pointed out in an ethical risk analysis. It is grossly misleading to describe risks as "voluntary" when for instance minors are among the risk-imposed. As one example of this, secondary smoking kills more than 100,000 children every year (Öberg et al. 2011). Their exposure is not voluntary in any meaningful sense of the word.

Meaningful participation in a decision also requires that one has access to the relevant information. It is often the decision maker who controls the information. The extent to which it is made available to the risk-exposed is an important parameter for the ethical analysis. It has sometimes been argued that the public should not be provided with full information about risks to public health and the environment, since such information might have negative psychological effects. For instance, Durodié has warned against "elevating risk awareness in the name of transparency and an individual 'right to know,'" since that right can lead to "nothing more than the promotion of unnecessary, unfounded, and unassuageable lifelong anxiety, bitterness, and cynicism" (Durodié 2003, p. 394). However, this is a strategy that has repeatedly failed miserably, for the simple reason that if information is withheld, then the public will find out that they are kept uninformed. Knowledge that one is not told the whole truth can give rise to more uncertainty and misconceptions than what the withheld information itself could have created, in particular, if it were presented in an informative and responsible way (Grill and Hansson 2005). In an ethical analysis of risk, the ways in which risk-relevant information is controlled, disseminated, or withheld will have to be investigated.

4. THE DECISION MAKERS AND THE BENEFICIARIES

Finally, let us turn to the relationship between decision makers and beneficiaries. The crucial question here is whether the decision makers benefit from (the activities or circumstances that lead to) other people's risk-taking. This they can do directly, for instance as a tobacco manufacturer, whose profits depend on consumers buying addictive, highly risk-inducing products. They can also do it indirectly, by depending on someone else who benefits directly from the risk-taking. An example of the latter is a newspaper that depends on advertising revenues from companies engaged in risk-inducing activities.

Decision makers with such double roles tend to have low credibility in the eyes of risk-exposed persons and the public in general. Unsurprisingly, it is difficult for a decision maker who gains from the risk exposure to obtain or retain the confidence of the risk-exposed. During the BSE (bovine spongiform encephalopathy, "mad cow disease") crisis in the 1990s the British meat industry chose to continue selling their products, and claimed that the risks were negligible. The public did not trust them, largely due to their strong economic interest in the matter. Other industries have had similar experiences. And obviously, the reservations of the public against such arrangements are justified. It is hardly a defensible system to leave decisions about risks to persons or organizations who have an economic interest in the risks being taken. In an ethical risk analysis this type of arrangement will always have to be pointed out.

Such arrangements are in fact so problematic that social structures lead-ing to them have often been subject to reform. There are at least four ways to avoid them. First, risk-benefiting decision makers can be made to pay for the risks so that they will no longer gain from them. In economic terms, this means that an activity with negative effects on others (negative externalities) should pay for these negative effects. This is done with various forms of eco-taxes, carbon credits, penalties, damages, etc.

Secondly, risk-benefiting decision makers can be controlled by other deci-sion makers who do not benefit from the risk. This can be done by providing the risk-imposed with legal means to limit or reduce the risks, for instance by letting employees appoint safety representatives with certain powers (Test et al. 2005; Chin et al. 2010; Walters 1995). More commonly, the controlling

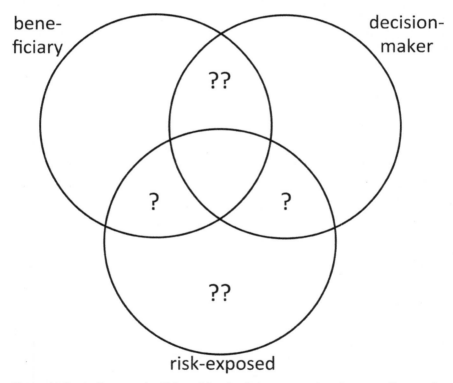

Figure 11.3 A diagram classifying risk roles into seven categories according to the distinctions explained in this chapter. The fields marked "??" are highly ethically prob-lematic. (One is a decision maker who does not run the risk but benefits from others doing so. The other is a risk-exposed person who neither receives any benefits from the risk being taken nor participates in decisions on the risk.) The fields marked "?" are also ethically problematic, but usually to a lower degree.

task is assigned to a government agency, such as an agency for environmental protection, workplace safety, food safety, radiation protection, etc. The credibility of such supervisory authorities depends to a high degree on their independence from the objects of their supervision.

The third method is to prevent persons or organizations from activities that would put them in the position of being risk-benefiting decision makers. Regulations against insider trading can be seen as an example of this.

The fourth and most drastic method is to prohibit the activity in question. Many illegal risk-inducing activities are typically carried out by risk-benefiting agents. Drug sale, pyramid schemes, and some forms of environmental pollution are examples of this.

A situation such as that depicted in figure 11.2c should always trigger a warning bell. It is usually not a good idea for decisions on risks to made by people who have something to gain but nothing to lose from risks in question.

5. CONCLUSION

The three-role model can be used to systematically describe and analyze major ethical issues in situations of risk. It can help us discover problematic features of the decision-making situation that we might not otherwise observe. In cases with only few persons or groups in the different risk roles the analysis can sometimes by summarized by classifying the situation into one of the categories shown in figure 11.2. In more complex cases, it may be more useful to place the various parties in the appropriate field in figure 11.3. For instance, a risk-exposed person who is neither benefited by the risk-taking nor a participant in decisions on it should be placed in the lowest field, whereas someone who has all three roles should be placed in the central field. As indicated in the figure, some positions in this diagram tend to be ethically problematic. The identification of such problematic positions (problematic risk roles) may be one of the most useful outcomes of an ethical risk analysis.

NOTES

1. The model for ethical risk analysis to be presented here has also been discussed in Hermansson and Hansson (2007), Hansson (2016), and Wolff (2010). For an application of the model, see Alverbro et al. (2011).

2. The problem of identifying those concerned by a social or technological measure has been called the stakeholder identification problem or the consenter identification problem (Thomas Long 1983; Schinzinger and Martin 1983).

REFERENCES

Alverbro, Karin, Göran Finnveden, and Per Sandin (2011) "Ethical Analysis of Three Methods for Destruction of Ammunition," *Risk Management* 13: 63–79.

Becker, M. H. (1986) "The Tyranny of Health Promotion," *Public Health Review* 14: 15–25.

Bryant, B., and Mohai, P. (eds.) (1992) *Race and the Incidence of Environmental Hazards*. Boulder: Westview Press.

Bullard, Robert D. (2001) "Environmental Justice in the 21st Century: Race Still Matters," *Phylon* 49: 151–71.

Burris S. (1997) "The Invisibility of Public Health: Population-level Measures in a politics of Market Individualism," *American Journal of Public Health* 87: 1607–10.

Chapman, Simon (1992) "Anatomy of a Campaign: The Attempt to Defeat the New South Wales (Australia) Tobacco Advertising Prohibition Bill 1991," *Tobacco Control* 1: 50–56.

Chin, Peter, Christopher DeLuca, Cheryl Poth, Ingrid Chadwick, Nancy Hutchinson, and Hugh Munby (2010) "Enabling Youth to Advocate for Workplace Safety," *Safety Science* 48: 570–79.

Doughterty, Colleen (2007) "The Cruel and Unusual Irony of Prisoner Work Related Injuries in the United States," *University of Pennsylvania Journal of Business and Employment Law* 10: 483–508.

Durodié, Bill (2003) "The True Cost of Precautionary Chemicals Regulation," *Risk Analysis* 23: 389–98.

Fischel, William A. (2001) "Why are There NIMBYs?" *Land Economics* 77: 144–52.

Gostin, Lawrence O. (2012) "A Framework Convention on Global Health: Health for All, Justice for All," *JAMA* 307: 2087–92.

Grill, Kalle and Sven Ove Hansson (2005) "Epistemic Paternalism in Public Health," *Journal of Medical Ethics* 31: 648–53.

Hansson, Sven Ove (2003) "Ethical Criteria of Risk acceptance," *Erkenntnis* 59: 291–309.

Hansson, Sven Ove (2005) "Extended Antipaternalism," *Journal of Medical Ethics* 31: 97–100.

Hansson, Sven Ove (2013) *The Ethics of Risk: Ethical Analysis in an Uncertain World*. New York: Palgrave Macmillan.

Hansson, Sven Ove (2014) "Food Risks," pp. 938–45 in Paul B. Thompson and David M. Kaplan (eds.), *Encyclopedia of Food and Agricultural Ethics*. Dordrecht: Springer.

Hansson, Sven Ove (2016) "Managing Risks of the Unknown," pp. 155–72 in Paolo Gardoni, Colleen Murphy, and Arden Rowell (eds.), *Risk Analysis of Natural Hazards*. Cham: Springer.

Hermansson, Hélène, and Sven Ove Hansson (2007) "A Three Party Model Tool for Ethical Risk Analysis," *Risk Management* 9(3): 129–44.

Long, Thomas A. (1983) "Informed Consent and Engineering: An Essay Review," *Business and Professional Ethics Journal* 3: 59–66.

Mill, John Stuart ([1859] 1977) *On Liberty* in *Collected Works of John Stuart Mill*, 33 volumes, John M. Robson (ed.), volume 18. Toronto: University of Toronto Press.

Mill, John Stuart ([1865] 1969) *Auguste Comte and Positivism* in *Collected Works of John Stuart Mill*, 33 volumes, John M. Robson (ed.), volume 10. Toronto: University of Toronto Press.

Needleman, H. L. (1998) "Childhood Lead Poisoning: The Promise and Abandonment of Primary Prevention," *American Journal of Public Health* 88: 1871–77.

O'Hare, M., L. Bacow, and D. Sanderson (1983) *Facility Siting and Public Opposition*. New York: Van Nostrand Reinhold Company Inc.

Öberg, Mattias, Maritta S. Jaakkola, Alistair Woodward, Armando Peruga, and Annette Prüss-Ustün (2011) "Worldwide Burden of Disease from Exposure to Second-Hand Smoke: A Retrospective Analysis of Data from 192 Countries," *Lancet* 377(9760): 139–46.

Okereke, Chukwumerije (2010) "Climate Justice and the International Regime," *Wiley Interdisciplinary Reviews: Climate Change* 1: 462–74.

Ringquist, E. J. (2000) "Environmental Justice: Normative Concerns and Empirical Evidence," pp. 232–56 in N. J. Vig and M. E. Kraft (eds.), *Environmental Policy: New Directions for the Twenty-First Century*. Washington, DC: CQ Press.

Saha, Robin, and Paul Mohai (2005) "Historical Context and Hazardous Waste Facility Siting: Understanding Temporal Patterns in Michigan," *Social Problems* 52: 618–48.

Schinzinger, R., and M. W. Martin (1983) "Commentary: Informed Consent in Engineering and Medicine," *Business and Professional Ethics Journal* 3: 67–78.

Shrader-Frechette, K. (2002) *Environmental Justice: Creating Equality, Reclaiming Democracy*. Oxford: University Press.

Taylor P. (1984) *Smoke Ring, The Politics of Tobacco*. London: Bodley Head.

Test, David W., Catherine H. Fowler, Wendy M. Wood, Denise M. Brewer, and Steven Eddy (2005) "A Conceptual Framework of Self-Advocacy for Students with Disabilities," *Remedial and Special Education* 26: 43–54.

Walters, David (1995) "Employee Representation and Occupational Health and Safety: The Significance of Europe," *Journal of Loss Prevention in the Process Industries* 8: 313–18.

Wolff, Jonathan (2010) "Five Types of Risky Situation," *Law, Innovation and Technology* 2(2): 151–63.

Part III

EMERGING TECHNOLOGIES

Chapter 12

Ethics of Emerging Technology

Philip Brey

This chapter surveys ethical approaches to emerging technology. In recent years, emerging technologies have become a major topic of study in the ethics of technology, which has increasingly focused its attention on early stage intervention in technology development. A number of specific approaches and methods have now been developed for the field, which in many ways is still in its infancy. The main problem for the ethics of emerging technology is the problem of uncertainty (Sollie, 2007): how to deal with the uncertainty of future products, uses, and consequences, and associated ethical issues that will result from an emerging technology. Several approaches to the ethics of emerging technology will be reviewed, which deal with this problem in different ways. Special attention will be paid to anticipatory approaches, which combine foresight analysis with ethical analysis. These approaches will be assessed and critically compared to alternative ethical approaches to emerging technology.

WHAT IS ETHICS OF EMERGING TECHNOLOGY?

A proper understanding of the ethics of emerging technology presupposes a proper understanding of what emerging technologies are. *Emerging technologies* are technologies that are new, innovative, and still in development, and are expected to have a large socioeconomic impact. They are new in the sense that they employ new concepts, methods, and techniques and cannot be subsumed under existing technologies. They are innovative in the sense that they promise new and potentially superior solutions to problems. They are still in development in that they are still largely a promise: no products or applications, or at least not many, have resulted from them, and few, if any, are marketed and used on a large scale. They are expected to have a large socioeconomic impact in that they are expected to generate significant economic value and activity, and have the promise to affect or transform one or more social or economic domains, such as education, health care, transportation, or the retail industry.

Importantly for our purposes, emerging technologies are still technologies in the making. They are not fully developed and entrenched in society. Though not a simple linear process, technological innovation involves different stages, which often begin with research (to investigate new phenomena, ideas, designs, or techniques), followed by development, production, marketing, and diffusion into society. A technology that has completed all these stages is sometimes called an *entrenched technology*. Such a technology is associated with a number of developed products, processes, procedures, or techniques that are widely used in society and have familiar uses and known impacts on society. Although new products based on the technology may still come out, they only represent incremental improvements on existing products, and do not involve radical innovation. Examples of entrenched technologies are automotive technology, satellite technology, antibiotics, polymer technology, radio technology, information technology, and nuclear technology.

Emerging technologies are still largely or wholly in the research and development (R&D) stage. They have not yet resulted in many products, and they have not yet generated a large socioeconomic impact. They are still partially a promise: to become a successful entrenched technology, further research may be needed, new innovative techniques and approaches may need to be developed or tested, methods may have to be developed to combine them with other technologies, new products and applications may have to be thought up, and their market success still has to be proven. Examples of emerging technologies are (at the time of writing) medical nanotechnology, synthetic biology, the Internet of Things, personal and service robots, augmented reality, and smart materials.

It can now be seen how the ethics of emerging technologies is different from the ethics of entrenched technologies. First, the ethics of entrenched technologies is able to address, evaluate, and direct a greater set of existing phenomena. The ethics of emerging technologies tends to have its focus on research and development of these technologies, as these are realities that can be assessed and redirected on the basis ethical assessments. The ethics of entrenched technologies can in addition ethically assess and recommend modifications of specific products, uses, regulations, and social impacts that are already in existence. Second, even if limiting itself to ethical assessments of research and innovation, the ethics of entrenched technology can draw from a wider range of data that are relevant to ethical analysis.

Different from the ethics of emerging technology, it can make use of data about existing products, uses, and social impacts. The ethics of emerging technologies can only make use of speculative data about future products, uses, and impacts. The ethics of entrenched technologies can arrive at better informed moral evaluations of, and prescriptions for, research and development.

In spite of the better epistemic position of the ethics of entrenched technologies and the broader range of topics that can be covered by it, there has been a big movement in recent decades toward the ethics of emerging technologies. This is the case because of one big advantage of the ethics of emerging technologies over that of entrenched technologies: the possibility of early intervention in innovation processes. Once billions have been spent to develop a technology in a particular way, and it becomes entrenched in society as a result, it is very hard to make fundamental changes to its overall design and embedding in society. The ethics of emerging technologies harbors the promise of early intervention when a technology is still malleable and there is still much room for choice in its development and social embedding. The price to be paid for this shift in focus is that the ethicist has a more limited range of empirical data to work with and is faced with significant uncertainties regarding future developments and impacts.

A further distinction relevant to the ethics of emerging technologies is that between stand-alone and enabling technologies. *Enabling technologies* are technologies that provide innovation across a range of products, industrial sectors, and social domains. They combine with a large number of other technologies to yield innovative products and services. Examples of enabling technologies are steam engine technology, glassmaking technology, integrated circuit technology, thermal energy storage technology, genetic engineering, and nanotechnology. In addition, there are also industry- or sector-specific enabling technologies, such as enabling technologies for smart mobile services, tissue engineering, sustainable architecture, and personalized medicine. *Stand-alone technologies*, in contrast, are technologies that yield specific products and services, and are often limited to one industrial sector and one application domain. Examples are quartz clock technology, ballistic missile technology, penicillin, and escalator technology.

The ethics of emerging technologies is focused in large part on emerging enabling technologies, which are expected to result in waves of innovations across different sectors in society and to raise a myriad of ethical issues in the process. Although emerging stand-alone technologies may also raise significant ethical issues, these are often more closely associated with specific products and services, so it is usually somewhat easier to subject them to ethical analysis of future products and associated uses and impacts.

TYPES OF APPROACHES

In the past ten to fifteen years, five distinct types of approaches to emerging technologies have emerged, which will be discussed below. Before they are discussed, it is worth noting that the ethics of emerging technology can be situated within a larger set of both qualitative and quantitative approaches to the assessment and guidance of emerging technology that have the intent of producing better outcomes for society. These include technology assessment (TA), futures studies, impact assessment, risk assessment, risk-benefit analysis, cost-benefit analysis and cost-utility analysis, and, as well as approaches focused on public and stakeholder engagement, democratization, and deliberative decision making. Many approaches in the ethics of emerging technologies seek a combination with one or more of these nonethical approaches, as one will see below.

Generic Approaches

A first approach, which I called the *generic approach* in Brey (2012a), focuses on broad features of an emerging technology that raise ethical issues, independently of and prior to any specific products, uses, or impacts. These are ethical issues that can be identified by considering inherent features of the technology, necessary conditions for its realization, or generic impacts that it is likely to have, regardless of how it will be developed in the future. Generic approaches rest on conceptual analysis and empirical observations of the general features of the technology. Sometimes, they can also involve projections of future impacts. A generic approach is, for example, taken in ethical critiques of genetic engineering that argue that manipulation of genomes is playing God because it amounts to designing new life, which should be done by God, and not by humans. Another example is criticizing an emerging technology because it involves at its core chemical or physical processes that produce toxic or harmful gases or substances as a byproduct, such as greenhouse gases, radiation, or carcinogens.

The generic approach has as an advantage over other approaches in that it does not have to concern itself much with future development and use of a technology and that it can limit itself to the technology as it already exists. It can therefore make reliable claims about the technology that involve little or no speculation about the future. A disadvantage of the generic approach is that it can only consider a small set of ethical issues in relation to emerging technologies: general ethical issues concerning the technology as it has developed so far.

Anticipatory Approaches

A second type of approach is an *anticipatory* or *foresight* approach (Brey, 2012a). Anticipatory approaches combine ethical analysis with various kinds of foresight, forecasting, or futures studies techniques, such as scenarios, trend analysis, Delphi panels, horizontal scanning, as well as various methods of TA. These techniques are used to project likely, plausible, or possible future products, applications, uses, and impacts that may result from the further development and introduction of an emerging technology. Ethical issues in these future applications and uses are subsequently identified and subjected to ethical analysis. Although anticipatory approaches may also be used to identify more general ethical issues as well, they are uniquely capable of identifying ethical issues in relation to projected future products, uses, and social consequences. Ethical analyses performed with them look as follows:

- Technology X is likely to lead to applications and uses that harm privacy. Therefore, it should be developed and introduced in such a way as to minimize such harms.
- Technology X may lead to applications in the military domain that are morally unacceptable. Therefore a strong regulation of X may be necessary to prevent such applications.
- Technology X will lead to products that may, in some societies, enhance socioeconomic inequalities. It therefore should be developed and introduced in a way that takes into account this moral issue.

Existing anticipatory approaches include ethical TA (Palm and Hansson, 2006); ethical impact assessment (Wright, 2010); anticipatory technology ethics (ATE) (Brey, 2012a, b); the ETICA approach (Stahl et al., 2010); the techno-ethical scenarios approach (Boenink, Swierstra, & Stemerding, 2010); and the moral plausibility approach (Lucivero, 2015; Lucivero, Swierstra, & Boenink, 2011). These approaches draw on TA (Palm and Hansson), impact assessment (Wright), and foresight and TA (Brey; Boenink, Swierstra, and Stemerding; Lucivero). Each of these approaches has its own unique selling points. For example, the ethical impact assessment approach is useful for innovation projects since it addresses the practical implementation of recommendations based on ethical assessments. The techno-ethical scenarios approach has the strength of addressing and studying moral change, and is capable of ethical analysis based on expected future moral values of stakeholders. The ATE approach is possibly the only approach that makes full use of foresight methods and presents a detailed methodology for combining these with ethical analysis. The moral plausibility approach, finally, proposes epistemic tools for critically assessing the plausibility of expectations about the future put forward by scientists and experts.

The strong point of anticipatory approaches is that they are the only ones capable of detailed and comprehensive forward-looking ethical analyses of emerging technologies. Their weak point is that they rely on information about the future that is to a degree uncertain and speculative. It is difficult to make reliable predictions, and foresight analyses have often been completely off in their projections of future developments, uses, and consequences of emerging technologies. Foresight analysts usually do not claim anymore to predict the future, but rather to describe plausible or possible futures. Even so, the unreliability of foresight analysis casts some doubt on its usefulness as a foundation for ethical assessment of emerging technologies. It should be noted, however, that foresight analyses tend to be more reliable if they concern the near future (e.g., one to five years, rather than thirty years from now), and that they can generate useful insights into potentialities, condition-alities, and dependencies concerning emerging technologies, even if they are not fully predictive.

Ethical Risk Analysis

Some approaches to emerging technologies focus on the risks that they can pose, including health, security, safety, economic, and environmental risks. These predominantly nonethical approaches include risk analysis and risk-benefit analysis. *Risk analysis* is the process of defining, assessing, analyzing, and managing risks (Haimes, 2015). It is often divided into *risk assessment*, which is the identification, evaluation and measurement of the probability and severity of risks, and *risk management*, which concerns decision making about risks. *Risk-benefit analysis* is the comparison of the risk of a situation to its related benefits. It aims to determine risk-benefit ratios, which are the ratio of a risk of an action to its potential benefits. A guiding principle is that actions should only be undertaken if the risk-benefit ratio is above one. For example, for an individual, the risk-benefit ratio of air travel is usually con-sidered to be above one, whereas the risk-benefit ratio of space travel has so far not been proven to be so.

Risk analysis and risk-benefit analysis are mostly quantitative approaches that do not make explicit use of ethical criteria. Ethical risk analysis has recently emerged to allow for risk analysis that takes into account ethical considerations (Hansson, this book; Asveld and Roeser, 2009). It investigates issues of responsibility, justice, autonomy, well-being, and others in relation to risk assessment and risk management. Ethical risk analysis of emerging technologies identifies risks in such technologies, morally evaluates them, and proposes risk management strategies that are justified from an ethical point of view. Similarly, ethical risk-benefit analysis takes into account ethi-cal issues in determining and utilizing risk-benefit ratios for risks and poten-tial benefits associated with emerging technologies.

Strictly speaking, ethical risk analysis and ethical risk-benefit analysis of emerging technologies are anticipatory approaches, because the calcula-tion of risks and potential benefits requires anticipation and estimation of probabilities of future consequences of the emerging technology. However, because of their unique focus on risk and on quantitative methods, they deserve their own category. A strong point of the two approaches is that they are able to provide quantitative, ethically grounded assessments of risks and benefits of emerging technologies. A weak point is that, like anticipatory approaches generally, they necessarily depend on projections of the future, and that quantitative determinations of risk and potential benefit will often be contentious. Another potentially weak point is the narrow focus on risks, which excludes other types of impacts that are deserving of moral consideration.

Experimental Approaches

Experimental approaches are based on the idea that emerging technologies bring with them many uncertainties regarding their consequences for society, and that these uncertainties often cannot be properly expressed as quantifiable risks and cannot be known or conjectured through foresight approaches because the consequences of emerging technologies are the unpredictable, emergent outcomes of the co-evolution of technology and society. Instead, we should see the introduction of a new technology into society as a process with inherently uncertain outcomes: as a social experiment. Conceiving of technologies as social experiments, we postpone the question "Is technology X morally acceptable?," which we for the most part cannot answer before the technology has been fully introduced into society. Instead, we try to answer the question "Is it ethically acceptable to experiment with technology X in society?"

The experimental approach of Van de Poel (2015) includes a framework for responsible experimentation with emerging technologies in society. Van de Poel bases his proposal on the ethical principles of respect for people, beneficence, and justice, and proposes a set of thirteen conditions for responsible experimentation based on these three principles. These are conditions such as there being no other reasonable means for gaining knowledge about the potential hazards, it being reasonable to expect social benefits from the experiment, hazards being contained as far as reasonably possible, the experiment being approved by democratically legitimized bodies, people being properly informed, and vulnerable experimental subjects being excluded or protected. The approach calls for an incremental introduction of emerging technologies so that an adaptive learning process is possible.

Participatory and Deliberative Ethical Approaches

An increasing number of approaches combine ethics with participatory, deliberative, and stakeholder approaches. Cotton (2014) makes the case for this combination as follows. Ethical assessment, he argues, is a too top-down, technocratic, and expertocratic exercise that fails to take into account the plurality of perspectives found in public responses to emerging technologies. Ordinary approaches to public and stakeholder engagement and deliberation are however too bottom-up, since they make assessments of emerging technologies subject to the opinions, prejudices, and unconsidered moral judgments of those participating, with no guarantee that ethical issues will be considered carefully, if at all. Therefore, an approach must be sought that combines the best elements of top-down and bottom-up approaches, which means a combination of ethics and participatory and deliberative approaches.

In principle, all previous approaches can be supplemented with participatory and deliberative approaches, and sometimes this possibility is made use of. I will focus here, however, on ethical approaches that are essentially participatory and deliberative. These approaches identify the public or the stakeholders as the ones who ultimately have to provide an ethical or ethically informed assessment of an emerging technology, and make moral decisions about its further development and use.

The ethicist has a supporting role in this process. One way in which the ethicist provides support is by developing approaches and tools for better inclusion of ethical principles and arguments in debates on emerging technologies. Another way is by developing ethical criteria for the organization of deliberative and decision-making processes, to ensure that relevant stakeholders are represented, and to avoid that power relations and unequal participation undermine a democratic deliberative process. Both approaches have their roots in discourse ethics (Habermas, 1991). Many authors use them both (Swierstra and Rip, 2007; Cotton, 2014; Keulart, Korthals, Schermer, and Swierstra, 2004).

An advantage of participatory and deliberative ethical approaches is that they include the opinions, viewpoints, and moral intuitions and judgments of different people in a way that could enrich ethical assessments. An advantage of stakeholder approaches in particular, is that including stakeholders in ethical deliberation and decision-making processes is more likely to lead to ethical outcomes, since they usually include actors that shape the future development and use of emerging technologies (technology developers, users, regulators, and other agents). A potential disadvantage of these approaches is that the ideal of serious moral deliberation under conditions of equality may be difficult to achieve. These approaches require that a substantial number of people are brought to the same table to engage in extensive moral deliberation in a way that follows the elaborate discourse rules of ethicists, moves the discussion beyond prevailing interests, and negates prevailing power relations that may distort the discussion. Even ordinary participatory and deliberative approaches have been difficult to realize in practice (Hagendijk and Irwin, 2006), and approaches that include ethical criteria face additional obstacles. Another potential disadvantage is that current approaches do not contain adequate methods for anticipating future ethical issues in relation to emerging technologies. Either the participants will have to engage in foresight themselves, and they risk lacking adequate expertise for this, or they will have to rely on foresight analyses by experts, in which case the approach effectively becomes a blend of anticipatory and participatory/deliberative ethical approaches.

In the remainder of this chapter, I will further discuss anticipatory approaches, for several reasons. Anticipatory approaches are the only ones that promise comprehensive, future-oriented ethical assessments of emerging technologies. They are more comprehensive than risk ethics approaches, and far more comprehensive than generic approaches, both of which they could subsume. The main competitors of anticipatory approaches are experimental and participatory/deliberative approaches. Experimental approaches are, however, only an interesting alternative if it is true that adequate foresight regarding future consequences of emerging technologies is impossible. So it merits investigation whether or not this is the case. If anticipatory approaches are capable of incorporating participatory and deliberative approaches, then they may moreover be more attractive than the stand-alone version of these approaches. So we will investigate this option as well.

ANTICIPATORY APPROACHES AND FORESIGHT

To what extent can future consequences of emerging technologies be known? Clearly, there are future consequences that can be known fairly reliably, and others that cannot. When several firms are in the process of developing household robots, for example, it can be predicted with some confidence that there will soon be household robots on the market, and that there will be people using them. If it is also known that these robots are being designed to collect and store personal information, then it can also be reliably concluded that they will introduce new privacy risks. On the other hand, whether there will be robots within the next thirty years that are in possession of superhuman intelligence and consciousness is something that probably cannot be known reliably. What these two examples suggest is that moderately reliable knowledge of future consequences of emerging technologies may be possible, if the time horizon is not too distant and if information is available about specific technological products that are in the planning and development stages.

Sometimes, it is possible to make predictions of future products and some of their consequences. But making reliable predictions is often not possible, and it is not what foresight analyses of emerging technologies usually try to do. Rather, they aim to identify *plausible* and *possible* futures. A possible future is one that could happen, and a plausible future is one that has a non-negligible likelihood to happen. Foresight analyses often explore multiple possible and plausible futures. The absence of concrete predictions does not make a foresight analysis worthless. The exploration of possible and plausible futures may provide valuable information. First, by giving glimpses of what *may* happen, it allows for better anticipation of the future than would be possible in a situation in which one has no idea what may happen. Second, by projecting possible future applications and uses of the technology and resulting consequences, it is possible to identify potential risks and benefits. It is likely, for example, that advanced 3D printers can be used to manufacture illegal weapons, from which it can be deduced that there is a significant risk that such printers will be misused in this way. It is also possible, and cases have been made, that nanoparticles have an adverse effect on the immune system. As long as this has not been conclusively investigated, this is a risk or uncertainty that can be associated with nanotechnology.

Next to being able to give us *some* anticipation of the future and helping us to identify potential risks and benefits, foresight analyses can also help us identify path dependencies, causal relations, contingencies, and constraints in the development and use of emerging technologies. They can, for example, help us systematically go through the consequences for the economy, the environment, and everyday life of a massive shift from vehicles with internal combustion engines to electric vehicles. Even if such a study is not predictive, it may help identify the path dependencies, constraints, and unintended consequences involved in such a shift. This helps in making better strategic choices possible. For ethical analyses, foresight analyses can show us path dependencies and contingencies that determine whether certain ethical issues will emerge or not, and will help us take steps to avoid undesirable effects.

A requirement for the identification of dependencies, constraints, and potential risks and benefits is that foresight analyses are logically valid and are based on empirically adequate generalizations. Implicitly, foresight analyses use empirical generalizations such as, "If a technological product *p* provides a service for which there is a need that is not provided equally well by other products, then, everything else being equal, people will aim to acquire *p*" and "People have a need for cheap and affordable transportation." Advances in foresight analyses of emerging technologies will require that good use is made of empirical generalizations gained from research in the field of science and technology studies (Hackett, Amsterdamska, Michael, & Wajcman, 2007), since this field has over the past forty or so years developed sophisticated, empirically adequate theories and models that capture lawlike relations in innovation, technology development, technology use, and the impacts of technology. Such models can be used to make realistic projections of future consequences of emerging technologies.

Foresight Methods

What follows is a brief and incomplete overview of tested foresight methods that can be used in anticipatory ethical studies of emerging technologies (cf. Giaoutzi & Sapio, 2013).

- *Horizon scanning* is the scanning or review of a broad range of data sources about the phenomenon about which one aims to gain foresight, in order to identify perspectives and trends that shed a light on future developments. The approach can take the form of a structured literature review or a bibliometric analysis. It can focus on existing foresight studies about the phenomenon, if any, but also on trends, expectations, and new developments and ideas collected from a variety of sources. It usually involves data from a wide variety of sources, including Internet sources, journals, databases, and various sorts of organizations (such as ministries, companies, NGOs, and research organizations).
- *Expert consultation* is a simple form of stakeholder engagement, in which experts with respect to the technology in question or specific impacts are consulted by means of interviews, a short workshop or a small survey. They are consulted about their expectations regarding possible, plausible, or likely future developments regarding the technology.[1]
- *Scenario methods* have become popular tools in foresight analysis, and are used in a wide variety of ways. An overview of current scenario approaches is offered by Börjeson et al. (2006). Scenarios are constructed by starting with the present and past, and projecting into the future. These are forward-looking scenarios. Backcasting scenarios instead look backward from a desired future. The objective of such scenarios is not to determine which futures are most likely to occur, but how to attain a particular future that is desirable. In pluralistic backcasting, multiple preferred futures are taken as starting points of the backcasting exercise. Scenarios are either concerned with what will happen (trend extrapolations, business as usual scenarios, probable scenarios), what could happen (forecasting, foresighting, strategic scenarios) and what should happen (normative scenarios such as those used in backcasting).
- The *Delphi method* is a method that involves an expert panel that fills out questionnaires with their forecasts on a topic in two or more rounds. They usually operate at a distance, although Delphi can also take place face-to-face. The experts enter their questionnaires anonymously, so as to allow for better judgments without undue influence from forceful or

high-status advocates. After each round, a facilitator anonymously summarizes the expert's forecasts from the previous rounds together with the reasons for their judgments, and the experts are encouraged to revise their earlier answers in light of these replies. After a number of rounds, a mean or median score or opinion is determined on the basis of the results in the final round. This method is based on the principle that decisions or forecasts of a structured group are more accurate than those of unstructured groups.

- *Trend analysis* involves the identification of trends: general tendencies or directions evident from past events, and increasing or decreasing in strength of frequency of observation. These trends are then used to predict future events. Trend analyses can be qualitative or quantitative, involving statistical analysis.
- *Relevance trees* are a normative forecasting method that originated in strategic planning. It starts with future needs or objectives, and then seeks to identify the conditions and actions required to meet them. A relevance tree is an analytic technique in which a broad topic is subdivided into increasingly smaller subtopics, thereby showing an increasing number of paths to the objective. It forecasts associated costs, probabilities, and durations for each element in the tree.
- *Roadmapping* is a collaborative foresight process in which a broad set of strategies and plans is developed to reach a common goal. Roadmapping may include any of the other foresight tools. It involves a collaboration network of multidisciplinary and sometimes competing experts. The roadmapping process emphasizes not only probable and preferred futures, but also uncertainties and challenges. The time horizon is often longer than traditional forecasts and plans (five–fifteen years or more). In roadmapping, trends, actions, challenges, and outcomes are commonly represented with graphical displays that are associated with support documents.
- *Participatory foresight.* In participatory foresight (Nikolova, 2014), citizen panels and other methods of citizen participation have a role in foresight analysis, often in combination with participation by experts and stakeholders. This is usually used in normative foresight analysis, in which citizens state their visions and preferences for particular futures and provide comments on scenarios and solutions presented by experts.

So do any or all of these approaches provide reliable insight into possible, plausible, or probable futures? It should be noted that traditional foresight analysis, which aimed at forecasting and prediction, has only had limited success. However, sophisticated methods have been developed in recent decades, and the shift from prediction to the mapping of plausible and possible futures and to normative foresight analysis has led to different standards for success. Nevertheless, a thorough epistemic assessment and testing of current foresight methods has not yet been performed, so it is difficult at this point to assess their reliability and soundness. As I argued earlier, foresight analysis has at least some value in mapping possible and plausible futures, and it may be further improved by better inclusion of insights from STS (science and technology studies). For this reason, it is an approach that is worth pursuing at this point, although further studies are needed to determine whether its limitations are so severe that in most cases alternative approaches to the ethics of emerging technologies are called for, in particular experimental methods as discussed above. It may also be best to combine anticipatory with experimental approaches, with experimental approaches entering into the equation at those moments when good foresight is not possible.

Combining Foresight, Ethics, and Public and Stakeholder Engagement

It has not been addressed so far how foresight analysis combines with ethical analysis. Let us first consider descriptive foresight analysis, which describes plausible futures that are based on mere anticipation and prediction rather than on a normative vision of the future. One way in which it can be combined with ethical analysis is by first having a separate stage of foresight analysis, after which the forecasted futures are studied for ethical issues that they may raise. A second way, which may be more effective for ethical analysis, is to first formulate particular moral values, principles, or issues, and then explore possible futures in relation to the emerging technology at issue in which they play a role. For example, in relation to the Internet of Things, one may explore various plausible future products and processes in which personal data is used so as to investigate possible implications for privacy. This is not an instance of normative foresight analysis, because the aim is not to work toward futures in which these values or norms are realized, but rather to limit the set of future developments that are studied to those relevant to or involving particular ethical principles or issues.

Normative foresight analysis, in which one sketches desirable futures and investigates how they can be reached, can be combined more directly with ethical analysis by including ethical criteria in the list of desirable qualities of the future. However, it is easy to include ethical criteria, but much more difficult to determine how they can be respected in the development and use of emerging technologies. Doing so will require much of the descriptive analysis and identification of ethical issues that is involved in descriptive foresight analysis. For example, one can do a normative foresight analysis of the Internet of Things in which one envisions a future Internet of Things where values like privacy, autonomy, and distributive justice are respected. But determining the attainability of this vision and the conditions that must be met will require identifying all the possible and plausible ways in which the technology may be developed and the ethical issues that they introduce, as is attempted in descriptive foresight analysis.

Anticipatory approaches can include stakeholder and public engagement in quite straightforward ways. Approaches based on descriptive foresight analysis can do so by presenting foresight analyses to stakeholders or members of the public and engaging with them in ethical assessments of the projected futures. Alternatively, they may be presented with both foresight analyses and ethical issues that have already been identified by ethical experts, and they are then asked to assess, weigh, and help resolve these ethical issues. In approaches based on normative foresight analysis, stakeholders and members of the public may be involved more directly in foresight analysis, and participatory foresight methods may be used to construct desirable futures for emerging technologies.

Anticipatory Technology Ethics

To illustrate the use of foresight analysis in an anticipatory approach, I will now discuss one particular approach, ATE (Brey, 2012a, b). I discuss this approach because in my admittedly subjective opinion, it is the only anticipatory approach that fully embraces foresight analysis and presents an extensive methodology for the assessment of emerging technologies. ATE is a method for comprehensive ethical assessments of emerging technologies. A comprehensive assessment is one in which the full range of plausible or possible ethical issues associated with an emerging technology, both generic ones and ones relating to particular products, applications or domains are identified and evaluated. ATE also allows for partial assessments, in which ethical issues are explored in relation to a particular value, product, application, or domain.

ATE analyses consist of three phases or stages: (1) foresight analysis; (2) identification of ethical issues; and (3) evaluation of ethical issues. After these three stages, there are optional stages that utilize the ethical evaluations for further action. These include a design feedback stage, in which the results of ethical analysis are used take identified ethical issues into account in the design and development of the technology, a responsibility assignment stage, in which responsibilities are assigned to different stakeholders for the ethical issues that have been identified, and a governance stage, in which governance recommendations are made for public policy.

ATE engages in foresight and ethical assessment at three levels of analysis: the technology; artifact; and application levels. The technology level is a level of description at which the general features of a technology are described, independently of any products or applications. This level centrally focuses on basic techniques that define the technology. For example, nuclear technology can be defined as the collection of techniques for the fission and fusion of atomic nuclei, and nanotechnology as the collection of techniques for manipulating matter on a scale of 1–100 nanometer. At the technology level, ethical issues of two sorts can be identified: generic ethical issues, of the sort discussed above in relation to the generic approach, and generic risks, which are across-the-board risks associated with techniques that are part of the technology when they are implemented in future products.

The artifact level is a level of analysis that focuses on ethical issues associated with usable products of a technology, which include technological artifacts (e.g., airplanes, x-ray imaging systems) and technological processes and procedures (e.g., food irradiation, nuclear well logging). These artifacts and procedures are studied for their ethical properties largely independently of, and prior to, particular uses of them in particular contexts. Just as it is sometimes possible to identify ethical issues in relation to techniques, prior to products and applications resulting from them, it is sometimes possible to identify such issues in artifacts. This is because particular technological solutions and designs may raise ethical issues that are not specific to a particular way of using them. For example, the internal combustion engine can be critiqued from the point of view of sustainability largely independently of particular uses of it in cars or other machines, because of its emission of greenhouse gases. Similarly, an app on a smartphone that automatically collects personal information and transmits it to the company behind it, or has the ability to do so, can be criticized for its risks to privacy, independently of how it is used by users or the company.

Finally, the application level, or use level, is concerned with particular uses of technological products, by particular types of users, and in particular contexts or domains. At this level, ethical issues are dependent on particular ways of using the artifact, and on the particular circumstances in which it is used, which jointly determine consequences or impacts. Ethical analysis focuses on ethical issues that emerge in particular ways of using technological products, in particular contexts or settings, or in relation to particular types of users. It may, for example, include ethical assessments of the use of cognitive enhancement for the elderly, or the use of drones in military contexts, or the use of 3D printers to make illegal or copyrighted products.

Ethical analysis in Ethical Technology Assessment (ETA) takes foresight analyses as inputs and initially aims to identify ethical issues that may be in play in the projected techniques, artifacts, uses, and impacts. It does so by cross-referencing the results of foresight analysis with ethical principles and issues. This can be done intuitively, on the basis of the expertise of the ethicists or the moral intuitions of stakeholders, or it can be done with the help of an ethical checklist or similar tool. Prior ethical studies may also be used in the process. At this identification stage, the objective is merely to flag and identify potential ethical issues. Subsequently, at the evaluation stage, a thorough ethical evaluation takes place, in which the ethical importance of the issue is further analyzed, and its conflicting values in these issues are weighed against each other, and possible ways of resolving them are explored.

CONCLUSION

This chapter reviewed current issues and approaches in the ethics of emerging technology. Five different categories of approaches were distinguished: generic, anticipatory, risk, experimental, and participatory and deliberative approaches. Strengths and weaknesses of each were reviewed. A further examination of anticipatory approaches was then undertaken, which involved review and assessment of foresight methods used in such approaches, the way in which they combine foresight analysis with ethical analysis, and the possibilities of combining such approaches with participatory and deliberative approaches. Some preliminary conclusions were drawn. However, the ethics of emerging technology is in many ways still in its infancy, and more work is needed to develop more sophisticated approaches, and to assess which approaches deliver the best results.

NOTE

1. Lucivero (2015) advocates that the ethicist or analyst should not be uncritical of the expectations of experts, particularly those of scientists and engineers, who tend to advocate positive visions of the technology that help them sell their ideas. She has developed an approach for assessing the epistemic plausibility of the projections of scientists.

REFERENCES

Asveld, L., & Roeser, S. (Eds.). (2009). *The Ethics of Technological Risk*. London: Earthscan Publishers.

Boenink, M., Swierstra, T., & Stemerding, D. (2010). Anticipating the Interaction between Technology and Morality: A Scenario Study of Experimenting with Humans in Bionanotechnology. *Studies in Ethics, Law, and Technology 4*(2), 1–38.

Börjeson, L., Höjer, M., Dreborg, K., Ekvall, T., & Finnveden, G. (2006). Scenario Types and Techniques: Towards a User's Guide. *Futures 38*(7), 723–39.

Brey, P. (2012a). Anticipatory Ethics for Emerging Technologies. *Nanoethics 6*(1), 1–13.

Brey, P. (2012b). Anticipating Ethical Issues in Emerging IT. *Ethics and Information Technology 14*(4), 305–17.

Cotton, M. (2014). *Ethics and Technology Assessment: A Participatory Approach.* Berlin: Springer-Verlag.

Giaoutzi, M., & Sapio, B. (Eds.). (2013). *Recent Developments in Foresight Methodologies.* New York: Springer.

Habermas, J. (1991). *Erläuterungen zur Diskursethik.* Frankfurt am Main: Suhrkamp.

Hackett, E. J., Amsterdamska, O., Michael, E. L., & Wajcman, J. (Eds.). (2007). *The Handbook of Science and Technology Studies, 3rd ed.* Cambridge, MA: MIT Press.

Hagendijk, R., & Irwin, I. (2006). Public Deliberation and Governance: Engaging with Science and Technology in Contemporary Europe. *Minerva 44*(2), 167–84.

Haimes, Y. (2015). *Risk Modeling, Assessment, and Management, 4th ed.* Hoboken, New Jersey: Wiley.

Keulartz, J., Schermer, M., Korthals, M., & Swierstra, T. (2004). Ethics in a Technological Culture: A Programmatic Proposal for a Pragmatist Approach. *Science, Technology and Human Values 29*(1), 3–29.

Lucivero, F. (2015). *Ethical Assessments of Emerging Technologies: Appraising the moral Plausibility of Technological Visions.* Dordrecht: Springer.

Lucivero, F., Swierstra, T., & Boenink, M. (2011). Assessing Expectations: Towards a Toolbox for an Ethics of Emerging Technologies. *NanoEthics, 5*(2), 129–41.

Nikolova, B. (2013). The Rise and Promise of Participatory Foresight. *European Journal of Futures Research 2*, 1–9.

Palm, E., & Hansson, S. O. (2006). The Case for Ethical Technology Assessment (eTA). *Technological Forecasting & Social Change 73*(5), 543–58.

Sollie, P. (2007). Ethics, Technology Development and Uncertainty: An Outline for any Future Ethics of Technology. *Journal of Information, Communications & Ethics in Society 5*(4), 293–306.

Stahl, B., Heersmink, R., Goujon, P., Flick, C., Van den Hoven, J., & Wakunuma, K. (2010). Identifying the Ethics of Emerging Information and Communication Technologies: An Essay on Issues, Concepts and Method. *International Journal of Technoethics 1*(4), 20–38.

Swierstra, T., & Rip, A. (2007). Nano-ethics as NEST-ethics: Patterns of Moral Argumentation About New and Emerging Science and Technology. *Nanoethics, 1*(1), 3–20.

Van de Poel, I. (2015). An Ethical Framework for Evaluating Experimental Technology. *Science and Engineering Ethics* (online article) 1–20. http://link.springer.com/article/10.1007%2Fs11948-015-9724-3#/page-1.

Wright, D. (2010). A Framework for the Ethical Impact Assessment of Information Technology. *Ethics and Information Technology 13*(3), 199–226.

Chapter 13

Designing Differently

Toward a Methodology for an Ethics of Feminist Technology Design

Diane P. Michelfelder, Galit Wellner,
and Heather Wiltse

In 2014, Apple released its much-anticipated HealthKit application, designed to let individuals use their iPhones to track an impressive range of data from their respiratory rates to the amounts of magnesium, sodium, and other minerals in their diet. To the bafflement of many, the application turned out not to have a way for women to be able to track their menstrual cycles (Lewis, 2014). A corporate culture dominated by men is the most frequently cited reason for this omission (see, e.g., Duhaime-Ross, 2014). Indeed, the underrepresentation of women managers and engineers in technology companies can certainly be one factor why technologies fall short of meeting women's needs and interests. Another, though, can be the absence of a systematic approach to thinking about gender in the course of making creative decisions that shape the process of technology design.

In this chapter, we make a proposal for addressing this absence by suggesting what a methodology for a feminist ethics of technology design might look like. While we intend for this methodology to apply to technological artifacts in general, our primary emphasis will be on the design of digital, and digitized, things. We hope that the thoughts presented here will not only add to the growing body of scholarship on the relations among ethics, gender, and technology, but also have an impact on working practices in companies that design and develop technologies.

Our chapter takes shape as follows. In the first, and background, section we highlight how material artifacts have been gendered in problematic ways, and identify why the rise of network-connected artifacts pose special risks in terms of reinforcing gendered social norms. From here, we turn to bring together, draw on, and analyze perspectives from feminist studies of technology, as well as feminist perspectives on ethics and technoscience, which explicitly discuss how the design process can result in gendered artifacts. Building on this analysis, we then turn to consider how it would be possible to design differently. We propose a methodology for a feminist ethics of technology design, one that is less a procedure than a dynamic set of resources for reflective activity, capable of offering different entry-points for analysis depending on the project. The understanding of methodology as a technology, as it were, plays a role in the content of our proposal. A methodology for a feminist ethics of technology design, we suggest, can serve not only to "de-gender" (Bath, 2009) technological artifacts where appropriate, but also to challenge some accepted practices within design as well as the conventional meaning of "designing" itself. We conclude with a summary amidst a note of caution.

1. BACKGROUND: GENDER NORMS AND TECHNOLOGY

In this section, we offer some background to highlight the need for a methodology for a feminist ethics of technological design, as well as to point to some considerations that such a methodology needs to address. We describe three ways in which technologies have been designed, intentionally or unintentionally, to embody and consequently reinforce gendered norms. In the next three sections, we will review the existing research on technologies and ethics through three angles: social norms representing beliefs and common activities; physical norms where technologies refer to the female body as different where it is similar or as similar where differences should be taken into account; and cognitive norms where female thinking and perceptions are regarded as different from those of men. Admittedly, in everyday life distinctions between these modes of embodiment cannot be easily drawn, and individual technologies cannot be easily separated from the sociopolitical and sociotechnical systems to which they belong (Johnson, 2010). We make these distinctions, here, however, for the sake of analytical clarity.

1.1 Technologies, Gender, and Social Norms

In her seminal article from 1976, Ruth Schwartz Cowan showed how the late industrial revolution transformed the roles of women in the family and society in the United States and Europe in the early decades of the twentieth century. But while the then-common research focused on the functional roles women played in the family context, Schwartz Cowan examined the household work (of middle-class American women) and the associated technological changes in household appliances, such as electric irons, electric washing machines, and modernized systems for heating hot water. The "industrialization of the home," she claimed, was accompanied not only by the disappearance of paid and unpaid servants, but also by the birth of the modern housekeeper who has performed all the chores without being paid. The new household technologies were advertised, not as a replacement of those workers but as an ideal to be pursued through self-labor. The social and the technological changes were intertwined. But unlike the classical Marxist model, in which the laborer is forced by the atomization of the work into a specialized role, the housewife was required to "generalize" by specializing in practically any aspect of everyday life, ranging "from scrubbing the bathroom floor to keeping abreast of the latest literature in child psychology" (p. 23). The gender bias was not limited to the marketing and usage phases. It started earlier at the design and development phases. Later research has studied the design processes of some domestic technologies such as the microwave oven, and found significant gendered assumptions back in the early stages of product conception and engineering, which worked to the disadvantage of women by reinforcing beliefs that they were less technologically competent than men (Cockburn, 1997; Cockburn and Ormrod, 1993). Hence, when analyzing the gender elements of a given technology, developers, designers, and researchers should not only look at the usage patterns but also reflect on the design phase and examine the underlying assumptions that led developers and system designers to make certain choices.

The Information and Communications Technology (ICT) revolution that surfaced in the 1980s has led scholars to ponder if and to what extent the relations between gender and technology can be different after the achievements of feminism in the 1960s and 1970s. Instead of technologies designed either for men (e.g., factory machinery, military technologies) or for women (e.g., home appliances), the ICT revolution carried a promise to refrain from a gender bias (e.g., Turkle, 1995). Alas, this promise did not materialize, partly due to the fact that as engineering evolved in Europe and in the United States, it did so as a predominately white male profession. This colored the technologies of the late twentieth century (Wajcman, 2009). Consequently feminist scholars categorized ICT as "masculine" (see e.g., Johnson, 2010). It should be noted that this type of explanation can be rooted in the same logic as "the fruit of the poisonous tree," a legal doctrine in the United States that describes evidence that was obtained illegally. In our context, this is an implicit assumption that if engineering is masculine, so are its results, that is, technologies.[1]

Interestingly, twenty-first-century technologies such as cell phones seem to escape (or avoid) being classified as masculine (Fortunati, 2009), and the (mostly sociological) research focuses on the ways in which existing gender biases are reflected in different usage practices for the same technology (e.g., Lemish & Cohen, 2005; Ling, 2001). Yet, sometimes gender biases manage to "sneak in" and shape technologies to be either masculine or feminine. Take for example, a cell phone application named "sex stamina tester" that aims to quantify sex. As early as the design phase, the gender bias emerges when the mobile handset is configured to measure the time length and types of movement during sexual encounters, and based on this data rates the act from the point of view of the male partner (Lupton, 2015). This focus on male performance reflects the stereotypical thinking of the predominantly male developers of this app. To be clear, technologies such as this are not inherently problematic, if they are explicitly designed for men; however, all too often they are designed to best serve men's needs but portrayed as being for "everyone." This results in a situation in which men are portrayed as the "normal" user, further reinforcing the humanist conception of (Western, white) man as the standard against which all others are measured and marked as "different."

1.2 Technologies, Gender, and Physical Norms

While technologies are frequently conceived as opening new possibilities, the last example of the cell phone app may lead us to talk of a "closing" that does not enable and that "hides" certain horizons. In gender and technology studies, there are many examples of such "closings," as technologies become gendered in the design process in terms of being "standardized" to reflect and to fit to the physical dimensions of a typical male body. Such gendering to male body norms can have many implications for women. At its worst, as in the well-publicized case where airbags were installed in automobiles after having previously been crash tested on dummies using assumptions about male body size (cf., e.g., Rosser, 2006), gendering design simply to male physical norms can have life-threatening implications for some women. Seatbelts tested on such dummies, originally designed for military use before being adopted by the automotive industry, led to the faulty belief that these were safe for pregnant women to use. In fact, though they often had to be worn in a way that posed a risk to fetal safety in case of an accident; and while in the United States and Europe seatbelts are now required to be tested to both male and female standards, this requirement does not yet extend to testing on pregnant crash test dummies (Schiebinger et al., 2011–2015).

In addition to bringing about disparate impacts on safety, gendering technologies to male physical norms can also result in disparate impacts on access: making technologies designed to such standards more accessible to men than to women. Standing out here as an example is a case much commented upon by feminist theorists, in which the U.S. Department of Defense tried to increase the number of women military pilots but was initially unsuccessful due to the fact that standard cockpit design excluded over two-thirds of women recruits (Johnson, 2010; Rosser, 2006; Webber, 1997). Corrina Bath (2009) brings up the example of early voice-recognition technologies, which, in being designed to recognize male voices, failed to recognize female voices due to their pitch. But even when technologies are intentionally "de-gendered" in one way in the design process so as to reflect neither male nor female physical norms, they can end up reflecting gender in others. A good case in point is "unisex" clothing. When such clothing was initially developed, it had the effect of making women's clothing more masculine and, in some cases, accentuating the sexual features of the physical body underneath the garments being worn (Paoletti, 2015). More recently, it was found that the design of an artificial heart was mainly for men, so it fits 86 percent of men but only 20 percent of women (Deng, 2014).

The quickly emerging development of social robots designed to interact with humans in hospitals, educational environments, and other sociotechnical settings strongly highlights the complexity of ethical issues associated with gendering technologies in the design process to reflect physical norms. Research in persuasive computing has pointed to the need for people to perceive social robots as trustworthy before accepting the information presented by these robots as believable, with results from one study showing that men and women took robots of the opposite sex to be more trustworthy, credible, and engaging (Siegel et al., 2009). For Siegel et al., the question is less whether or not social robots should reflect physical gender, and more one of how to optimize such gendering, for example, through "dynamically modifying" the robot so it could appear to be male or female depending on the preferences of the person with whom it was interacting (Siegel et al., 2009, p. 2,568). They also point out that in some situations a person's health or safety may depend on accepting what a robot says. But from a feminist perspective, the need to assign robots gender for the sake of making people become more "used" to interacting with them raises a number of questions. Is the entry of social robots into everyday social life the kind of introduction that ought to be "smoothed over" by fitting robots into the gender binary? What are the implications of the design team led by MIT roboticist Cynthia Brazeale saying about Jibo, its tabletop social robot, that it is "very much a boy," even though its design reflects masculinity only in its voice (Team Jibo, 2015)? To what extent does designing gender into social robots perpetuate gender stereotypes and gender inequality within society? Or, might it have the opposite impact, if more robots for caregiving settings were designed with male characteristics and more "rescue robots" were designed to reflect female forms (cf. Datarro, 2015)? And, if sociable robots were designed without typical gender markers, how might this have an influence over human-human social interactions and performance of gender identities in the future?

1.3 Technologies, Gender, and Cognitive Norms

Technologies can also be gendered so as to consciously or unconsciously reflect current social norms and assumptions related to cognitive differences between men and women, potentially leading to what Batya Friedman (1996) has called "preexisting bias" being incorporated within the designed product. Such preexisting bias might not only involve perceived differences between men and women with respect to reasoning skills, but also differences between the sexes involving attention, memory, perception, judgment formation, and other skills and abilities. The Netatmo company released in 2014 a wearable bracelet, named June, with a UV sensor transmitting to a smartphone a notification alerting its user when to put on sunscreen. It was targeted exclusively toward women, even though, if survey findings on this matter are to be trusted, men are arguably more at risk for overexposure to sunlight since they are less likely to use sunscreen in the first place. Such an example of a wearable device can be interpreted as embodying a preexistent cognitive bias that women are more in need of being "reminded" in this particular context. On a wider scale, the potential for preexisting cognitive biases to become incorporated into technology design has implications for what kinds of activities become monitored by fitness trackers, how the data arising from these activities get tracked using these devices, and, on a larger scale, to what degree gender becomes non-transparently embedded in technology development that supports the so-called Quantified Self. Machine learning algorithms, for example, work behind the scenes and are invisible to end users. In an ethnographic investigation of the Quantified Self movement, Nafus and Sherman (2014, p. 1786) have called attention to how these algorithms, based on the data they receive from users, may learn from how people "enact social categories" such as gender online. These findings can be implemented on a wider scale and may end up reinforcing a "soft biopolitics," which narrows possibilities by limiting what advertisements people see.

Likewise, digitized objects such as computer software can also be "gendered" with respect to cognitive norms. An example of this can be found in a study by C. Huff and J. Cooper (1987, cited by Friedman, 1996) in which programmer/educators were asked to design software to help three groups of students: girls, boys, and a mixed group, learn how to use commas. Given the choice between whether their work was shaped as a game or a learning tool, programmers for the boy students designed their software as a game, while those designing for girls identified their work as a "learning tool." Despite the fact that most of the designers were women, the program for the mixed group was framed to be a game, and so according to the researchers reflected "male bias" (Huff and Cooper, 1987).

By means of these examples, we can see that just as there is a complexity of issues associated with gendering technologies in the design process to reflect physical norms, the issues associated with designing technologies to reflect gendered cognitive norms are equally complicated. Such design (as in the first example of wearable bracelet) can reflect gender bias, when it starts from the assumption that forms of cognition traditionally associated with men are superior to those traditionally associated with women, and shapes technologies so as to reflect that point of view. It can also reflect gender bias (as in the second example of teaching boys through games), when it begins with the assumption that men and women have different but equally valuable ways of paying attention, processing information, making judgments, and so on. Both, though, carry the potential with them of continuing gender stereotypes about cognition. They also point to potential risks of taking the results of studies on cognitive differences between the sexes and/or surveys of potential users into account in the design process, even when designers may be interested in doing this in order to push back against female stereotypes. In a paper for UNESCO, the designer Klaus Schroeder commented that when women users were asked to provide feedback on the design of a mobile telephone headset, they expressed concern that wearing a headset sent a signal that they were "not fully available for the people around them" (2010, p. 10). Here, it seems, designers face a dilemma: on the one hand, taking this feedback into consideration in the final design seems like the ethically responsible thing to do. It also fits within the dominant tradition of user-centered design, which points toward supporting people's behaviors and choices, rather than imposing the designer's own preferences. On the other hand, to uncritically act on the basis of this feedback might also be a way of going against the best interests of women, by reinforcing social expectations that they constantly need to be available to others. For a designer working within a company setting and so needing to produce products that people will buy, going against the preferences of consumers, and so the financial interests of the company, might seem irresponsible; then again, through working to "educate the market," the company might shape consumer perceptions and preferences in relation to its products in ways that enable it to become a market leader (and further reinforce these norms). We will come back to this dilemma in the next section of this chapter.

dilemma #1

2. FEMINIST PERSPECTIVES

Although some gendered aspects of technologies are readily apparent, others are more subtle. There are also multiple angles and perspectives that can be taken. For more help with identifying problematic gender aspects of technologies, and conceptual tools for more nuanced analysis, we now turn to analyze perspectives connected to three areas of theoretical inquiry: feminist studies of technology; feminist ethics; and feminist technoscience. This move will let us expand our analysis beyond individual technologies themselves to the consideration of more pervasive underlying dynamics, found in prevailing cultures of technology development, that tend to materialize and reinforce certain problematic gender dynamics and stereotypes.

From here we can raise the question: But what would be a better alternative? In this section, we begin to ask this question and to establish a theoretical basis for the methodology section to follow. As noted earlier, we hope that this methodology could be helpful to designers, who could treat it as one way forward when it comes to reducing the questionable gendering of technologies in the ways described above.

2.1. Feminist Studies of Technology

Do apps, cockpits, consumer electronics, household devices, and other technologies discriminate because they don't consider women to be equal to men, or because women are different from men but their difference is not taken into account? Here we can identify a basic split between two strands of feminism—liberal and radical: the former regards women and men to be equal and usually approaches technologies with the assumption that some technologies are predesigned either for women or for men and hence discriminate women; and the latter strives to reveal the differences between genders and hence asserts that women's interests and needs are not well served by certain technologies, which are presumed to be neutral.

This split is elaborated by Judy Wajcman (2009) as two stages in the research of gender and technology. The mission of the early research, she explains, was to expand the notion of technology to include not only "the usual suspects" of industrial machinery and military weapons but also everyday technologies such as modern bathtubs (Schwartz Cowan, 1976) and microwave ovens (Cockburn, 1997). Such studies aimed to deconstruct the sociocultural identification of technology with masculinity which dated back to nineteenth century's emergence of engineering as a male profession. In the next stage, gender studies of technology shifted from asking "how women can be more equitably treated within and by" a given technology, to the question of how a certain technology "apparently so deeply involved in distinctively masculine projects can possibly be used for emancipatory ends" (Wajcman, 2009, p. 4). In other words, "The problem was not only men's monopoly of technology, but also the way gender is embedded in technology itself" (Wajcman, 2009, p. 4).

Wajcman's notion of "technofeminism" (2009) covers both strands and denotes how technological innovation is saturated in gender relations and is not the product of rational neutral professionals. Technology is therefore both the source and the consequence of gender relations so that gender and technology co-shape each other. The co-shaping process is endless, as gender—understood as performative—and technology—understood as socially constructed and constantly domesticated—cannot be regarded as pre-given notions or as stable constructs.

Another important analytical tool is offered by Wendy Faulkner (2001), who distinguishes between gender *in* technology and gender *of* technology. The *in* proposition refers to the ways in which technologies are developed to include in them certain gender biases or built to produce certain forms of such biases. The *of* proposition indicates an association with gender that has not necessarily material implications in the technological artifact, yet the artifact is being marketed to a specific gender. The latter can be exemplified in the usage of "male" and "female" in the electromechanical professional literature to describe certain parts. According to this classification, Schwartz Cowan describes the *of* and Weber's study of the cockpit is concerned with the *in*.

Faulkner's *in* proposition is further elaborated by Bath (2009), who maps four approaches in the design process that might lead to "gendered computational artifacts": (1) the "I-methodology" that assumes technology as neutral; (2) implicit gendered assumptions and the gendered distribution of labor, which are inscribed into computational artifacts; (3) gender stereotypes reflected in technology; and (4) decontextualization and disputable epistemological and ontological assumptions pretending to be gender-neutral. In her article Bath offers ways to "de-gender" technologies for each of the four mechanisms: (1) to seek the gender differences, physical and social, as well as cultural, age, etc., through usability tests and other user-centered design methods; (2) to attribute equal competencies to female and male users and to upgrade women's work and empower the female workers when their work is "invisible" or regarded as low rank; (3) to conceive gender and technology as social and unstable constructs, thereby allowing users to reflectively engender themselves and perform their gender identity; and (4) to question basic assumptions like what is the female body, emotions, etc. Although Bath's methodological framework is originally intended for the development of ICTs, we believe that it is useful also for other technological domains. In section 3, we offer a critical assessment of Bath's approach, prior to describing our own methodological view.

2.2 Feminist Ethics

Since this chapter aims at developing a methodology for a feminist ethics of technology design, it makes sense to support it, at least in part, on developments in feminist ethics. Much as the "I-methodology" (Oudshoorn, Rommes, and Stienstra, 2004) results in technologies being designed for male users rather than for all, Western philosophical ethics has historically taken a parallel track, summed up well by Virginia Held's observation that "ethics . . . has not been a search for universal, or truly human guidance, but a gender-biased enterprise" (1990, p. 323). Turning now to feminist ethics, we can see it as being a heterogeneous field marked by a diversity of points of view, much as feminist theory. For instance, in their contribution to *The Stanford Encyclopedia of Philosophy,* Tong and Williams (2009) include eleven different strands of thought under the larger heading of feminist ethics; Rosser (2006), in her lucid and comprehensive overview of the relationships among feminist theories, design, and use, identifies ten. Here we will concentrate on just three of these approaches as they relate to ethics: liberal feminism; radical feminism; and the feminist ethics of care. By limiting our discussion to these three approaches of feminist ethics, we are not casting doubt on the value of the others. Rather, we are taking a pluralist, pragmatic approach and suggesting that these three theories, despite the profound differences among them and even within each one taken separately, arguably offer the broadest, most useful support in terms of justifying the methodology for the technological design we aim to propose here.

Liberal feminism, as Rosser points out (2006, p. 14), is primarily interested in bringing about increased equality for women and in eliminating unjust discrimination that impedes the ability of women to have equal opportunities and equal rights. These, and the freedoms that go with them such as personal autonomy (contested, but still valued within liberal feminism) and freedom of mobility, from the perspective of liberal feminism provide essential support for a good life, which has the potential of coming within reach through self-discovery and self-actualization. Liberal feminism would be concerned about all the ways identified here in which technological design can be gendered (as would the other two forms of feminism as well), but it would be especially concerned with how technologies can be gendered to male physical standards. Such gendered design, highlighted in the previous section with the examples of cockpit design, seatbelts, and artificial hearts, can have a direct impact on making some opportunities more difficult for women to access, exploit, and use. In addition, instances where it would be responsible to take the physical differences between males and females into account in the design process but where instead the focus ends up being on designing to male physical standards—as for example, in the case of unisex clothing or the more serious case of the artificial heart, which was designed to fit the bodies of most men but only a minority of women's. This is in spite of the fact that in the United States, over 40 percent of those who experience heart failure are female (see, e.g., Deng, 2014). This could arguably be seen as violating women's healthcare rights. The liberal feminist approach provides a basis at least in part for Bath's "de-gendering" methodology, as she too takes equity to be an important value for at least some technologies to reflect, primarily technologies designed for women's use rather than that of the general population (Bath, 2009, p. 4). We will discuss this limitation further in the next section.

Even if the need for equal rights and equal opportunities were to be recognized in technological design through de-gendering or re-gendering so as to support innovations that offered equal physical accessibility for/usability to women, there would still be more work to do in order to avoid designing to certain social or cognitive gender norms. While problems associated with technologies unfairly gendered to physical norms can be solved with the introduction of different technologies or by simply changing the dimensions of the physical artifact, designing to mitigate social or cognitive stereotypes about women is a more complex matter, and rests on different theoretical bases with regard to feminist ethics. Radical feminism, for instance, would question why it is that technologies keep being brought onto the market only to have to be modified at a later point to better "fit" women, not only physically but also with respect to other needs and interests. Alison Jaggar (1983) contrasts well the distinction between radical feminism and other forms of feminism in observing that "radical feminism shows how, in contemporary society, distinctions of gender structure the whole of life." Such structuring, radical feminism contends, subordinates women to men; "distinctions of gender" are distinctions that feed the maintenance of stereotypes and the oppression of women (1983, p. 85) and (it is here where the goals of liberal and radical feminism come together) put obstacles in the way of women being free to affirm themselves and to achieve their full potential. But, unlike with respect to physical norms, here there are no "quick fixes." Designing technologies so as to avoid reinforcing problematic prevailing social norms regarding women brings with it a number of complexities, as it is important to look out not only for how these norms might be reproduced in the designed object itself, but also for how the object might act to reproduce gender structures in particular contexts of use.

For one, this would involve being mindful, in the design process, of Cockburn's observation that "if in some sense we 'gender' artifacts, so do we gender skills" (Cockburn and Ormrod, 1993, p. 2). For example, Amazon promotes its Echo technology as being able to read children's bedtime stories aloud from Kindle books and also to place an order for pizza to be delivered. To reflect on whether this functionality reinforces social norms, developers would need to think beyond the apparently non-gendered character of these functionalities to look at matters such as where the Echo is most likely to be located in the home, who would be most likely to give Echo commands, for whom it would be most likely to free up labor rather than creating more, and what impacts its connection to the Alexa voice-service (which makes the Echo respond to commands with a woman's name and speak in a female-sounding voice) have on traditional gendered divisions of work within the home.

While the perspective of the feminist ethics of care is quite different from that represented by radical feminism, with reference to the design process it echoes the latter in speaking to the need to look critically and broadly at possible conditions of use for the object being designed. The starting point for feminist care ethics is the idea that ethical decision making is always context-dependent, and that the individuals who make moral decisions are "fundamentally social creatures whose existence is primarily structured by relationships with others" (Michelfelder and Jones, 2016), in particular relationships that are characterized by dependency, vulnerability, and reliance. As a result, being a moral agent in such circumstances often means caring about and addressing the needs of others; doing this well involves a "register" of cognition where the thinking is informed by relational feelings and attitudes such as empathy, compassion, and trust. While care ethics has sometimes been faulted for being a form of essentialism and so working to maintain gender stereotypes, Virginia Held and others have stressed that caring as a fundamental moral activity is within the reach of anyone, gender notwithstanding (Tong and Williams, 2014).

It is this latter emphasis on nonessentialism that allows feminist care ethics to contribute to a methodology for a feminist ethics of technology design, particularly where the design at stake may involve including cognitive gender norms, such as those discussed in section 1.3. While no justification can be found in feminist care ethics for embedding norms that imply the superiority of a "male" way of judging, perceiving, paying attention, etc., this approach to ethics wouldn't necessarily object, for instance, to the development of computer software that took advantage of the differences in learning processes between women and men. But, before embedding such gender differences in a designed product, responsible developers, thinking from the perspective of a feminist ethics of care, would need to ask a number of questions. What would be the advantage of taking this design direction? Are these perceived differences based in a false essentialism? On trustworthy empirical research? On the expressed preferences of potential users? If the latter, to what degree are these preferences "adaptive" ones? If adaptive, should they be respected in the design process, given that they are choices women have autonomously made (see, e.g., Khader, 2011)? Might these choices, reflected in design, support women as they pursue lives marked by self-discovery and self-actualization?

In these questions, we can find echoes of some of the methodological principles involved in empathic design, which, through conversation with consumers over a period of time, seeks to innovate, based not only on how consumers use products but also on how they feel about them (Postma et al., 2012). Connecting the ways in which technologies can be gendered to reflect social and cognitive norms to feminist ethical perspectives discloses a need for designers to look critically and thoughtfully at not only user experiences but also the social contexts in which they occur and the cognitive assumptions they involve, as taking user experiences and potential product uses at face value may inadvertently result in reinforcing biases and misperceptions. Similarly, and just as importantly, this also discloses a need for designers to critically reflect on how they themselves, as gendered users of technology, are situated within social contexts and are influenced by cognitive norms and assumptions. Later we will explore further both these methodological points.

2.3 Feminist Technoscience

Feminist technoscience is a strand of scholarship that grew out of feminist critiques of the supposed objectivity and purity of science, pointing instead to the inherent situatedness of scientific practices and close interrelationships with technological tools that both participate in these practices and are seen to be their outcomes as the application of basic knowledge. The term technoscience emphasizes the inseparability of this relation between science and technology (Ihde, 2009). The feminist perspective further underlines the societal entanglements and political and ethical accountability of both scientific and technological development practices (Åsberg & Lykke, 2010). Rather than aiming for objective knowledge as the goal (even if elusive or unobtainable), it celebrates what Donna Haraway refers to as the "privilege of partial perspective," a "feminist objectivity" that entails "situated knowledges" and the associated responsibility for one's position (Haraway, 1988). Suchman (2002) extends this orientation in order to conceptualize "located accountabilities" in technology production, recognizing the extended networks of many actors involved in technology production and use and the multiple accountabilities thus entailed in technology development processes. Of course, this is much easier said than done though; and knowledge that is objective, impartial, universal, and so on is still viewed as the ultimate (even if elusive or unobtainable) goal.

These views of knowledge and technology production practices emphasize their contingencies and situatedness in particular (social) contexts and networks of other actors. They thus suggest that we cannot understand what a technology "is" just by looking at it as a thing in itself, but must rather take a broader view that encompasses these other dynamics and contexts, if we are to understand its character and consequences. However, we can go even further than that by drawing on the work of theoretical physicist and feminist technoscience scholar Karen Barad (2003, 2007), who develops insights from quantum physics into a position she calls "agential realism" that sees entities and agencies mutually constituting each other through their "intra-actions." In this view there are no such things as separate, independent entities. Rather, the basic ontological unit is phenomena, and it is through intra-actions within phenomena that "agential cuts" are made that separate subject and object, and agencies are (re)configured. This is a performative understanding of identity and matter that Barad connects to Judith Butler's conception of the materialization of gender.

What does this mean for how gender is implicated in the design of technologies, if it is not "hardwired" but rather something that emerges over time and is performed through intra-actions? This is a problem articulated and taken up by van der Velden and Mörtberg (2011), who point out that script analysis (one of the main tools used so far in order to identify gender issues in technologies) is based on a separation of design and use. They use a set of case studies from their own design research practices—one about classifying local knowledges in a computer system in a Maasai community in Kenya, the other about the effects of an inflexible IT system on a civil servant's work in Sweden—to point to the emergent effects of design decisions and to complicate understandings of the relations among designer, user, and use. They then develop a strategy of "ungendering design" that "is based on the idea that every inscription of gender is or will be problematic at one time, because we can never foresee the effects when an artifact gets new meaning or when it is altered or ignored" (p. 15).

There is, then, a temporal expansion of analytic frame required that parallels the expansion from isolated technology to network of actors and infrastructures. In fact, especially in the case of interactive computational technologies, this temporal form may be even more significant, since we in many instances can really understand what a thing is and does only through interactions that unfold over time; and yet, the fact that traditional notions of form in design emphasize the visual—and thus viewing things from a particular, frozen, distanced perspective—works against exploring these crucial aspects of temporal form (Redström, 2013).

One particular strategy for expanding conceptions of design temporally and in terms of who participates is to recognize acts of design that occur during use—in other words, innovative acts that change what it is possible to do with a designed thing, but occur on the side of use rather than during the formal design process (Oudshoorn and Pinch, 2003; Redström, 2008). We can also think of the "artful integrations" (Suchman, 2002) that are necessary for a technology to become useful in a particular context, and the more local acts of participatory design that might help to decenter what are traditionally thought of as the sources of innovation where futures are made, and who participates (Ehn, Nilsson, and Topgaard, 2014).

A technology is thus not something that can be isolated and validly assessed at (only) one particular moment in time, because both the technology and its effects unfold over time. Design is not something that occurs only in a design studio or technology company lab, but is rather an ongoing process of (re)configurations enacted in many locations that blur distinctions between design and use. What, then, does this mean for technology assessment and, indeed, for locating the accountability of designers? Certainly embedded scripts matter, and ones that are problematic should not be supported. Yet we also must recognize that scripts are only one part of an ongoing story that is continuously unfolding. And while it is indeed important to expand conceptions of where design activity takes place and who does it, we must also recognize that design as a profession was called into being by industrialization (Dilnot, 2014) and is (at least typically) done in service of particular clients (Nelson and Stolterman, 2012). Designers thus work within a set of interwoven and powerful interests that constrain what they are actually able to do.

Echoing insights from feminist technoscience, we can thus say that technology design is never innocent, dislocated, or impartial; but it is also not all-powerful, and the things it produces are never fixed in terms of their effects, meanings, or forms. Perhaps this inherent openness points to a way forward: to seeing the gendering or ungendering of design as an ongoing process of (re)configurations, rather than something that occurs at some originating moment of design. Designers have a very significant role and corresponding responsibility, to be sure; and design is inherently a process of world and (hopefully) future-making—a rather grand and weighty enterprise requiring careful consideration. Yet, as Barad (2003, 2007) shows, the world is continuously becoming; that becoming is characterized by constraints, but also openness. When we think about how to design differently, this responsibility needs to be taken as a basic assumption.

3. DESIGNING DIFFERENTLY: TOWARD A METHODOLOGY OF AN ETHICS OF FEMINIST TECHNOLOGY DESIGN

Having diagnosed the situation of gendered norms as being deeply implicated in and reinforced by much technology development, the next logical step is to ask how things might be done differently. However, before continuing, it is worth noting the shift that is entailed when moving from assessment of existing technologies and associated practices to the design of technologies that do not yet exist and the envisioning of anticipated associated practices and effects.

3.1 Design and Assessment

While any assessment is in some ways open-ended in terms of what can be known and in the particular perspectives of those doing the analysis, the openness of design is of a rather different order. Perhaps this is why there have been more deconstructive feminist studies of technologies than practical implementations of feminist methods in design (Rommes, Bath, and Maass, 2012).

Design is an act of making a new, purposeful addition to the world, of bringing into existence that-which-does-not-yet-exist in order to serve a particular purpose (Nelson and Stolterman, 2012). It is inherently future-oriented and future-making (Yelavich and Adams, 2014), even as it is also a historical project of world-making (Fry, Dilnot, and Stewart, 2015). Although designers may have certain intentions for how a given designed thing will be used and the purposes it will serve, these do not foreclose the many other possibilities for what may actually happen once it is put out into the world. Design is thus a matter of making things with the intention that they will be useful and usable, and that they will make sense (Krippendorff, 1989) aesthetically and semantically for particular contexts and types of users. But it is also, fundamentally, a process of making and becoming, where what emerges and comes into being can never be precisely or entirely known in advance. This is true of the design process itself and, even more so, of what a thing actually becomes and what dynamics develop once a designed thing is released into the world.

This leaves us, then, with a certain complexity and difficulty when it comes to adequately assessing technologies and their effects in relation to design. Specifically, we can identify two major issues. First, since any designed thing is made to serve a particular purpose, it follows that *evaluation of a designed thing should be undertaken in relation to that intention and purpose.* Now, this is not to say that there are not extremely valid critiques of technologies that can still be made—not least in relation to gender—on the basis of clearly bad intentions, glaring and avoidable oversights, entrenched prejudices and discrimination that become manifest in designed things, etc. We can also note the effects that particular technologies have, and on this basis argue that things should be done differently. It is not appropriate to simply look at a technology that is designed for a very specific purpose and user group (say, e.g., twenty-year-old men serving in the U.S. Marines) and say that it is discriminatory because it is not well suited to sixty-year-old women; however, if a technology is effectively designed for twenty-year-old men but with the intent and claim that it is universally usable, then there is clearly a problem. Thus, we must in our analysis keep (at least) a double view: an orientation to the particular purpose a designed thing was intended to serve, but also the ways in which designed things can materialize and reinforce (problematic, pervasive) gender dynamics and power structures. Second, *design and use are open-ended, intertwined processes, and it is impossible to know precisely what consequences a designed thing will have in the world* (Oudshoorn and Pinch, 2003). This means that, rather than an isolated technology, a more suitable unit of analysis is often human-technology relations. It also means perhaps shifting our thinking from doing a technology assessment as a part of a design process that can be "checked off" when complete, to an orientation directed toward following and caring for the consequences things actually have in the world with a view to how insights gained can feed back into ongoing (re)configurations.

3.2 A Methodology for Designing Differently

In section 2.1, we described the elements of the methodology developed by Bath in her pioneering work (2009) in feminist technology design in computer science. Bath presents her work as a "basic methodology" that needs to be filled out by both feminist theory and empirical evidence. While the feminist theory presented in this chapter could be seen as helping to complete Bath's framework, our project is more accurately seen as critically building upon what Bath has already done. Taken as a whole, her methodology matches specific problems in the gendering of technologies with their antidotes, found in particular theories of design. Gender biases created by the "I-methodology" can for instance in Bath's view be countered through the approach of user-centered design. Our methodology builds upon Bath's but differs from it in several ways. First, we wonder whether there is necessarily a one-to-one correspondence between particular ways in which technologies are gendered and theories of design that can be used for "de-gendering" purposes. Second, we caution against accepting theories of design at face value for their potential to contribute to a methodology for "designing differently." As we have pointed out, adopting the approach of user-centered design may lead to reinforcing gender bias and stereotypes. Lastly, as we will discuss briefly in this section, we believe that this critical eye, when it comes to developing a methodology for a feminist ethics of technology design, needs to be extended to the process of design itself.

Moreover, when it comes to actual design work, overly prescriptive methods are rarely used (or useful). According to Stolterman (2008),

> It seems as if (interaction) design practitioners are inclined to appreciate and use: (i) precise and simple tools or techniques (sketching, prototypes, interviews, surveys, observations, etc.), (ii) frameworks that do not prescribe but that support reflection and decision-making (design patterns, ways of using prototypes, styles of interaction, etc.), (iii) individual concepts that are intriguing and open for interpretation and reflection on how they can be used (affordance, persona, probe, etc.), (iv) high-level theoretical and/or philosophical ideas and approaches that expand design thinking but do not prescribe design action (reflective practice, human-centered design, experience design, design rationale, etc.). (p. 63)

In this spirit, and because we want our work to be useful for design, we here present examples and approaches that we hope can contribute to developing (design) sensitivities, competences, and character (Nelson and Stolterman, 2012) with respect to issues of gender.

There have been a number of attempts to take an explicitly feminist approach to technology development, building in feminist "scripts" rather than ones with problematic gender norms. These include designing feminine/feminist values and perspectives into technologies (Rasmussen and Petersen, 2011) and games (Fullerton, Morie, and Pearce, 2007), as well as developing technology to support social justice (Dimond, Dye, LaRose, and Bruckman, 2013), and using critical game design for social and political critique or intervention (Flanagan, 2009). Building on a perspective of considering use qualities that emerge in the gestalt of interaction with artifacts (Löwgren and Stolterman, 2004), qualities of feminist interaction that have been suggested are "pluralism, participation, advocacy, ecology, embodiment, and self-disclosure" (Bardzell, 2010, p. 1305).

More speculative and critical design projects have sought to more directly tackle issues of gender and their relations to designed things. One such case is the "Andro-Chair" that was designed using a gender-critical approach to enable men to experience something at least similar to what women experience in gynecological chairs, and to uncover the gender norms that are involved in their design (Sundbom, Ehrnberger, Börjesson, and Hertz, 2015). These projects are not intended to be mass produced, but rather to pose questions and provoke reflection through objects serving as "design props" that materialize particular fictions and thereby enable speculation about possible (as well as existing) realities (Dunne and Raby, 2013). They also serve as examples (albeit extreme ones) that might help us to think about how design can be done from a critical feminist perspective.

Although speculative and/or more academic or artistic projects such as the Andro-Chair can be designed with the intent to challenge existing (problematic) norms, the situation in more mainstream industrial design is rather more complicated. Indeed, the general orientation toward "user-centered design" that has been dominant for decades advocates a design process that takes into account the intended users' actual practices, desires, cultural norms and references, aesthetic preferences, and so on. This is a framework that has not only helped to produce many "user-friendly" products, but has also thereby been quite successful commercially. Thus, designing products that would not be in line with or even challenge existing norms would go against deeply ingrained and in many ways quite successful strategies of industrial design. From the perspective of wanting to not perpetuate and/or actively disrupt problematic gender norms through design, this poses a dilemma for which there are no easy solutions—particularly for designers whose choices are constrained by the larger systems within which they work (Jones, 1992).

In addition to considering the (feminist) qualities that emerge in the use of particular artifacts, we can also consider the processes by which they are created. Women have often been excluded from processes of technology development, so in this light participatory design that includes women and other stakeholders who are typically marginalized (as well as efforts to get more women into tech and design fields) can be seen as a feminist move.

Another somewhat different strategy for reconfiguring (gendered) relations in and of design is to redefine and reconceptualize what actually counts as innovation and design. This is something that feminist historians of industrial design have done as a means of critiquing and countering the absence of women in dominant design historical narratives (Buckley, 1986; Sparke, 2010). They pointed to consumption as an important dimension of design, which made it possible to bring women into the picture since they were frequently the intended users of the objects of industrial design. Another angle was to include craft practices in narratives of design, since these were typically the only means of production accessible to women (Buckley, 1986). This and other kinds of related "research on the actual work involved in putting technologies into use highlights the mundane forms of inventive yet taken for granted labor, hidden in the background, that are necessary to the success of complex sociotechnical arrangements" (Suchman, 2009). This research serves to more equitably distribute attribution for contributions made in processes of technological development, and particularly in ways that can recognize the roles of women.

Perspectives from the tradition that is referred to variously as participatory, collaborative, collective, or co-design also emphasize design processes that unfold over time, and that have central political aims of enabling democratic participation in addressing shared matters of concern (Binder et al., 2015). Here, designers often act as catalysts and facilitators, designing open-ended platforms and infrastructures that can evolve over time and allow others to do things, rather than designers themselves creating finished products. Working within this tradition, Lindström and Ståhl (2015) point to the need to consider the temporal aspect that is central in design (but obscured through the primarily spatial figurations of networks and similar) and the entangled collectives that can emerge over time and space in co-design. They propose "patchworking" as a figure that captures this dynamic, especially as it relates to their "Threads" project—a traveling exhibition in the format of a traditional "sewing circle" that traveled around rural Sweden. In these sewing circle gatherings, participants embroidered SMS messages in fabric, either by hand or through a custom sewing machine set up to pull messages directly from a phone and do the embroidering automatically. This project began at a time when mobile phones had quite limited space, which often required that SMS messages be deleted in order to free up space. Embroidering a certain SMS message was thus a way of preserving it in another form, and this process also encouraged participants to talk about their reasons for choosing particular messages and about the role of these technologies in their lives. Through this collaborative making, it was thus possible to engage participants with issues surrounding the role of new technologies in society. Rather than producing a material product as the outcome, this work initiated a platform that reached many people and traveled and evolved over the years as others also came to be involved in organizing it, sometimes taking it in new directions; it was a project of design as infrastructuring and creating material conditions in which publics could emerge through working with specific matters of concern (Latour, 2005).

At this point we have considered a broad range of possible problematic intersections of technologies and gender, as well as potential avenues of intervention and ways of actively designing differently. One notable dynamic in the progression of the chapter, as we have attempted to open up these issues, is the many ways in which we have expanded from a perhaps typical conception of design as a predominately white male activity. We have called attention to the networks of multiple actors who are involved in processes of technology development, and the creative (design) acts of appropriation and integration on the side of use; to the inherent openness of design that becomes apparent as interactions, meanings, practices, and effects emerge and evolve over time; and to processes of design that seek to actively critique and subvert gender norms as well as enable participation and diversity. Thus, while we can point to some specific things to consider during design processes, an ethics of feminist technology design might be better conceived as a diverse set of sensitivities, commitments, and modes of engagement—more tactics than strategy (de Certeau, 1984). Moreover, responsibility does not begin and end with the formal design process and designers, but is rather an ongoing accountability we all have in relation to our (technological) choices and practices.

4. CONCLUSION

In conclusion, we turn to the cautionary note promised at the beginning of this chapter. The methodological tactics we have developed here address only one piece of the puzzle and ongoing challenge when it comes to opening up the processes and outcomes of technology development such that they become more inclusive and thoughtful with respect to gender. We all know that technologies have unintended consequences. They may be designed to counteract negative gender norms but end up promoting them for reasons invisible in advance, even to the most discerning eye. Technologies are also "multi-stable" with respect to use (Ihde, 1990); a point Johnson puts succinctly by noting that "designing artifacts for gender equity cannot . . . determine equitable gender relations" (Johnson, 2010, p. 48). The way a technology is advertised and, more broadly, the way it is marketed can serve to subvert the intentions of designers to develop more gender-inclusive technologies. And—to return to the Apple Watch example with which we began this chapter—the persistent underrepresentation of women in engineering design and leadership roles in technology companies (see for instance, Ashcraft and Blithe, 2010; Gellman and Wells, 2016) represents a substantial obstacle to taking women's needs and interests as seriously as those of men in the development of new technologies. Even here, it is important to keep in mind that solving the underrepresentation problem is not just a matter of bringing more women into engineering design fields, as women can be brought into these roles to address "the women's perspective." Such "inclusion" could put them in the position of needing somehow to represent the interests of all women as well as framing, and so "gendering" their role as "female designers."

Still, the need to be cautious about the impact that a methodology for a feminist ethics of design can have when taken by itself does not take away from the importance of contributing to its construction. As Sarah Kember has shown, by means of algorithms that sort individuals as either male or female, face-recognition technologies can be used for both surveillance and marketing purposes (2013, p. 4). The first purpose can support existing social norms regarding gender, while the second can do the same for socially embedded perceptions regarding cognitive differences between men and women. In one of a series of experiments conducted by Datta et al. (2015), the researchers found that those who identified themselves as female on Google's AdSettings page and then searched for job openings were shown more ads for lower-paying positions than were those who identified themselves as male. Outsourcing cognitive tasks to "smart" devices can also reinforce gender-specific social norms. The fact that everyday life activities of both women and men are becoming more and more dependent on algorithmically driven, "smart" technologies adds a special urgency to the project we are engaged with here.

The perspective we have developed in this chapter could be called a methodology of vigilance. It suggests designers need to be mindful to take a multiperspectival approach to their own work, an approach that focuses on the object to be designed, the sociotechnical context of its use, the designers' own identities as gendered users of technologies, and the overall process of design itself. Perhaps through expanding our conceptions of the processes, products, and actors involved in technology design we can, rather than simply removing responsibility from designers, recognize the distribution of entangled accountabilities that are spread across a variety of actors and time scales. In the end, we are all responsible for the world we choose to make, together.

NOTE

1. The "masculine positioning" of ICT is not limited to the development of technologies. It also leads to narrating a certain history in which the role women played in the development of ICT was marginalized. In the history of software, for example, it took some efforts to "reveal" Ada Lovelace who cooperated with the well-known Charles Babbage and highlight her achievements (Plant, 1997). Such a positioning of ICT has evolved into the "masculization" of the departments of computer sciences (Ensmenger, 2015), accompanied by a decline in the number of female students and female programmers—See NPR's podcast: "When Women Stopped Coding," October 17, 2014, http://www.npr.org/sections/money/2014/10/17/356944145/episode-576-when-women-stopped-coding. Interestingly, in the 1970s the number of women in these departments was not negligible, and so was not influenced by the history of engineering, which came to dominate only at later stages.

REFERENCES

Åsberg, C., & Lykke, N. (2010) Feminist Technoscience Studies. *European Journal of Women's Studies, 17*(4), 299–305. doi:10.1177/135050681037769.

Ashcraft, C., & Blithe, Sarah. (2010) *Women in IT: The Facts.* National Center for Women and Information Technology. http://www.ncwit.org/sites/default/files/legacy/pdf/NCWIT_TheFacts_rev2010.pdf.

Barad, K. (2003) Posthumanist Performativity: Toward an Understanding of How Matter Comes to Matter. *Signs, 28*(3), 801–31.

Barad, K. (2007) *Meeting the Universe Halfway: Quantum Physics and the Entanglement of Matter and Meaning.* Durham: Duke University Press.

Bardzell, S. (2010) Feminist HCI: Taking Stock and Outlining an Agenda for Design. *Proceedings of CHI 2010*, 1301–10.

Bath, C. (2009) Searching for Methodology: Feminist Technology Design in Computer Science. *GICT 2009 Proceedings.* http://www.informatik.uni-bremen.de/soteg/gict2009/proceedings/GICT2009_Bath-geloescht.pdf.

Bath, C. (2014) Searching for Methodology: Feminist Technology Design in Computer Science. In W. Ernst & I. Horwath (Eds.), *Gender Studies: Gender in Science and Technology: Interdisciplinary Approaches* (pp. 57–78). Wetzlar: Transcript Verlag. Retrieved from www.oapen.org/download?type=document&docid=46325.

Binder, T., Brandt, E., Ehn, P., & Halse, J. (2015) Democratic Design Experiments: Between Parliament and Laboratory. *CoDesign, 11*(3–4), 152–65. doi:10.1080/15710882.2015.108124.

Buckley, C. (1986) Made in Patriarchy: Toward a Feminist Analysis of Women and Design. *Design Issues, 3*(2), 3–14. doi:10.2307/151148.

Cockburn, C. (1997) Domestic Technologies: Cinderella and the Engineers. *Women's Studies International Forum, 20*(3), 361–71.

Cockburn, C., & Ormrod, Susan. (1993) *Gender and Technology in the Making.* Sage Publications Ltd.

Datta, A., Tschantz, Michael Carl, & Datta, Anupam. (2015) Automated Experiments on Ad Privacy Settings: A Tale of Opacity, Choice, and Discrimination. *Proceedings on Privacy Enhancing Technologies,* (1), 92–112.

Datarro, L. (2015) Bot Looks Like a Lady: Should Robots have Gender? *Slate.* February 4. http://www.slate.com/articles/technology/future_tense/2015/02/robot_gender_is_it_bad_for_human_women.html.

de Certeau, M. (1984) *The Practice of Everyday Life.* Berkeley and Los Angeles: University of California Press.

Deng, M. (2015) One Size Fits Few: Artificial Hearts Leave Many Out (Op-Ed). *LiveScience.* September 4. http://www.livescience.com/52093-artificial-hearts-too-large-for-many-to-receive.html.

Dilnot, C. (2014) Debate: No Future. *Companion to DRS 2014: Design's Big Debates.* June 17. Umeå: Umeå University.

Dimond, J. P., Dye, M., LaRose, D., & Bruckman, A. S. (2013) Hollaback!: The Role of Collective Storytelling Online in a Social Movement Organization. In *Proceedings of the 2013 Conference on Computer Supported Cooperative Work* (pp. 477–89). San Antonio, Texas, USA.

Duhaime-Ross, A. (2014) Apple Promised an Expansive Health App, So Why can't I Track Menstruation? *The Verge.* September 25. http://www.theverge.com/2014/9/25/6844021/apple-promised-an-expansive-health-app-so-why-cant-i-track.

Dunne, A., & Raby, F. (2013) *Speculative Everything: Design, Fiction, and Social Dreaming.* Cambridge, MA; London, England: The MIT Press.

Ehn, P., Nilsson, E. M., & Topgaard, R. (Eds.) (2014) *Making Futures: Marginal Notes on Innovation, Design, and Democracy.* Cambridge, MA; London, England: The MIT Press.

Ensmenger, N. (2015). "Beards, Sandals, and Other Signs of Rugged Individualism": Masculine Culture within the Computing Professions. *Osiris, 30*(1), 38–65.

Flanagan, M. (2009) *Critical Play: Radical Game Design.* Cambridge, MA: MIT Press.

Fortunati, L. (2009) Gender and the Mobile phone. In G. Goggin, & L. Hjorth, *Mobile Technologies: From Telecommunications to Media* (pp. 23–34). New York, London: Routledge.

Friedman, B. (1996) "Value-Sensitive Design." *Intersections.* November–December: 17–23.

Fry, T., Dilnot, C., & Stewart, S. C. (2015) *Design and the Question of History.* London: Bloomsbury.

Fullerton, T., Morie, J., & Pearce, C. (2007) A Game of One's Own: Towards a New Gendered Poetics of Digital Space. In *Proceedings DAC.* Perth.

Gellman, L., & Wells, Georgia. (2016) Progress is Hampered for Women in Tech Jobs. *Wall Street Journal*, 23 March: B1; B7.

Haraway, D. (1988) Situated Knowledges: The Science Question in Feminism and the Privilege of Partial Perspective. *Feminist Studies 14*(3), 575–99. doi:10.2307/3178066.

Heeter, C., Egidio, R., Mishra, P., Winn, B., & Winn, J. (2009) Alien Games: Do Girls Prefer Games Designed by Girls? *Games and Culture, 4*(1), 74–100.

Held, V. (1990) Feminist Transformations of Moral Theory. *Philosophy and Phenomenological Research, 50* (Autumn Supplement): 321–44.

Huff, C., & Cooper, J. (1987) Sex Bias in Educational Software: The Effect of Designers' Stereotypes on the Software they Design. *Journal of Applied Social Psychology,* 17: 519–32.

Ihde, D. (1990) *Technology and the Lifeworld.* Bloomington, IN: Indiana University Press.

Jaggar, A. (1983) Feminist Politics and Human Nature. Totowa, New Jersey: Rowman & Allanheld.

Johnson, Deborah G. (2010) Sorting Out the Question of Feminist Technology. In *Feminist Technology,* pp. 36–54. Lynda L. Layne, Sharra L. Vostral, and Kate Boyer, Eds. Urbana, IL: The University of Illinois Press.

Jones, J. C. (1992) *Design Methods* (second ed.). New York: Van Nostrand Reinhold. (Original work published 1970).

Kember, S. (2013) Gender Estimation in Face Recognition Technology: How Smart Algorithms Learn to Discriminate. *Media Fields Journal,* 7: 1–10.

Khader, S. J. (2011) *Adaptive Preferences and Women's Empowerment.* Oxford: Oxford University Press.

Krippendorff, K. (1989) On the Essential Contexts of Artifacts or on the Proposition that "Design is Making Sense (Of Things)". *Design Issues 5*(2), 9. doi:10.2307/151151.

Latour, B. (2005). From Realpolitik to Dingpolitik. In *Making Things Public: Atmospheres of Democracy* (pp. 14–43). Cambridge, Massachusetts / London, England: ZKM | Center for Art and Media Karlsruhe / The MIT Press.

Lemish, D., & Cohen, A. A. (2005). On the Gendered Nature of Mobile Phone Culture in Israel. *Sex Roles, 52*(7/8).

Lewis, T. (2014) "Apple's Health App Tracks Almost Everything, Except Periods." *Livescience.* September 26. http://www.livescience.com/48040-apple-healthkit-lacks-period-tracker.html.

Lindström, K., & Ståhl, Å. (2015) Figurations of Spatiality and Temporality in Participatory Design and After—Networks, Meshworks and Patchworking. *CoDesign: International Journal of CoCreation in Design and the Arts, 11*(3–4), 222–35. doi: 10.1080/15710882.2015.108124.

Ling, R. (2001). "We Release them Little by Little": Maturation and Gender Identity as Seen in the Use of Mobile Telephony. *Personal and Ubiquitous Computing, 5*(2), 123–36.

Löwgren, J., & Stolterman, E. (2004) *Thoughtful Interaction Design: A Design Perspective on Information Technology.* Cambridge, MA: The MIT Press.

Lupton, D. (2015) Quantified Sex: A Critical Analysis of Sexual and Reproductive Self-Tracking Using Apps. *Culture, Health & Sexuality, 17*(4), 440–53.

Michelfelder, D., & Jones, Sharon. (2016) From Caring About Sustainability to Developing Care-ful Engineers. *New Developments in Engineering Education for Sustainable Development.* Eds. Walter Leal Filho and Susan Nesbit. Dordrecht: Springer Press.

Nafus, D., & Sherman, Jamie. (2014) This One Does Not Go Up to 11: The Quantified Self Movement as an Alternative Big Data Practice. *International Journal of Communication* 8: 1784–94.

Nelson, H. G., & Stolterman, E. (2012) *The Design Way: Intentional Change in an Unpredictable World* (second ed.). Cambridge, MA; London, England: The MIT Press.

Oudshoorn, N., Rommes, Els, & Stienstra, Marcelle. (2004) Configuring the User as Everybody: Gender and Design Cultures in Information and Communication Technologies. *Science, Technology, & Human Values 29*(1), 30–63.

Oudshoorn, N., & Pinch, Trevor. *How Users Matter: The Co-Construction of Users and Technology (Inside Technology)*. Cambridge, MA: MIT Press, 2003.

Paoletti, Jo B. (2015) *Sex and Unisex: Fashion, Feminism, and the Sexual Revolution.* Bloomington, IN: Indiana University Press.

Plant, S. (1997) *Zeros + Ones: Digital Women + The New Technoculture.* New York: Doubleday.

Postma, C., Pelgrim, Elly Zwartkruis, Daemen, Elke, & Du, Jia. (2012) Challenges of Doing Empathic Design: Challenges from Industry. *International Journal of Design 6*(1), 59–70.

Rasmussen, M. K., & Petersen, M. G. (2011) Re-scripting Interactive Artefacts with Feminine Values. *Proceedings of the 2011 Conference on Designing Pleasurable Products and Interfaces*. Milano, Italy.

Redström, J. (2008) RE:Definitions of Use. *Design Studies, 29*(4), 410–23. doi:10.1016/j.destud.2008.05.001.

Redström, J. (2013) Form-Acts: A Critique of Conceptual Cores. In R. Mazé, L. Olausson, M. Plöjel, J. Redström, & C. Zetterlund (Eds.), *Share this Book: Critical Perspectives and Dialogues About Design and Sustainability* (pp. 17–28). Axl Books.

Rommes, E., Bath, C., & Maass, S. (2012) Methods for Intervention: Gender Analysis and Feminist Design of ICT. *Science, Technology, & Human Values, 37*(6), 653–62.

Rosser, Sue V. (2006) Using the Lenses of Feminist Theories to Focus on Women and Technology. In *Women, Gender, and Technology,* pp. 13–46. Mary Frank Fox, Deborah G. Johnson, and Sue V. Rosser, Eds. Urbana, IL: The University of Illinois Press.

Schiebinger, L., Klinge, I., Sánchez de Madariaga, I., Paik, H. Y., Schraudner, M., & Stefanick, M. (Eds.) (2011–2015) Pregnant Crash Test Dummies: Rethinking Standards and Reference Models. *Gendered Innovations in Science, Health & Medicine, Engineering and Environment.* www.genderedinnovations.stanford.edu.

Schroeder, C. (2010) Gender Dimensions of Product Design. *United Nations Division for the Advancement of Women. Science, Technology and Society Expert Group Meeting.* Paris, France: 28 September–1 October. http://www.un.org/womenwatch/daw/egm/gst_2010/Schroeder-EP.13-EGM-ST.pdf.

Schwartz, Cowan, R. (1976). The "Industrial Revolution" in the Home: Household Technology and Social Change in the 20th Century. *Technology and Culture*, 1–23.

Siegel, M., Breazeal, C., & Norton, M. I. (2009) Persuasive Robotics: The Influence of Robot Gender on Human Behavior. *The 2009 IEEE/RSJ International Conference on Intelligent Robots and Systems*, pp. 2563–68. http://dx.doi.org/10.1109/IROS.2009.5354116.

Sparke, P. (2010) The Architect's Wife, Introduction to as Long as it's Pink: The Sexual Politics of Taste. In G. Lees-Maffei & R. Houze (Eds.), *The Design History*

Reader (pp. 355–59). London and New York: Bloomsbury. (Original work published 1995).

Stolterman, E. (2008). The Nature of Design Practice and Implications for Interaction Design Research. *International Journal of Design, 2*(1), 55–65.

Suchman, L. (2002) Located Accountabilities in Technology Production. *Scandinavian Journal of Information Systems, 14*(2), 91–105.

Suchman, L. (2009) *Agencies in Technology Design: Feminist Reconfigurations.* Retrieved from https://www.researchgate.net/publication/27336947_Agencies_in_Technology_Design_Feminist_Reconfiguration.

Sundbom, C., Ehrnberger, K., Börjesson, E., & Hertz, A.-C. (2015) The Andro Chair: Designing the Unthinkable-Men's Right to Women's Experiences in Gynaecology. In *Proceedings of Nordes 2015: Design Ecologies.*

Team, J. (2015) "Jibo's Name: How did We Pick It?" *Jibo Blog.* June 25. http://blog.jibo.com/2015/06/25/jibos-name-how-did-we-pick-it/.

Tong, R., & Williams, Nancy. (2014) Feminist Ethics. *The Stanford Encyclopedia of Philosophy.* Ed. Edward N. Zalta. http://plato.stanford.edu/cgi-bin/encyclopedia/archinfo.cgi?entry=feminism-ethics.

Turkle, S. (1995) *Life on the Screen: Identity in the Age of the Internet.* New York: Touchstone.

van der Velden, M., & Mörtberg, C. (2011) Between Need and Desire: Exploring Strategies for Gendering Design. *Science, Technology & Human Values*, 1–21. doi:10.1177/016224391140163

Wajcman, J. (2009) Feminist Theories of Technology. *Cambridge Journal of Economics*, 1–10.

Weber, R. N. (1997) Manufacturing Gender in Commercial and Military Cockpit Design. *Science, Technology & Human Values, 22*(2), 235–53.

Yelavich, M., & Adams, B. B. (Eds.) (2014) *Design as Future-making.* London: Bloomsbury.

Chapter 14

Value-Sensitive Design and Responsible Research and Innovation

Judith Simon

Value-sensitive design (VSD) refers to a field of research addressing the inscription of values in technologies in general and information and communication technologies (ICT) in particular. In this chapter, VSD, a term originally proposed by (Friedman et al. 2006) is used as an umbrella term encompassing also similar approaches developed by other proponents, such as *values in design* (Knobel & Bowker 2011), *values at play* (Nissenbaum 2005; Flanagan et al. 2008), and *disclosive computer ethics* (Brey 2000, 2010).

VSD departs from the observation that in the process of designing technologies, societal values are often unintentionally inscribed into these technologies and that resulting technologies in return may promote or demote certain values, for example, justice, fairness, or privacy. The crucial idea behind VSD as a research approach and a methodology is then to turn this insight into a research question: If values are often unconsciously imparted in the process of designing and developing technologies, can we steer this inscription more reflexively, that is, can we intentionally embed desired values into technologies? In line with this goal of embedding desired values into technologies, proponents of VSD have developed concrete methodologies to guide the design and development of technological artifacts that promote the values desired by the various stakeholders who are or can be affected by these technologies.

VSD, therefore, (a) aims at steering technology design and development to attune to shared societal values and (b) promotes the early inclusion of various direct and indirect stakeholders into the process of technology design and development. As such VSD appears to be particularly suited to support and feed into initiatives promoting more "Responsible Research and Innovation" (RRI).

RRI as a term refers to both strategic efforts of national and international funding bodies, most notably the European Commission (EC)[1] to better align the process and the outcomes of research and innovation with the values, needs, and expectations of society, as well as to the academic discourse which has formed around these strategic initiatives (e.g., Grunwald 2011; Koops et al. 2015; Oftedal 2014; Owen et al. 2013a; von Schomberg 2013; Simon 2015; Stilgoe et al. 2013; Timmermans & Stahl 2013; or van den Hoven et al. 2014).

Linking RRI and VSD therefore, appears to be only a consequential result: VSD can support RRI by providing a concrete methodology to both assess societal values, needs, and expectations and to implement desired values into technologies. Moreover, RRI can benefit from the lessons learned in VSD as a research field, in particular with regards to the pitfalls of stakeholder inclusion and the performativity of value inscription. Accordingly, RRI as a strategy should learn from VSD as a research field and methodology (van den Hoven 2013; Simon 2016). In return, RRI can provide ample opportunity for VSD to be further applied, developed, and refined in highly diverse research settings stretching beyond ICT design.

1. VALUE-SENSITIVE DESIGN

VSD as an interdisciplinary field of research has its roots within the social science and humanities as well as within computer science. Within computer science, the fields of social informatics, computer supported cooperative work, and participatory design were of particularly high relevance for the emergence and shaping of VSD. Within philosophy, it has been in particular the discourse within computer ethics that has shaped and has been shaped by VSD. Computer ethics as a rather young philosophical discipline deals with the nature and the social consequences of computer technologies, the formulation and justification of ethical norms regarding their usage (Moor 1985), as well as with the professional responsibilities of computer scientists, software engineers, and programmers (Bynum & Rogerson 2004). In recent years, the focus of analysis has shifted from the *usage* of computer technologies toward their *design and development* (Johnson 2009; Brey 2010), opening up the possibility to analyze the role of values in the design and development phases of technologies.

The starting point for VSD as a research initiative is usually attributed to Batya Friedman's seminal book *Human Values and the Design of Computer Technology* (Friedman 1997). In this anthology Friedman, together with renowned scholars from computer science, philosophy, anthropology, and sociology opens up questions regarding the unintentional and intentional inscription of values into IT artifacts. Friedman's hypothesis is that social and moral values are inevitably imported into technologies during the design and development phases. Usually missing during these design and development phases, however, is a critical reflection upon this unconscious inscription of values: Which values and whose values are being inscribed into a technology and how does this happen? How are and how should decisions be made in case of value conflicts?

1.1. Values and Valuing

A central notion in VSD is of course that of values. What are those values that we aim to inscribe into technologies? Although the notion of values is frequently used in everyday life, what is meant by values is far from clear. Even within the academic discourse, definitions and conceptualizations of "value" differ profoundly between and even within disciplines. Mitcham, for instance, differentiates between economic, social scientific, and philosophical perspectives on values (Mitcham 2005). Within philosophy, debates concern the intension as well as the extension of values, the differences between shared values and personal values, between values as norms and values as feelings, etc. (Mitcham 2005).

Regarding VSD in particular, Friedman and her colleagues, define values quite broadly as something that "a person or group of people consider important in life" (Friedman et al. 2006: 349). Thus, the notion of "values" in VSD normally refers not to economic valuation, but to societal values, that is, values as socially shared judgments about what and who is how important. In many articles on values and technologies, authors shy away from addressing the general notion of "value" at all, and instead, focus only on specific values that they consider relevant for the technologies they are analyzing or designing, such as privacy, justice, sustainability, trust, and so on.

Understanding societal values as *shared* judgments does in no way imply that values are *universally shared*—quite the contrary. If values are judgments about what is important in life, it is clear that such judgments might and often do differ between different persons and groups. And then the question arises of *whose values* are considered relevant and whose values are ignored or even antagonized. Values are always someone's values, the shared judgments of some group as opposed to another. Accordingly, when values are inscribed into technologies—irrespective of good or bad intentions—it is always a process of imposing one's view on others. As such, technology design is embedded into a context of existing power relations and potential power disparities, while at the same time it may provide the means to either consolidate or challenge existing networks and relations of power.

Moreover, by being solidified in artifacts, value judgments, possible biases, and power relations are often rendered invisible. It is in particular this combination of invisibility and enduring impact, which makes a proper analysis of values in technologies all the more relevant.

Finally, it must be noted that the relationship between values and technologies must be understood as dynamic and performative. By stating that "values and valuing are as much a challenge to science as science is to values," Mitcham (2005) stresses the bidirectional relationship between values and science. Adopting the same view on technology implies that technology design is not only influenced by societal values, but also can influence and change societal values in return. The direction of the relationship is at the heart of the debates around the question of technological determinism versus social constructivism (Kline 2001).

1.2. Morality or Neutrality?

According to Philip Brey (2000, 2010) one of the central tasks of VSD consists in rebutting the widespread belief that technologies are neutral. Defendants of the neutrality thesis claim that technologies, such as a hammer or nuclear fission are in themselves neutral and thus cannot be assessed ethically. Only their usage—to beat a nail into the wall or slay someone, to generate electricity or build a bomb—is morally loaded and scrutable to ethical analysis.

While this neutrality thesis has some plausibility with regard to the hammer, which appears equally suited as a tool and a weapon, the neutrality already becomes less convincing in the case of nuclear energy, since it can be argued that nuclear technology in itself already encompasses options for action and consequences that are morally charged (Jonas 1979; Mumford 1964).

Within VSD, artifacts and technologies are understood as inherently morally loaded, in so far as they promote or demote specific values. This does not imply that technologies are moral agents or have moral responsibility, but rather that already the design and not only the usage of technologies can have moral consequences. Thus, not only usage, but also technology design must be assessed from an ethical perspective.

Brey (2010) defines embedded values as a specific form of embedded consequences of technologies, since values are not merely inscribed, they often lead to new sociotechnical realities. Distinguishing central and peripheral uses of technology, he defines embedded consequences as those which normally manifest in central forms of technology use, that is, in all those situations in which the user does not actively prevent such consequences. With this definition, Brey seeks to avoid technological determinism and to acknowledge that there are degrees of freedom in the usage of technologies. Thus, technologies are not neutral and do promote and demote specific values. As such, they have indeed a potentially lasting impact on sociotechnical realities. Nevertheless, users are not entirely determined in their usage of artifacts and have some flexibility to subvert design intentions in their usage. Clearly, the amount of freedom and flexibility differs profoundly between different technologies. The possibility for subversion may be lower the more autonomous artifacts are, the more deeply they are embedded in critical infrastructures, and the more obligatory their usage is. Accordingly, such types of technologies require all the more attentiveness to the values embedded in them.

The neutrality thesis has of course received earlier criticism both within philosophy of technology and Science and Technology Studies (STS). Landon Winner's "The politics of artefacts" is probably one of the most seminal articles in this context. Drawing on a wide range of case studies, ranging from the mechanical tomato harvester and cotton spinning mills over automobile assembly teams and Baron Haussmann's restructuring of Paris to the most famous example of the design of parkway bridges in New York, Winner (1980: 121) argues that technologies are by no means neutral, but have political properties by embodying "specific forms of power and authority" (Winner 1980: 121).

Winner's empirical starting point for his analyses on the politics of artifacts has been the observation that the parkway bridges in New York are "extraordinarily low" (Winner 1980: 123). The person in charge of building those bridges was Robert Moses, "legendary political entrepreneur, who has shaped the physical form of New York in this century and beyond as no other person" (Joerges 1999: 412). Departing from this seemingly innocent empirical observation about the height of the parkway bridges, Winner argues that Moses *intentionally* had those bridges built that low to "discourage the presence of buses on his parkways." By this trick, he was able to "limit access of racial minorities and low-income groups to Jones Beach, Moses's widely acclaimed public park" (Winner 1980: 124). Winner argues that due to his social and political power as a city planner, Moses was able to intentionally inscribe his values and prejudices into technology, in order to achieve certain societal effects.

Almost twenty years later, this seemingly straightforward story was refuted by Bernward Joerges, who claimed that Winner's story about the parkway bridges, while being a "highly successful parable" (Joerges 1999: 416), is unfortunately counterfactual. Based on correspondences with U.S. civil engineers, Joerges asserts that commercial traffic was forbidden on the parkways in general, and that since the transport situation on Long Island was already good, there was no reason to waste the money on building higher bridges. Hence, Joerges concludes that *"Moses could hardly have let buses on his parkways, even if he had wanted differently"* (Joerges 1999: 419, italics in original).

Despite his thorough critique of Winner's story as a rhetorical device, Joerges concludes that Winner's story serves a purpose "to resituate positions in the old debate about the control of social processes via buildings and other technical artifacts—or more generally, about material form and social content" (Joerges 1999: 411). What was so seductive about Winner's case is that he delivered a simple and strong case for the *inscription of societal values into technology and the societal effects of such biased technologies*. This insistence on the political character of artifacts and the possibility of social engineering through technology hit the zeitgeist of critical science and technology scholars. Winner initiated a discussion about the politics of artifacts by refuting the assumption that technologies are neutral or that they follow some innertechnological rationality. Instead he stressed the societal environment with all its values, prejudices, and assumptions that get inscribed into these artifacts. In Moses's case—and that makes this specific example even more seductive—there seemed to have been this powerful man who *intentionally* inscribed his views into technology, who quite literally carved his racial prejudices and societal inequalities into stone, made them durable and solidified them in artifacts, and ensured their enduring societal impact.

The inscription of values into technologies is also a crucial topic for other researchers within STS in general and Actor–network theory (ANT) in particular. Drawing on his analyses of the nonhuman agency of automated door closers and the beeping reminders to put on seat belts in cars, Latour (1992: 157), for instance, argues that by now "we have been able to delegate to non-humans not only force . . . but also values, duties, and ethics. It is because of this morality that we humans behave so ethically, no matter how weak and wicked we feel we are."

According to Latour, this sociotechnical distribution of both competences and morality, a morality shared between human and nonhuman agents, is the reason why we as humans behave ethically. Thus, our human morality resides in part on the morality of machines, artifacts, and artificial agents. The question of whether artifacts can exhibit agency, what exactly artificial agency amounts to, and what the implications of such artificial agency could be for morality, accountability, and responsibility is still hotly debated within STS (e.g., Barad 2007; Suchman 2007) as well as within philosophy of technology and computing (e.g., Floridi 2013; Simon 2015). Moreover, in regard to (partially) autonomous systems, such as drones, self-learning algorithms, or self-driving cars, these issues are not only conceptually interesting, but also of increasing legal and political relevance.

Also situated within ANT, Madeleine Akrich (1992) argues that the creation of technological objects must be understood as an interplay between the technical and the social, between inside and outside of the technological artifact and that we shall avoid falling victim to either technological or social determinism. Already, in 1992, she investigated what happens when artifacts start to travel, that is, when artifacts are used in contexts different from the ones intended or even imagined. Analyzing the use of photoelectric lighting kits in specific African regions, she shows how reciprocal adaptions occur between a technological artifact and its new environment and thus delivers an early case of what Nissenbaum and Friedman (1997) have labeled "emergent bias," that is, biases which may occur if technologies are used in a context very different from their context of development.

Even if her case studies emphasize the degrees of freedom users have to appropriate, modify, or even subvert artifacts, Akrich nonetheless concludes that design decisions remain important, because they set the limits and affordances to the usage of the technical objects. In Akrich's own words: "Although users add their own interpretations, so long as the circumstances in which the device is used do not diverge too radically from those predicted by the designers, it is likely that the script will become a major element for interpreting interaction between the object and its users" (Akrich 1992: 216).

In conclusion, we should acknowledge the political character of technological artifacts. Decisions made in technological design and development set affordances and limits and thus have consequences that go beyond the look-and-feel of technological artifacts. Even if artifacts can be used in ways other than those intended by their designers, even if defaults can be changed or subverted, the construction delivers keys for interpretation, which have to be actively circumvented to be undone. Further, we have seen that the intentionality of the designer is not a necessary prerequisite for the politics of technologies. Indeed, intentionality may even be the exception, and most inscriptions of values and stereotypes may occur rather implicitly. Finally, the term "inscription" should be used with caution, since it may overrate both human intentionality and the effectiveness of social engineering through technology, thus ignoring the complexities and performativity of sociotechnical relations.

1.3. Value-Sensitive Design as a Methodology

The goal of VSD is twofold: on the one hand, it aims at supporting *critical analyses of existing technologies* regarding the values and disvalues that have been—intentionally or unintentionally—embedded into them. As such, VSD may be used to (a) assess whether or not desired values, for example, privacy or fairness, have indeed been achieved through technology design;

and (b) identify disvalues, for example, by showcasing biases in technologies (Nissenbaum & Friedman 1997) that may discriminate against certain user groups or other direct or indirect stakeholders affected by a specific technology. Thus, a crucial task of VSD is to serve as an *analytical tool* to open up valuation processes within technology design and development that are usually blackboxed or neglected.

On the other hand, VSD offers a concrete *methodology for how to intentionally inscribe desired values into the design of new hardware, software, data bases, algorithms, and so on.* This methodology of VSD consists in an iterative integration of three steps: conceptual-philosophical,[2] empirical, and technical investigations (Friedman et al. 2006; Flanagan et al. 2008). The *conceptual-philosophical investigations* encompass not only the identification of relevant values, but also the identification of relevant direct and indirect stakeholders. By including indirect stakeholders into the arena of analysis, VSD aims at countering the frequent neglect of nonusers in technology design, that is, of groups which may not use a technology themselves, but who are nonetheless affected by it (Wyatt 2005; Oudshoorn and Pinch 2005b). Relevant questions at this stage are (a) the characteristics of the different stakeholders; (b) the ways in which they are affected by the use of technologies; (c) the relative importance of different values; and (d) the trade-offs between conflicting values.

The *empirical investigations* make use of a diversity of quantitative and qualitative research methods from the social sciences to analyze how people actually conceive and prioritize different values, which role these play in the actual actions, and so on. It is at this stage, that a *performative understanding of sociotechnical systems* is taken seriously, because in such an iterative, empirical methodology, usage and appropriation of technological artifacts can be observed and it can further be analyzed whether the values intended in the design process are fulfilled, amended, or subverted.

The *technical investigations* as described by Friedman et al. (2006) consist of two parts. The first focuses on the role values play in existing technologies and is in principle similar to previous analytic approaches, only with a decided focus on the technology itself. The second concerns the proactive design of systems to support values identified in the conceptual and empirical phases of investigation.

In the case of digital technologies, inscribing values normally means inscribing them into software code. However, it is essential to distinguish different ways of inscribing such values into a code. To use the example of value-sensitive game design (cf. Flanagan et al. 2008), it becomes evident that values, such as cooperation, gender equity, or diversity can be expressed at various instances and stages of software development. Different values can be inscribed into the content of a game, for example, the character representation, the game plot, and so on, or into the game structure, for example, through incentives and the reward mechanisms. According to Flanagan et al. (2008), in the former case, the values are expressed, while in the latter they are materially embodied. Moreover, value judgments may also play a role in decisions on the very background system of the game, for example, with regard to data storage and data protection impacting for instance on the value of privacy. While these background decisions may have no relation to the game design per se and may be mostly hidden from the users' perception and easily overlooked in ethical analyses, they are nonetheless an important arena in which value judgments are essential, as numerous cases of data breaches have recently shown.

Since 1997, VSD has established itself as a vibrant and growing field of research, especially in the United States, where many of the early proponents of VSD are situated, but also in Europe. Throughout the years, VSD has been applied to the analysis and design of numerous and highly diverse technologies, ranging from early works on search engines (Introna & Nissenbaum 2000a, 2000b) cookies, plasma screens, and simulation tools for urban planning (Friedman et al. 2006), over game design (Flanagan et al. 2007, 2008) and robotics in care settings (Wynsberghe 2012) or e-democracy initiatives (Simon 2012), to recent projects on health data and personal genomics.[3]

Moreover, many proponents of VSD are also involved in science policy, for example, by participating in the Values in Design Council, a multidisciplinary team that works alongside the National Science Foundation's Future Internet Architecture Initiative (FIA) in the United States, or by promoting RRI on the level of the European Commission and the research and innovation funding of its member states.

2. RESPONSIBLE RESEARCH AND INNOVATION

2.1. RRI as a Political Goal and Concept

While responsibility in research, development and innovation has been both requested and promoted for some time, in particular with regard to developments in nanotechnology (cf. Timmermans and Stahl 2013), the discourse around the specific notion of RRI has only emerged in the last few years. Within Europe, the emergence of this discourse is closely tied to the adoption of research funding initiatives promoting RRI both at national and EU levels. The European Commission in particular has proposed RRI as a strategy to shape research and innovation practices within the EU Framework Programme Horizon 2020.[4]

According to the European Commission,[5] RRI "is an approach that antici-pates and assesses potential implications and societal expectations with regard to research and innovation, with the aim to foster the design of inclusive and sustainable research and innovation." More specifically, "Responsible Research and Innovation (RRI) implies that societal actors (researchers, citi-zens, policy makers, business, third sector organizations, etc.) work together during the whole research and innovation process in order to better align both the process and its outcomes with the values, needs and expectations of society." Within Horizon 2020, RRI is practically implemented by a focus on the following issues: (a) public engagement, (b) open access, (c) gender, (d) ethics, and (e) science education.[6]

2.2. RRI as an Interdisciplinary Field of Academic Discourse

Besides these research policy aims, and partly as a result of them, a vibrant and expanding field of research has emerged, which aims at bringing the concept of RRI to life. In addition to proponents from within the European Commission (e.g., von Schomberg 2013), it has been in particular research-ers from the fields of technology assessment (TA) (e.g., Grunwald 2011, 2014), philosophy (e.g., Koops et al. 2015; Oftedal 2014; Simon 2015; van den Hoven 2013, 2014), and STS (e.g., Owen et al. 2013b; Stilgoe et al. 2013), who have contributed to the notion of RRI by (a) elaborating on and specifying central concepts, (b) providing case studies, and (c) drawing on lessons learned in their disciplinary histories to avoid potential pitfalls of RRI, for example, regarding the dangers of ignoring power disparities in participatory processes. The research work on RRI as well as the number of actors involved have steeply increased in recent years, with the *Journal of Responsible Innovation* being one of the major publishing venues. In the following, some of the most influential accounts of RRI will be briefly presented.[7]

As noted above, one of the strongest proponents of RRI has been the European Commission, which is currently fostering RRI through numerous research projects and initiatives in Horizon 2020. The Commission's position on RRI as introduced above has certainly been shaped by various researchers, particularly those participating in RRI expert groups (e.g., Jakobs et al. 2013). One of the earliest and most influential proponents of RRI from within the European Commission has been René von Schomberg, although he stresses that his views on RRI represent his personal opinion and not the official EC position on RRI. In a widely cited article, Schomberg embeds RRI into the context of the so-called grand challenges[8] our contemporary societies are facing and argues that "RRI should be understood as a strategy of stakehold-ers to become mutually responsive to each other and anticipate research and innovation outcomes underpinning the 'grand challenges' of our time for which they share responsibility" (Schomberg 2013: 51).

He argues that while there are formal procedures to assess the risks of technologies, there is no equivalent assessment of the benefits of technologies nor even a normative baseline for such an assessment. Yet, should not the benefits of technologies also be taken into account when deciding about public funding priorities, especially in times of shrinking budgets? Schomberg claims that the EU human rights charter can provide normative anchor points for such positive impact assessment. Based upon these considerations, Schomberg (2013: 9) defines RRI as a "transparent, interactive process by which societal actors and innovators become mutually responsive to each other with a view to the (ethical) acceptability, sustainability and societal desirability of the innovation process and its marketable products (in order to allow a proper embedding of scientific and technological advances in our society)."

Schomberg importantly acknowledges that innovation and technology development are normally the result of collective action. Accordingly, any ethical approach toward responsibility must take this collective and distributed agency into account. He writes: "Modern 'Frankensteins' are not intentionally created by a single actor, but (if they arise), are more likely to result from the unforeseen side effects of *collective action*. . . . An ethics focused on the intentions and/or consequence of actions of individuals is not appropriate for innovation. There is a collective responsibility both for the right impacts and negative consequences, whether these impacts are intentional or not" (Schomberg 2013: 59f).

Already in 2009, that is, five years before the adoption of RRI in Horizon 2020, the Dutch Research Council started funding projects on Responsible Innovation, resulting in an impressive amount of Dutch research and case studies on RRI (cf. van den Hoven et al. 2014; Koops et al. 2015). Van den Hoven (2013, 2014) presents the Dutch context of RRI and shows how research funding initiatives promoting RRI are embedded into a strong tradition of critical technology design rooted in STS, participatory TA, and applied ethics of technology within Dutch academia.

Showcasing what he calls "two Dutch failures in innovation" (van den Hoven 2014: 8), the introduction of smart meters and a new electronic patient record system, van den Hoven argues that early consideration of values in the design process may not only lead to morally better outcomes, but also to economically better outcomes. Both initiatives have been rejected by the Dutch parliament due to concerns regarding privacy, security, and data protection. Van den Hoven argues that if privacy and security as crucial values had been taken into account from the onset of the technology development, these failures could have been prevented, not only leading to better products but also to the acceptance of the innovations and more overall satisfaction among the stakeholders involved. Crucially, acceptance in itself should not be the main goal of RRI. RRI in general and the application of VSD in particular are meant to improve the quality of products and their consideration of societal values, so that this acceptance is also more justified and normatively appropriate.

Armin Grunwald, as a professor in technology ethics and head of the largest German research institute for technology assessment (TA), embeds RRI into the context of TA, arguing that TA with its extensive experience in assessment, foresight, and evaluation procedures, as well as in actor involvement, is one of the main roots of responsible (research and) innovation (Grunwald 2014). Delineating a short history of TA, he distinguishes four partially overlapping branches of TA that aim at adding reflexivity to technology governance, namely: (1) TA as policy advice (e.g., parliamentary TA); (2) TA as medium for participation (e.g., participatory TA); (3) TA as a means of shaping technology (e.g., constructive TA); and (4) TA in innovation processes. According to Grunwald, responsible innovation draws upon this body of experience from TA, but extends its scope of considerations to ethical issues in general and reflections about responsibility attribution in particular.

Distinguishing the sociopolitical, moral, and epistemic dimensions of responsibility, Grunwald argues that issues of responsibility in science and technology should best be described as a four-place relation: *someone* assumes responsibility for *something* relative to a *body of rules* and relative to the *quality of available knowledge* (Grunwald 2014: 23). Grunwald diagnoses an epistemological blindness in many debates around responsibility in science and technology and thus argues that the epistemic dimension of responsibility, that is, the availability and quality of knowledge for decision making, must be accounted for more carefully. Grunwald's contribution to RRI is one of the few examples which opens up the concept of responsibility for some philosophical inspection. Delineating the historical emergence of debates around responsibility in relation to scientific and technological progress, Grunwald endorses an understanding of responsibility that is tied to individual or collective human actors (e.g., the engineers) as decision makers in science and technology (governance). Given contemporary developments in technology (e.g., regarding artificial agents), it can, however, be argued that we need to develop novel accounts of responsibility that can also capture sociotechnically distributed agency in highly complex and dynamic environments and the implications of such hybrid agency for the attribution of accountability and responsibility (cf. Simon 2015; Floridi 2013).

Another influential and early account on RRI has been provided by Richard Owen et al. (2013b). According to these authors, RRI is "a collective commitment of care for the future through responsive stewardship of science and innovation in the present" (Owen et al. 2013b: 36). In developing their framework for RRI, they stress the future-oriented, that is, the prospective and anticipatory aims of RRI, and argue that not only the products of innovation, but the very purpose of innovation must also be subjected to critical reflection.

Outlining the shortcomings of traditional forms of regulation via market forces or legal regulation alone, they propose the notions of care and responsiveness as their philosophical cornerstones, portraying them as two dimensions of prospective responsibility, which may be well suited for the governance of complex and dynamic innovations. Legal regulation in particular, as an evidence-based form of intervention requiring both existing knowledge and norms, is often "poorly equipped to govern areas of novel science and technology which are highly uncertain in terms of their current and future impacts, or which, by virtue of their novelty, have no historical precedent" (Owen et al. 2013b: 32).

In contrast, *responsiveness* stresses the need to be both adaptive, that is, responsive to changes, and deliberative, that is, responsive to various views and framings by different stakeholders, while *care* emphasizes the orientation toward our collective goals for the future, that is, what we collectively want and do not want science and innovation to bring about.

As a result of their investigations, the authors propose four dimensions of RRI, namely, that the responsible process of innovating entails a collective and continuous commitment to be (a) *anticipatory,* that is, to use appropriate methodologies to reflect upon the impact of innovations; (b) *reflective*, that is, to reflect upon the purposes, motivations and impacts of research and innovation; (c) *deliberative*, that is, to engage with and listen to a wide variety of stakeholders; and (d) *responsive*, that is, to influence the trajectory and pace of innovation through participatory and anticipatory governance.

Finally, Bernd Carsten Stahl and his colleagues have specifically focused on RRI in the field of ICT research and innovation (Stahl et al. 2013). Stressing the relational nature of responsibility as a form of social ascription, they argue that RRI should be understood as a meta-responsibility, that is, as a responsibility for responsibilities. According to them, "RRI can define socially desirable consequences that existing responsibilities can work toward and develop responsibility relationships that ensure that the achievement of such desired aims is possible" (Stahl et al. 2013: 202).

3. CONCLUSIONS

VSD and RRI clearly are well aligned in their goals and should thus learn and benefit from each other. On the one hand, VSD offers a well-tested methodology stressing stakeholder involvement and an acknowledgment of societal values that can be employed to support responsibility in technology design. On the other hand, RRI can, as a research strategy, offer new opportunities for projects to apply and further develop VSD, for example, by expanding the field of application beyond ICT design or by refining central concepts or methodologies.

Within the academic discourse around RRI, methods as well as central concepts (e.g., responsibility, reflexivity or participation) are continuously being refined. It remains to be seen, however, whether these nuances can be kept up in the broader application field of RRI. What needs to be avoided is that RRI turns into yet another check-box, which research applicants need to fill out in order to be eligible for funding. Thus, we need an understanding of RRI that is theoretically sound, while at the same time being practically useful and inspiring for implementation in different contexts for research and innovation.

To conclude, if applied well, both approaches, VSD and RRI, can enrich each other and support research as well as technology design and development in becoming more responsible and value-sensitive. However, for these goals to be achieved, we need to ensure first of all a deep integration of humanities, social sciences, and the techno-scientific disciplines throughout the whole course of research and innovation. Moreover, ethical analyses and a deep concern for societal values should be at the very core of research and innovation projects and not merely an add-on. Finally, in promoting different forms of public engagement in research and innovation, we must be highly attentive to power disparities and vulnerabilities of the different stakeholders involved. Otherwise we may run the risk that RRI in general and stakeholder involvement in particular, can be misunderstood as a tool to fabricate acceptance and misused to flatten public debate and controversy about research and innovation.

NOTES

1. Please refer to: https://ec.europa.eu/programmes/horizon2020/en/h2020-section/responsible-research-innovation (last access: August 7, 2016).

2. Friedman et al. (2006) label this phase "conceptual investigations," while Flanagan et al. (2008) label it "philosophical mode." Since the two methodologies are highly similar, I do not further distinguish between them and use the notion philosophical-conceptual investigations.

3. Projects of the Values in Design Lab at UC Irvine: http://evoke.ics.uci.edu/#gallery.

4. It should be noted, however, that programs with different titles (e.g., *Responsible Innovation*), but similar aims have already been part of earlier framework programs and that several projects on RRI have received funding under FP 7.

5. Please confer: https://ec.europa.eu/programmes/horizon2020/en/h2020-section/responsible-research-innovation (last access: August 7, 2016).

6. For an overview of currently funded projects focusing on RRI as well as further resources on RRI, please confer the *Responsible Research and Innovation in ICT Platform*: http://www.rri-ict-forum.eu/view/Main_Page. This platform has been developed within the RRI-ICT Forum project, which "aims at analysing, supporting and promoting the contribution of Social Sciences and Humanities (SSH) to, and the Responsible Research and Innovation (RRI) approach in ICT research and innovation under H2020." http://rri-ict.eu/about-rri-ict/ (last access: August 7, 2016).

7. Please note that some authors refer to "Responsible Innovation " only instead of "Responsible Research and Innovation" in some of the publications cited below. For the purpose of this article, no distinction between the terms is used and the abbreviation RRI will be used consistently.

8. According to the Lund declaration, these challenges are "global warming, tightening supplies of energy, water and food, ageing societies, public health, pandemics, and security" (Lund Declaration 2009: 1).

REFERENCES

Akrich, M. (1992). The De-scription of Technical Objects. *Shaping Technology/ Building Society: Studies in Sociotechnical Change*. Eds. W. E. Bijker and J. Law. Cambridge, MIT Press: 205–24.

Barad, K. (2007). *Meeting the Universe Halfway: Quantum Physics and the Entanglement of Matter and Meaning*. Durham, Duke University Press.

Brey, P. (2000). Disclosive Computer Ethics. *Computers & Society*: 10–16.

Brey, P. (2010). Values in Technology and Disclosive Computer Ethics. *The Cambridge Handbook of Information and Computer Ethics*. Ed. L. Floridi. Cambridge, Cambridge University Press: 41–58.

Bynum, T. W. and S. Rogerson, Eds. (2004). *Computer Ethics and Professional Responsibility*. Malden, Blackwell Publishing.

Flanagan, M., D. Howe, and H. Nissenbaum (2007). Design Method Outline for Activist Gaming. *Worlds in Play*. Eds. S. d. Castell and J. Jenson. New York, Peter Lang Publishers: 241–48.

Flanagan, M., D. C. Howe, and H. Nissenbaum (2008). Embodying Values in Technology: Theory and Practice. *Information Technology and Moral Philosophy*. Eds. J. v. d. Hoven and J. Weckert. Cambridge University Press: 322–53.

Floridi, L. (2013). Distributed Morality in an Information Society. *Science and Engineering Ethics* 19(3): 727–43.

Friedman, B., ed. (1997a). Human Values and the Design of Computer Technology. Cambridge: Cambridge University Press.

Friedman, B., and H. Nissenbaum (1997). Bias in Computer Systems. *Human Values and the Design of Computer Technology*. Ed. B. Friedman. Cambridge: Cambridge University Press: 21–40.

Friedman, B., P. H. Kahn, and A. Borning (2006). Value Sensitive Design and Information Systems. *Human-Computer Interaction in Management Information Systems: Foundations*. Eds. P. Zhang and D. Galletta. New York, M.E. Sharpe: 348–72.

Grunwald, A. (2011). Responsible Innovation: Bringing together Technology Assessment, Applied Ethics, and STS Research. *Enterprise and Work Innovation Studies* 7: 9–31.

Grunwald, A. (2014). Technology Assessment for Responsible Innovation. *Responsible Innovation 1: Innovative Solutions for Global Issues*. Eds. J. Van den Hoven, N. Doorn, T. Swierstra, B.-J. Koops, and H. Romijn. Heidelberg, Springer: 15–31.

Introna, L., and H. Nissenbaum (2000). The Public Good Vision of the Internet and the Politics of Search Engines. *Preferred Placement—Knowledge Politics on the Web*. Ed. R. Rogers. Maastricht, Jan van Eyck Akademy: 25–47.

Introna, L., and H. Nissenbaum (2000). Shaping the Web: Why the Politics of Search Engines Matters. *The Information Society* 16: 169–85.

Jacob, K., M. J. van den Hoven, L. Nielsen, F. O. Roure, L. Rudze, J. Stilgoe, K. Blind, A.-L. Guske, and C. Martinez Riera (2013). *Options for Strengthening Responsibile Research and Innovation: Report of the Expert Group on the State of Art in Europe on Responsible Research and Innovation*. Luxembourg, European Commission: 78.

Joerges, B. (1999). Do Politics Have Artefacts? *Social Studies of Science* 29(3): 411–31.

Johnson, D. G. (2009). *Computer Ethics: Academy and the Internet*. Upper Saddle River, NJ: Pearson.

Jonas, H. (1979). Das Prinzip Verantwortung: Versuch einer Ethik für die technologische Zivilisation. Frankfurt a.M.

Kline, R. R. (2001). Technological Determinism. *International Encyclopedia of the Social and Behavioral Sciences*. Eds. N. J. Smelser and B. Baltes: 15495–98.

Knobel, C., and G. C. Bowker (2011). Computing Ethics—Values in Design. *Communications of the ACM* 54(7): 26–28.

Koops, B.-J., I. Oosterlaken, H. Romijn, T. Swierstra, and J. van den Hoven, Eds. (2015). *Responsible Innovation 2: Concepts, Approaches, and Applications*. Heidelberg, Springer.

Latour, B. (1992). Where are the Missing Masses? The Sociology of a Few Mundane Artifacts. *Shaping Technology/Building Society: Studies in Sociotechnical Change*. Eds. W. E. Bijker and J. Law. Cambridge, MIT Press: 225–58.

Mitcham, C. (2005). Values and Valuing. *Encyclopedia of Science, Technology, and Ethics*. Ed. C. Mitcham. Detroit, MI, Macmillan Reference. 4.

Moor, J. H. (1985). What is Computer Ethics? *Metaphilosophy* 16(4): 266–79.

Mumford, L. (1964). Authoritarian and Democratic Technics. *Technology and Culture* 5(1): 1–8.

Nissenbaum, H. (2005). Values in Technical Design. *Encyclopedia of Science, Technology and Ethics*. Ed. C. Mitcham. New York, Macmillan: lxvi–lxx.

Oftedal, G. (2014). The Role of Philosophy of Science in Responsible Research and Innovation (Rri): The Case of Nanomedicine. *Life Sciences, Society and Policy* 10(5).

Oudshoorn, N., and T. Pinch (2005b). How Users and Non-users Matter. *How Users Matter: The Co-Construction of Users and Technology*. Eds. N. Oudshoorn and T. Pinch. Cambridge, MIT Press: 1–28.

Owen, R., J. Bessant, and M. Heintz, eds. (2013). *Responsible Innovation: Managing the Responsible Emergence of Science and Innovation in Society*. London, Wiley.

Owen, R., J. Stilgoe, P. Macnaghten, M. Gorman, E. Fisher, and D. Guston (2013). A Framework for Responsible Innovation. *Responsible Innovation: Managing the Responsible Emergence of Science and Innovation in Society*. Eds. R. Owen, J. Bessant and M. Heintz. London, Wiley: 27–50.

Simon, J. (2012). *E-Democracy and Values in Design*. Proceedings of the XXV World Congress of IVR—Law, Science and Technology, Frankfurt.

Simon, J. (2015). Distributed Epistemic Responsibility in a Hyperconnected Era. *The Onlife Manifesto: Being Human in a Hyperconnected Era*. Ed. L. Floridi, Springer: 145–59.

Simon, J. (2016). Values in Design. *Handbuch Medien—und Informationsethik*. Ed. J. Heesen. Stuttgart, Metzler.

Suchman, L. A. (2007/2009). *Human-Machine Reconfigurations: Plans and Situated Actions*. Cambridge: Cambridge University Press.

Stilgoe, J., R. Owen, and P. Macnaghten (2013). Developing a Framework for Responsible Innovation. *Research Policy* 42: 1568–80.

Stahl, B. C., G. Eden, and M. Jirotka (2013). Responsible Research and Innovation in Information and Communication Technology: Identifying and Engaging with the Ethical Implications of ICTs. *Responsible Innovation: Managing the Responsible Emergence of Science and Innovation in Society*. Eds. R. Owen, J. Bessant, and M. Heintz. London, Wiley: 199–218.

Timmermans, J., and B. Stahl (2013). *Annual Report on the main trends of SiS, in particular the trends related to RRI*. http://www.great-project.eu/deliverables_files/deliverables05, Governance of Responsible Innovation GREAT – 321480.

van den Hoven, J. (2013). Value Sensitive Design and Responsible Innovation. *Responsible Innovation: Managing the Responsible Emergence of Science and Innovation in Society*. Eds. R. Owen, J. Bessant and M. Heintz. London, Wiley.

Van den Hoven, J., N. Doorn, T. Swierstra, B.-J. Koops, and H. Romijn, eds. (2014). *Responsible Innovation 1: Innovative Solutions for Global Issues*. Heidelberg, Springer.

Van den Hoven, J. (2014). Responsible Innovation: A New Look on Technology and Ethics. *Responsible Innovation 1: Innovative Solutions for Global Issues*. eds. J. Van den Hoven, N. Doorn, T. Swierstra, B.-J. Koops, and H. Romijn. Heidelberg, Springer.

Von Schomberg, R. (2013). A Vision of Responsible Innovation. *Responsible Innovation: Managing the Responsible Emergence of Science and Innovation in Society*. Eds. R. Owen, J. Bessant, and M. Heintz. London, Wiley.

Wyatt, S. (2005). Non-Users Also Matter: The Construction of Users and Non-Users of the Internet. *How Users Matter: The Co-Construction of Users and Technology*. Eds. N. Oudshoorn and T. Pinch. Cambridge/MA, MIT Press: 67–80.

Winner, L. (1980). Do Artifacts Have Politics? *Daedalus* 109(1): 121–36.

Wynsberghe, A. (2012). *Designing Robots with Care: Creating an Ethical Framework for the Future Design and Implementation of Care Robots*. PhD dissertation, Twente University.

Part IV

ETHICAL REFLECTIONS

Chapter 15

The Ethics of Doing Ethics of Technology

Sven Ove Hansson

As ethicists we analyze the ethical aspects of what other researchers do, but we seldom devote much effort to the ethics of our own activities. The present chapter aims to show that we should pay much more attention to it, and to summarize the main issues that such ethical self-reflection should address.

1. OUR CHOICE OF RESEARCH TOPICS

The number of technological artifacts and practices in current use is staggering, and only a small selection of them has been subject to ethical scrutiny. A good argument can be made that the ethics of technology should focus on the practically most important ethical issues that technology gives rise to. However, that does not seem to be the case. Critics have argued that too much emphasis is put on issues whose practical relevance is uncertain, for instance, on "speculative nanoethics" that refers to hypothetical future developments in nanotechnology with little relevance for the nanotechnology that is available or under development (Nordmann 2007; Nordmann and Rip 2009; Grunwald 2010). On the other hand, many technologies with prominent ethical problems have received scant attention by ethicists. This applies to automobile technology that has a death toll of more than a million persons every year (Hansson 2014), and to technologies that are essential for the welfare of large populations in developing countries, such as sanitation, water supply, agricultural, and food-making technologies. In short, the ethics of technology has its focus on a small selection of technologies in affluent societies, and it has very little to say on the role of technology in the daily lives of the underprivileged populations of the world.

This is certainly not due to a lack of technology-related issues in less prosperous countries that can be better understood with the help of ethical analysis. Instead, the distribution of funding seems to be a large part of the explanation. The (fairly small) sums available for studies in the ethics of technology are predominantly meant for problems in the industrialized countries. Individual researchers cannot be criticized for focusing their work on topics that attract funding. However, there are reasons for ethicists of technology, as a community, to bring up this issue in contacts with funding agencies and others who can influence for which purposes funding is made available.

2. CAN ETHICAL RESEARCH HAVE NEGATIVE CONSEQUENCES?

Potential negative consequences of research are major topics in the research ethics of most other disciplines. It is generally agreed that researchers should not build weapons of mass destruction, invent technologies that endanger the natural environment, or develop new methods of psychological manipulation. What about ethics? Perhaps we need not worry, since ethical research always contributes to social improvement? Isn't it obvious that clarifications and reflections on ethical issues will have a positive effect—or at least not a negative one—on social decision making?

Unfortunately the empirical evidence does not support such an optimistic view on the effects of ethical studies. Judging by the research that has been reported, knowing and adhering to ethical principles need not promote moral behavior (Batson et al. 2001). To the contrary, training in moral reasoning can even facilitate immoral behavior by making rationalizations for such behavior more accessible (Valdesolo and DeSteno 2008; Mercier 2011). In politics, moral convictions can stand in the way of compromises and even foster extremism (Ryan 2014). As one researcher noted:

> In fact, moral judgment can be extremely destructive: moral condemnation reduces economic efficiency, incites political extremism, damages close relationships, radicalizes terrorists, motivates sexual-orientation hate crimes, and blocks medical services for pregnant women, people addicted to drugs, and HIV patients. (DeScioli 2016)

In face of the empirical evidence, it cannot be taken for granted that ethical reflection or discussion always has a positive ethical impact. Potentially, even the act of labeling an issue as ethical, or deciding to discuss it in ethical terms, may have untoward ethical consequences. For instance, it has been hypothesized that when an issue is treated as ethical, this can make people less willing to compromise. It can also induce them to turn for advice to the persons they take to have moral expertise, often religious authorities (Hansson 2017).

Moral philosophers often discuss, and occasionally endorse, standpoints that most people consider to be morally repulsive. Arguably, a seminar presentation defending torture or infanticide is not expected to have any negative effects on society. However, if the same standpoints are presented in public forums we cannot take it for granted that there will be no such effects[1] (Hansson 2017). Just as a bacteriologist must seriously consider if a new strain of bacteria with potentially dangerous properties can be used in warfare, we as ethicists have to seriously consider whether our arguments can be used for immoral purposes. The naïve view that research in ethics always has ethically good consequences has to be replaced by serious ethical reflections of the same type that we recommend other researchers to engage in.

3. HUMAN SUBJECTS

In social research, the treatment of human subjects is usually the most important ethical issue. Increasingly (and for very good reasons) researchers in ethics perform empirical research, usually in the form of questionnaires, interviews, and focus groups. Sometimes, we ask our subjects quite sensitive questions, for instance, about illicit or dangerous uses of technologies. Whenever human subjects are involved we have to abide by the same ethical (and in some countries legal) requirements as other researchers, which includes submitting our research plans to an ethical review board.

Three of the major concerns in research on human subjects are informed consent, privacy, and risk. A subject's approval can only count as informed consent if she has received accurate information about the purpose and the nature of the research that she will contribute to, and fully understood that information. It is also essential that she can withdraw from participation at any time, without being subject to any disadvantages. (This excludes arrangements where subjects are required by their employers to be research subjects.)

Privacy issues arise when researchers collect sensitive personal information, for instance about health, religion, sexual orientation or experiences, or criminal actions. Subjects who are asked such questions should be guaranteed anonymity, either with anonymous questionnaires or with a system for safe storage and handling of the questionnaires.

Research performed by ethicists usually does not expose subjects to risk. However, if you bring up sensitive or traumatic issues in research interviews, you may in some cases provoke severe psychological reactions. This may occur, for instance, if you interview survivors of a serious accident. In all such cases, it is necessary to make sure that interviewees will have access to adequate help should the need arise.

4. CONFLICTS OF INTEREST

In some areas of applied ethics, consultancy is quite common. This applies in particular to business ethics and medical ethics. Consultants in business ethics develop ethical codes and construct criteria for ethical investment, ethical advertising, and fair trade. In medical ethics, consultancy is predominantly performed in clinical settings, but sometimes companies in the pharmaceutical and medical technology industries hire ethicists to help them in the development and clinical introduction of their products. In the ethics of technology, consultancy seems to be less common. Obviously, wherever ethical consultancy takes place, it can give rise to conflicts of interest.

There are also other types of arrangements than consultancy that can potentially give rise to conflicts of interest. For instance, ethicists involved in value-sensitive design (VSD) will be cooperating with companies in the development phase of new products. In this way, ethical considerations can have an influence in the design phase of new technologies, which is usually the phase when most of the ethically important decisions are made. However, as so often happens, influence comes with responsibilities and potentially also with conflicts of interest. A major issue is of course the risk of financial dependency. It is highly advisable to avoid situations where an ethicist's private economic situation depends on what conclusions she draws on the issues she investigates.

Other cooperations than those with industry can be problematic for similar reasons. For instance, many ethicists work in academic research projects devoted to the development of some new technology (usually at an early stage, before the design of actual products). Just like industrial cooperations, such projects can offer ethicists unique possibilities to study new technologies and to make sure that ethical considerations are taken into account at the right point in time in their development. But just as in cooperations with industry, the ethicists' independence and integrity have to be considered carefully beforehand.

The researcher's integrity is an issue in all kinds of research, but in ethics it is even more precarious than in most other disciplines. There are at least two reasons for this. First, ethicists are supposed to understand the requirements of ethics better than other researchers. They are expected to satisfy the requirements of ethics for about the same reasons that Anglicists are supposed to write their research papers in impeccable English. Secondly, the lack of agreement on what is "right" in ethics makes it difficult to determine whether an ethicist's work is biased or not. The best response to these difficulties is to apply even stronger procedural criteria than in other disciplines to avert potential threats to integrity. The following are three components in a strategy to avoid the damaging effects of conflicts of interest:

1. When deciding what types of funding, cooperations, or other arrangements are compatible with your credibility as an ethicist, do not ask yourself "Would this arrangement have a negative impact on my integrity and independence?" Instead, ask "Are there colleagues on whose integrity and independence this arrangement would have a negative impact?" If the answer to the latter question is yes, then you have a strong reason not to enter into that arrangement.
2. Be open about your potential conflicts of interest, and include a statement about them in all publications where they are relevant. If you prefer not to be open about a funding or cooperation, then that is a strong reason to refrain from it.
3. The role as an impartial ethical adviser is usually not compatible with that of a spokesperson or a propagandist for a company or other special interest. If you want to have the former of these roles, you will need to draw a sharp line against the latter.

5. BEING AN ETHICAL EXPERT

Ethicists are often called upon to act as experts in ethical issues. The role as an ethical expert is often unpaid, and it is (at least in most cases) different from that of being a consultant. Ethicists act as experts for instance when interviewed in media and when serving in public or academic committees.

Is it at all possible to be an expert in ethical issues? In traditional, pre-modern societies it was usually assumed that "there is a universally valid ethical canon and those who do not subscribe to it are simply mistaken" (Kovács 2010, p. 770). In such a perspective, the notion of ethical expertise was unproblematic. Those who knew the ethical canon, usually the religious authorities, were qualified to tell everyone else what is morally right and wrong, and others had better rely on their expertise. However, in modern societies the dominant view, also among ethicists, is that there is no generally recognized ethical expertise in that sense. (Such expertise would be difficult to combine with democracy: cf. Lagerspetz 2008, p. 21.) The claim to expertise of professional ethicists is much more modest. According to the current consensus, ethicists are experts in ethical concepts and in the implications and interrelations of ethical standpoints. With this expertise they can act as educators and facilitators, supporting others in their efforts to make morally sound judgments, but they cannot dictate what the decision should be.

Kevin Elliott (2006) has summarized the task of ethical expertise as that of promoting autonomous decision making by the public and its representatives. Ethical experts should make decision makers better equipped to make decisions conforming with their own values, not those of the experts. In order to achieve this, the expert should clarify the nature of the problem, provide concepts to analyze it and show what standpoints there are and where they can lead. This means that different standpoints should be presented, as well as their weaknesses and strengths. This will provide the decision makers with a "moral cartography" (Crosthwaite 1995), but not tell them what they must do.

In controversial public issues, it is common for the contestants to recruit scientific experts of their own who support their respective opinions. The result is often a confused discussion that blurs the distinction between policy issues and issues to be decided by experts (Wagner 1995). Partisan ethical advocacy is problematic for the same reason. Like anyone else, ethicists can contribute to public debates in policy issues, but it is important to make it clear when one acts as an expert respectively as a private citizen with an opinion.

6. MISCONDUCT IN RESEARCH

By scientific misconduct is meant that a researcher distorts the research process by, for instance, fabrication or grossly misleading presentation of data, illicit appropriation of the work of other researchers, or misleading presentation of the research process.

Until recently, ethics research did not deal much with data, but this has changed through the increasing use of questionnaires, interviews, and other empirical methods. As in other disciplines, truthfulness in the management of data is of paramount importance. The most serious wrongdoings usually involve the outright fabrication or falsification of data. There are also somewhat less serious misdemeanors that are probably more common. In the treatment of nonquantitative data, such as answers to open questions in interviews, it is often tempting to select answers that support your favorite hypothesis, while not mentioning other answers that point in the opposite direction. Obviously, this is a temptation to be resisted. In the statistical treatment of quantitative data there are sometimes reasons to exclude extreme answers that seem to depend on misunderstandings of the question or are irrelevant for some other reason. The exclusion of such outliers has to be done with caution and—most importantly—it has to be truthfully reported in the publication.

Once you have entered your data into a statistical software program it is easy to try out a large number of calculations. Usually, if you try sufficiently many of them, you will find a number of statistically significant correlations. However, this could also happen if you performed a similar search for correlations on a collection of random numbers. This is called the "multiple testing problem." For example, suppose that you distribute a questionnaire with about one hundred questions to three groups of engineers. Due to the effects of chance you will probably find several statistically significant differences between the groups. Suppose that you select two or three of these that you find particularly interesting, and adjust the introductory part of your article to create the impression that you started out with hypotheses that these results confirmed. This would severely mislead the readers. There is no simple solution to the multiple testing problem, but the following five pieces of advice should be of some help:

1. Report all statistical tests that you have performed, including those that yielded no interesting results.
2. Ask a statistician for advice before doing any statistical testing, and preferably before collecting the data. There are statistical means to reduce the risk of incorrect conclusions due to multiple testing.
3. Examine (with the statistician's help) the coherence of the correlations you find. If they exhibit an incoherent pattern then that is a reason to be cautious in interpreting them.
4. Pay close attention to the size of the observed effects. Small effects should usually be interpreted with caution even when they are statistically significant, since they can be caused by small errors in the procedure.
5. When reporting your study, do not create the impression that your results confirmed a prior hypothesis, unless this was really the case.

The fifth of these items may very well be the one that is most often violated. Often, this is not done on purpose, but is rather the effect of wishful thinking. Typically, the problematic statements are written into the introductory part of the paper. (Introductions are almost always written after the data has been collected.) The best way to avoid this problem is to write down the research questions and hypotheses of the research beforehand, circulate this text among the researchers in the collaboration and reach an agreement on it before the data is collected.

7. PLAGIARISM

Plagiarism is the wrongful appropriation of someone else's work in one's own (oral or written) presentation. Plagiarism is wrongful to the colleagues whose work is purloined. Some forms of plagiarism also distort the records of science in other ways, for instance by giving readers the incorrect impression that there are two independent investigations yielding the same result when there is in fact only one.

There are two major forms of plagiarism—the illicit appropriation of words and the illicit appropriation of contents. We can call them word-snatching and contents-snatching. Word-snatching, the verbatim copying of a text, is the most effortless but also the most risky of the two forms of plagiarism. The original text is usually available on the Internet (or will become so later), and can easily be found. Unfortunately word-snatching is nevertheless still common, also in ethics. In the last few years, several articles have been withdrawn from ethics journals due to this form of plagiarism (Hansson 2015).

More cunning plagiarists do not copy others' texts verbatim. Instead they take data, ideas, and arguments from others, and express them in their own words. Already Cicero was already complaining of thieves stealing philosophical ideas—he said that they "generally change the labels on the items they have taken" (Cicero, *De Finibus* 5.25.74, 2001, p. 142). This form of plagiarism is usually more difficult to discover than word-snatching. It is also more difficult to discover in ethics than in most other disciplines, and that for two reasons. First, it is often difficult to determine whether an idea in moral philosophy is new or just a new formulation of an old idea. Secondly, there are still some moral philosophers (and other philosophers) who write in a style of "thinking from scratch," deliberately omitting references to the previous literature. Wittgenstein is the most well-known modern philosopher who wrote in that way. Although a sourceless style of writing may have literary merits, it is unsuitable for scholarly communication and often causes problems for those who use it (as it did for Wittgenstein, see Hintikka 1993).

Of course, all cases of similarity of ideas are not plagiarism. There are at least two other possible explanations. One is independent discovery, and the other is cryptomnesia. Cryptomnesia is the illusion of believing that one creates something new when one is in fact recreating what one has read or heard. Psychological experiments have confirmed the reality of cryptomnesia; we tend to remember others' ideas but believe them to be our own (Brown and Halliday 1991; Marsh and Bower 1993; Marsh, Landau, and Hicks 1997; Defeldre 2005). Many of us know this from our own experience: it is often difficult to remember the origin of ideas, and all too easy to believe that ideas with forgotten sources must be one's own. Cryptomnesia is probably the cause of many similarities between ethical and other philosophical texts that may at first glance look like the effects of plagiarism (Hansson 2008).

The best way to avoid such "involuntary plagiarism" is to

1. Avoid presenting old ideas under new names. If you find good reasons to do so, mention the old name and its origin, and explain why you do not use it.

2. Before publishing a new idea, make a careful literature search to find out if someone else has come up with the same idea, or something similar to it, before you.
3. Make notes when you read so that you can easily track the origin of the ideas you are working with.
4. Ask knowledgeable and well-read colleagues for advice.

8. DUPLICATE PUBLICATION

By duplicate publication is meant the publication of one's own text in more than one place. (The term "self-plagiarism" is common but misleading.) There are several forms of reuse of one's own text, some of which are acceptable whereas others are not. Two forms are always unacceptable. One of them is publication of the same data in two places without clearly stating in at least one of these publications that the same data is used. This is inappropriate for the same reason as plagiarism of someone else's data: readers can get the impression that there are two independent data sets in support of a claim or a hypothesis, when there is in fact only one.

The other clearly unacceptable form is the publication of the same (or nearly the same) text in two different journals, without a clear statement in the last publication that it is a republication. When such a duplication is discovered, the second journal can be expected to withdraw the paper. However, there are also cases when it is legitimate to republish the same or a slightly modified text. Sometimes journal articles are republished in a thematic anthology or a book collecting works by the author. Sometimes publications in conference proceedings or (in particular) report series are considered to be preliminary versions, and a final, sometimes only slightly changed, version is published in a journal. Chapters from an unpublished PhD thesis are treated in the same way. In all these cases, it is strongly recommended to clarify the relation between the two publications in the one that is published last.[2]

There are also cases when the reuse of small parts of a text is not only acceptable but also recommended. If you use the same method in two articles, it is an advantage if you also describe it in the same words. Changing the description can confuse readers and create the wrongful impression that there was some difference.

9. AUTHORSHIP

Who should be listed as author of an article? Authorship practices differ between disciplines. Ethicists often cooperate with colleagues from other disciplines, and in such cases mutual adjustments may be needed. However, there are also principles that are common to all academic disciplines. They can be summarized as follows: *To be coauthor of a paper you must satisfy two criteria. First, you must have made an important scientific contribution to the paper. Secondly, you must take responsibility for the text as a whole to the extent that your own competence is sufficient to do so.*

An author does not have to take part in the actual writing of the article, but in order to satisfy the second of these criteria she must have read through it carefully enough to take responsibility for all aspects of it that fall within her own area of expertise. In cooperations involving several disciplines some of the authors may lack the competence needed to assess all aspects of the paper, but that does not diminish their responsibility for the aspects that they are able to assess.

Notably, none of the following conditions qualifies a person for authorship:

• being the supervisor of a student who is one of the authors
• being the leader of a participating research group
• being head of the department or unit where the research took place
• having contributed funding, research material, or other resources

The order between author names follows practices that differ between disciplines. In all disciplines, the person who has done most of the work is normally the first author. In some disciplines, the person who has led the work is usually the second author, whereas in other disciplines she is usually the last author. If it is not clear to the reader who has done what, then it is a good idea to make a short statement—for instance in a footnote that clarifies the division of labor and responsibilities between the authors.

10. ETHICAL CODES

Ethicists often tell members of other professions that proactive ethical reflections on their professional tasks and responsibilities will help them to deal with difficult issues if and when they arise. Ethical codes have a central role in such ethical reflections. It has often been pointed out that the process of writing and discussing the code is at least as important as the end product, the code itself. In January 2014 the American Society for Bioethics and Humanities adopted what was probably the first code of ethics for an ethical or philosophical profession (ASBH 2014). There is currently no code of ethics for ethicists of technology. Perhaps there should be?

NOTES

1. These are real examples. On philosophical defense of infanticide, see Glock 2011 and Hansson 2017.

2. This is a suitable occasion to mention that some parts of this chapter are based on Hansson 2017.

REFERENCES

ASBH (2014) *Code of Ethics and Professional Responsibilities for Healthcare Ethics Consultants*, http://asbh.org/uploads/publications/ASBH%20Code%20of%20 Ethics.pdf.

Batson, C. Daniel, and Thompson, Elizabeth R. (2001) "Why don't moral people act morally? Motivational considerations," *Current Directions in Psychological Science* 10:54–57.

Brown, A.S., and Halliday, H.E. (1991) "Cryptomnesia and source memory difficulties," *American Journal of Psychology* 104:475–90.

Cicero (2001) *On Moral Ends*. Cambridge Texts in the History of Philosophy, ed. J. Annas, transl. R. Woolf. Cambridge: Cambridge University Press.

Crosthwaite, Jan (1995) "Moral expertise: A problem in the professional ethics of professional ethicists," *Bioethics* 9:361–79.

Defeldre, A.-C. (2005) "Inadvertent plagiarism in everyday life," *Applied Cognitive Psychology* 19:1033–40.

DeScioli, Peter (2016) "The side-taking hypothesis for moral judgment," *Current Opinion in Psychology* 7:23–27.

Elliott, Kevin C. (2006) "An ethics of expertise based on informed consent," *Science and Engineering Ethics* 12:637–61.

Glock, Hans-Johann (2011) "Doing good by splitting hairs? Analytic philosophy and applied ethics," *Journal of Applied Philosophy* 28:225–40.

Grunwald, A. (2010) "From speculative nanoethics to explorative philosophy of nanotechnology," *Nanoethics* 4:91–101.

Hansson, Sven Ove (2008) "Editorial: Philosophical plagiarism," *Theoria* 74:97–101.

Hansson, Sven Ove (2014) "Making road traffic safer: Reply to Ori," *Philosophical Papers* 43:365–75.

Hansson, Sven Ove (2015) "The ethics of doing philosophy," *Theoria* 81:93–96.

Hansson, Sven Ove (2017) "The ethics of doing ethics," *Science and Engineering Ethics*, in press.

Hintikka, Jaakko (1993) "Ludwig's apple tree: On the philosophical relations between Wittgenstein and the Vienna circle." In F. Stadler et al. (eds.) *Scientific Philosophy: Origins and Developments*, pp. 27–46. Dordrecht: Kluwer.

Kovács, József (2010) "The transformation of (bio)ethics expertise in a world of ethical pluralism," *Journal of Medical Ethics* 36:767–70.

Lagerspetz, Eerik (2008) "Ethical expertise in democratic societies," In V. Launis and J. Räikkä (eds.) *Genetic Democracy*, pp. 21–29. Springer.

Marsh, R.L., and Bower, G.H. (1993) "Eliciting cryptomnesia: Unconscious plagiarism in a puzzle task," *Journal of Experimental Psychology: Learning, Memory, and Cognition* 19:673–88.

Marsh, R.L., Landau, J.D., and Hicks, J.L. (1997) "Contributions of inadequate source monitoring to unconscious plagiarism during idea generation," *Journal of Experimental Psychology: Learning, Memory, and Cognition* 23:886–97.

Mercier, H. (2011) "What good is moral reasoning?" *Mind and Society* 10:131–48.

Nordmann, A. (2007) "If and then: A critique of speculative nanoethics," *Nanoethics* 1:31–46.

Nordmann, A., and Rip, A. (2009) "Mind the gap revisited," *Nature Nanotechnology* 4:273–74.

Ryan, Timothy J. (2014) "Reconsidering moral issues in politics," *Journal of Politics* 76:380–97.

Valdesolo, P., and DeSteno, D. (2008) "The duality of virtue: Deconstructing the moral hypocrite," *Journal of Experimental Social Psychology* 44:1334–38.

Wagner, Wendy E. (1995) "The science charade in toxic risk regulation," *Columbia Law Review* 95:1613–723.

Index

About the Contributors

Anthony I. Akubue is professor of environmental and technological studies at St. Cloud State University, Minnesota, USA. He is member of the International Technology and Engineering Educators Association (ITEEA), Minnesota Technology and Engineering Education Association, and Epsilon Pi Tau (the International Honorary for Professions Fraternity for Education in Technology). He received the Paul T. Hiser Exemplary Publication Award for the best article in *The Journal of Technology Studies* in 2001 ("Gender Disparity in Third World Technological, Social, and Economic Development"). He has been the keynote speaker at several conferences in both the United States and Nigeria. He has published articles in international journals on appropriate technology, technology transfer, deforestation, technology and sustainable development, and has also contributed newspaper articles on a variety of topics. He has served on many commissions and boards, including St. Cloud Human Rights Commission, St. Cloud Hospital Board of Directors, Catholic Charities of Central Minnesota, Tri-County Action Program, Great River Regional Library Trustee Board, Mission Office Board, and Christ Church Parish Council. He published the textbook *Technological and Socio-economic Development: A Third World Challenge* in 2006.

Philip Brey is full professor of philosophy of technology at the University of Twente in the Netherlands, and scientific director of the 4TU Centre for Ethics and Technology (www.ethicsandtechnology.eu), a research center that spans four universities in the Netherlands and includes over sixty researchers. He has published extensively in the areas of ethics of technology, philosophy and ethics of information technology, and responsible research and innovation. He is president of the International Society for Ethics and Information Technology, a former president of the Society for Philosophy and Technology, and a member of the editorial board of ten leading journals in his field. He currently coordinates the EU-funded project SATORI (budget 4.7 M€; satoriproject.eu) on European standards for ethical assessment of research and innovation.

Michael Davis, PhD, University of Michigan 1972, is senior fellow at the Center for the Study of Ethics in the Professions and professor of philosophy, Illinois Institute of Technology, Chicago, USA. Before coming to IIT in 1986, he taught at Case-Western Reserve, Illinois State, and the University of Illinois at Chicago. Since 1991, he has held—among other grants—four from the National Science Foundation to integrate ethics into technical courses. Davis has published more than 200 articles (and chapters) and authored seven books, including: *Thinking Like an Engineer* (1998); *Ethics and the University* (1999); and *Profession, Code, and Ethics* (2002). He has also edited or coedited five other books: *Ethics and the Legal Professions* (1986); *AIDS: Crisis in Professional Ethics* (1994); *Conflict of Interest in the Professions* (2001); *Engineering Ethics* (2005); and *Ethics and the Legal Profession,* 2nd ed. (2009). Among his current interests is finding ways to study the concept of profession in cultures that lack a word for it.

Sven Ove Hansson is professor in philosophy at the Royal Institute of Technology, Stockholm, Sweden. He is member of the Royal Swedish Academy of Engineering Sciences (IVA) and former president of the Society for Philosophy and Technology. He is editor in chief of *Theoria* and of the two book series *Philosophy, Technology and Society* and *Outstanding Contributions to Logic.* His research includes contributions to moral and political philosophy, the philosophy of risk, decision theory, logic, and the philosophy of science and technology. He is the author of well over 300 refereed journal papers and books chapters. His recent books include *The Ethics of Risk: Ethical Analysis in an Uncertain World* (2013), *Social and Ethical Aspects of Radiation Risk Management* (edited with Deborah Oughton, 2013), *The Role of Technology in Science: Philosophical Perspectives* (edited, 2015), and *The Argumentative Turn in Policy Analysis: Reasoning about Uncertainty* (edited with Gertrude Hirsch Hadorn, 2016).

Gertrude Hirsch Hadorn is an adjunct professor at the Department of Environmental Systems Science, Swiss Federal Institute of Technology (ETH), Zurich. She has worked in environmental ethics and in the philosophy of environmental and sustainability research with case studies in the fields of climate change and ecology and has articles in *Ecological Economics, Environmental Science and Policy* and *WIREs Climate Change.* She has contributed to the methodology of transdisciplinary research, and has worked on values in science, the epistemology of computer simulations, and the analysis of uncertainty in decision making. She is the leading editor of the *Handbook of Transdisciplinary Research* (2008) and coeditor of *The Argumentative Turn in Policy Analysis: Reasoning about Uncertainty* (edited with Sven Ove Hansson, 2016). She is member of the Scientific Board of the interdisciplinary journal *GAIA*, and she was vice president of the Swiss Academy of Sciences in 2001–2006.

Diane P. Michelfelder is professor of philosophy at Macalester College, St. Paul, Minnesota, USA. Her primary areas of research inquiry are the philosophy of technology and the philosophy of engineering. She has been actively involved in the creation and development of fPET: The Forum on Philosophy, Engineering, and Technology, and served as the president of the Society for Philosophy and Technology in 2007–2009. Currently, she is Co-Editor-in-Chief of that society's journal, *Techné: Research in Philosophy and Technology*. Her work has been published there as well as in *Science and Engineering Ethics, AI & Society, Philosophy and Technology, Engineering Studies, and Ethics and Information Technology*, among others. Her most recent books are *Philosophy and Engineering: Reflections on Practice, Principles, and Process* (2013, edited with Natasha McCarthy and David E. Goldberg), and *Philosophy and Engineering: Exploring Boundaries, Expanding Connections* (2016, edited with Byron Newberry and Qin Zhu).

Payam Moula is a PhD student in philosophy at the Royal Institute of Technology, Stockholm, Sweden. His research is within the field of applied ethics with a particular focus on the ethics of biotechnology. He also has interests in political philosophy.

Jessica Nihlén Fahlquist is a researcher at the Centre for Research Ethics and Bioethics at Uppsala University, Sweden. Her research focuses on ethical aspects of risk in the context of technology and public health, and she has a particular interest in notions of moral responsibility. She has published articles on public health ethics, the philosophy of risk, the ethics of technology, and environmental ethics. Nihlén Fahlquist received her PhD in philosophy at the Division of Philosophy at the Royal Institute of Technology in Stockholm in 2008. In the periods 2007–2011 and 2012–2015, she was a postdoctoral researcher at the Philosophy Department of Delft University of Technology.

Christine Rösch has a PhD in agricultural science and is head of the research unit Sustainability and Environment at the Institute for Technology Assessment and Systems Analysis (ITAS) of the Karlsruhe Institute of Technology (KIT), Germany. Since 2009, she is the representative of the topic "Environment and Technology" of the KIT center "Humans and Technology," and since 2012 she is deputy representative of the KIT competence area

"Technology, Culture, and Society." She was head of the topic "Sustainability Monitoring" of the Helmholtz Alliance "ENERGY-TRANS" in 2011–2016. Her research includes contributions to technology and sustainability assessment in theory and practice as well as applied systems and impact analysis in the fields of bio-economy, energy, and technology. She is project leader of several research projects with European and national funding, and member of the national and regional bioeconomy network.

Robert Rosenberger is associate professor of philosophy in the School of Public Policy at the Georgia Institute of Technology, USA. His research is devoted to the phenomenology of technology, studying issues such as laboratory imaging, educational simulation, traffic policy, interface design, and homelessness. In an unexpected turn, during the early part of 2016, he spent time as the world's leading expert on phantom vibration syndrome, that is, the feeling that your is phone vibrating when it hasn't actually done so. Rosenberger is editor in chief of the book series *Postphenomenology & the Philosophy of Technology*, and has edited the books *Postphenomenological Investigations* (coedited with Peter-Paul Verbeek, 2015) and *Philosophy of Science: 5 Questions* (2010). He is currently completing a polemical pamphlet critiquing anti-homeless design and policy, tentatively titled *Guilty Technology*.

Per Sandin is senior lecturer in bioethics and environmental ethics at the Swedish University of Agricultural Sciences, Uppsala, Sweden. He received his PhD in philosophy from the Royal Institute of Technology, Stockholm, in 2005. He has written extensively on applied ethics, the philosophy of risk, and the precautionary principle.

Judith Simon holds a chair in ethics and information technology at the University of Hamburg. Previously she has been employed at the IT University Copenhagen, the University of Vienna, the Karlsruhe Institute of Technology, the Institute Jean Nicod (CNRS/ENS) in Paris, and the Research Centre Jülich. Simon holds a PhD in philosophy from the University of Vienna and an MA in psychology from the Free University of Berlin. She serves as co-editor of the journals *Philosophy & Technology* and *Big Data & Society* as well as on the executive boards of the *International Association for Computing and Philosophy* and the *International Society for Ethics and Information Technology*. Her research interests include the philosophy of computing, computer ethics, philosophy of science and technology, sociotechnical epistemology, science and technology studies, technology assessment, value-sensitive design, and responsible research and innovation.

Stefan Strauß is a researcher at the Institute of Technology Assessment (ITA) at the Austrian Academy of Sciences in Vienna. In his research he explores the interplay between information technology and society with a particular focus on the related impacts on political processes, identity construction, security, surveillance, and privacy. Further research interests include information and computer ethics and the philosophy of information. He has been involved in several European research projects e.g., on privacy, security and surveillance, cloud computing, e-democracy and identity, and security of critical infrastructures. He authored a number of publications on ICT-supported participation, digital identity, security and privacy. Most of his recent papers deal with the implications of big data.

Galit Wellner, PhD, is assistant professor at the NB School of Design Haifa, Israel. She is also a lecturer at Tel Aviv University and Bezalel Academy of Art and Design. Galit studies digital technologies and their interrelations with humans. She graduated from the STS department at Bar-Ilan University in 2014. Her book *A Postphenomenological Inquiry of Cellphones: Genealogies, Meanings and Becoming* was published in 2015. She was a guest-editor in *Techné*, editing "Celling While Driving" (2014) and "Techno-Anthropology" (2015), and she has published several peer-reviewed articles and book chapters. She is one of the lead authors of the Israeli National Ecosystem Assessment. Galit was the vice-chair of Israeli UNESCO's Information for All Program (IFAP), a board member of the FTTH Council Europe, and a founder of a start-up. Before that, she worked for hi-tech companies and start-ups in strategic marketing. Galit holds LLB and LLM from Tel Aviv University.

Heather Wiltse is assistant professor at Umeå Institute of Design, Umeå University, Sweden, where she is also currently serving as director of PhD studies. Her research centers round trying to understand and critique the role of (digital) things in experience and society in ways that can inform design, and it sits at the intersection of design studies, philosophy of technology, and critical technology studies. She has published and presented refereed work in philosophy of technology, science and technology studies, human-computer interaction, and design research. She is currently writing a book in collaboration with Johan Redström, to be published by Bloomsbury, that investigates and articulates what has become of things as computational processes, dynamic networks, and contextual customization now emerge as factors as important as form, function and material were for designing, using, and understanding objects in the industrial age.

Lightning Source UK Ltd.
Milton Keynes UK
UKHW041914160119
335678UK00001B/172/P